THE
REFERENCE
SHELF

ETHICS IN POLITICS
AND GOVERNMENT

edited by ANNE MARIE DONAHUE

THE REFERENCE SHELF

Volume 61 Number 2

THE H. W. WILSON COMPANY

New York   1989

THE REFERENCE SHELF

The books in this series contain reprints of articles, excerpts from books, and addresses on current issues and social trends in the United States and other countries. There are six separately bound numbers in each volume, all of which are generally published in the same calendar year. One number is a collection of recent speeches; each of the others is devoted to a single subject and gives background information and discussion from various points of view, concluding with a comprehensive bibliography that contains books and pamphlets and abstracts of additional articles on the subject. Books in the series may be purchased individually or on subscription.

Library of Congress Cataloging-in-Publication Data

Main entry under title:

Ethics in politics and government.
(The Reference shelf ; v. 61, no. 2)
Bibliography: p.
1. Political ethics—United States. 2. Political ethics. I. Donahue, Anne Marie. II. Series.
JK468.E7E84 1989   172'.0973   89-8876
ISBN 0-8242-0781-5

Printed in the United States of America

CONTENTS

IV. Character, Moral Judgment, and Ethical Leadership

Bibliography

PREFACE

The Founding Fathers harbored few illusions about the virtue of the men who would make and execute the laws of the new nation. In a speech delivered to the Virginia ratifying convention in 1788, James Madison warned against the idea that "we are to place unlimited confidence in them [legislators], and expect nothing but the most exalted integrity and sublime virtue." He went on to argue that the citizens, not their leaders, were ultimately responsible for the success of the American experiment:

> To suppose that any form of government will secure liberty or happiness without any virtue in the people is a chimerical idea. If there is sufficient virtue and intelligence in the community, it will be exercised in the selection of these men. So that we do not depend on their virtue, or put confidence in our rulers, but in the people who are to choose them. . . .

Two hundred years later, the American people give increasing evidence of dissatisfaction with at least some of the choices they have made. Public opinion polls show that confidence in government has been declining since the late '50s, when it stood at about 80 percent. According to a study by *Public Opinion* magazine (April/May 1985), those expressing a great deal of confidence in Congress had fallen to 28 percent by 1984. The public's growing disillusionment with government is often attributed to a rise in malfeasance of office. Disclosure of the cover-up surrounding the Watergate burglary during Richard Nixon's administration fueled fears that politicians could not be trusted, and scandals involving elected officials, government employees, and political appointees have erupted regularly since then.

In 1987 the Iran-contra affair again generated widespread criticism of senior government officials. Revelations that profits from a secret arms sale to Iran had been used illegally to fund the Nicaraguan contras revived debate over the morality of the use of covert procedures in the conduct of foreign policy. Section I of this volume is devoted to discussion of that debate's central issues of the roles of honesty and accountability in securing national interests. The following two sections consider issues involving ethics in the executive and legislative branches. The final section focuses on the dilemmas of ethical leadership and the consideration of various approaches to promoting ethics in politics and government.

5

I would like to thank the authors and publishers who granted their permission to reprint the material in this collection. Special thanks are due to Maggie Pax, Dr. John Donahue, Lynn Shipley, Margit Conrad, and David Brittan.

ANNE MARIE DONAHUE

March 1989

I. MORAL PRINCIPLE AND FOREIGN POLICY

EDITOR'S INTRODUCTION

Although references to principle are frequent in the rhetoric of diplomacy and international politics, many American scholars and policy makers believe that ethics should play no part in the making of U.S. foreign policy. As the United States emerged as a world power, opinion on the place of morality in foreign policy split into two broad schools of thought.

The Idealist school maintains that nations can promote justice, peace, and international harmony through the application of reason, law, and moral principle. Dominant during the tenure of President Woodrow Wilson, Idealist views found expression in the 1928 Kellogg-Briand Pact, which outlawed war as an instrument of national policy.

Wilsonian Idealism had been all but extinguished by the end of World War II. Since then, policy and opinion have tended to reflect the tenets of the Realist school, influenced by the ideas of theorists such as St. Augustine, John Calvin, Edmund Burke, and James Madison. In the Realist view, the perils of world politics and the lack of internationally recognized moral standards dictate that ethical concerns must be subordinated to the pursuit of national interest.

George Kennan, one of the leading contemporary Realists, updates and clarifies the doctrine he has championed for nearly fifty years in the first selection, "Morality and Foreign Policy," an article that appeared in *Foreign Affairs*. In the next piece, "Exorcising Wilson's Ghost," reprinted from *The Washington Quarterly*, George Weigel maintains that the Realist/Idealist debate has centered on a reductive conception of morality and he proposes a foreign policy approach founded on both prudence and ethical principle.

The Realist approach attracted much criticism after the Vietnam war, and Idealist views underwent something of a revival during the presidency of Jimmy Carter, who emphasized respect for human rights in U.S. foreign relations. But the perception that American power had eroded in the '70s undermined Carter's popularity and fueled enthusiasm for Ronald Reagan. Condemning those who "blame America first" and promising to stand firm against the Soviet adversary, President Reagan viewed his landslide election victory as a mandate for a more assertive foreign policy. During his first term, Congress approved a massive military buildup and the Reagan Doctrine of U.S. support for anti-communist insurgencies became national policy. Charles Krauthammer's article, "Morality and the Reagan Doctrine," printed in *The New Republic,* examines major objections to the Reagan administration's approach to dealings with foreign nations.

In the last piece on this aspect of the topic, the congressional committees investigating the Iran-contra arms sale and diversion of funds present their executive summary of these events and their conclusions.

MORALITY AND FOREIGN POLICY[1]

In a small volume of lectures published nearly thirty-five years ago, I had the temerity to suggest that the American statesmen of the turn of the twentieth century were unduly legalistic and moralistic in their judgment of the actions of other governments. This seemed to be an approach that carried them away from the sterner requirements of political realism and caused their statements and actions, however impressive to the domestic political audience, to lose effectiveness in the international arena.

These observations were doubtless brought forward too cryptically and thus invited a wide variety of interpretations, not excluding the thesis that I had advocated an amoral, or even immoral, foreign policy for this country. There have since been demands, particularly from the younger generation, that I should make clearer my views on the relationship of moral considerations to American foreign policy. The challenge is a fair one and deserves a response.

[1] Reprint of an article by George F. Kennan, Professor Emeritus at the Institute for Advanced Study, Princeton. Reprinted by permission of FOREIGN AFFAIRS, 1985/86 (vol. 64, no. 2, pp. 205–218). Copyright © 1985 by the Council on Foreign Relations, Inc.

II

Certain distinctions should be made before one wanders farther into this thicket of problems.

First of all, the conduct of diplomacy is the responsibility of governments. For purely practical reasons, this is unavoidable and inalterable. This responsibility is not diminished by the fact that government, in formulating foreign policy, may choose to be influenced by private opinion. What we are talking about, therefore, when we attempt to relate moral considerations to foreign policy, is the behavior of governments, not of individuals or entire peoples.

Second, let us recognize that the functions, commitments and moral obligations of governments are not the same as those of the individual. Government is an agent, not a principal. Its primary obligation is to the *interests* of the national society it represents, not to the moral impulses that individual elements of that society may experience. No more than the attorney vis-à-vis the client, nor the doctor vis-à-vis the patient, can government attempt to insert into the consciences of those whose interests it represents.

Let me explain. The interests of the national society for which government has to concern itself are basically those of its military security, the integrity of its political life and the well-being of its people. These needs have no moral quality. They arise from the very existence of the national state in question and from the status of national sovereignty it enjoys. They are the unavoidable necessities of a national existence and therefore not subject to classification as either "good" or "bad." They may be questioned from a detached philosophic point of view. But the government of the sovereign state cannot make such judgments. When it accepts the responsibilities of governing, implicit in that acceptance is the assumption that it is right that the state should be sovereign, that the integrity of its political life should be assured, that its people should enjoy the blessings of military security, material prosperity and a reasonable opportunity for, as the Declaration of Independence put it, the pursuit of happiness. For these assumptions the government needs no moral justification, nor need it accept any moral reproach for acting on the basis of them.

This assertion assumes, however, that the concept of national security taken as the basis for governmental concern is one rea-

sonably, not extravagantly, conceived. In an age of nuclear striking power, national security can never be more than relative; and
to the extent that it can be assured at all, it must find its sanction
in the intentions of rival powers as well as in their capabilities. A
concept of national security that ignores this reality and, above
all, one that fails to concede the same legitimacy to the security
needs of others that it claims for its own, lays itself open to the
same moral reproach from which, in normal circumstances, it
would be immune.

Whoever looks thoughtfully at the present situation of the
United States in particular will have to agree that to assure these
blessings to the American people is a task of such dimensions that
the government attempting to meet it successfully will have very
little, if any, energy and attention left to devote to other undertakings, including those suggested by the moral impulses of these
or those of its citizens.

Finally, let us note that there are no internationally accepted
standards of morality to which the U.S. government could appeal
if it wished to act in the name of moral principles. It is true that
there are certain words and phrases sufficiently high-sounding
the world over so that most governments, when asked to declare
themselves for or against, will cheerfully subscribe to them, considering that such is their vagueness that the mere act of subscrib-
ing to them carries with it no danger of having one's freedom of
action significantly impaired. To this category of pronouncements belong such documents as the Kellogg-Briand Pact, the Atlantic Charter, the Yalta Declaration on Liberated Europe, and
the prologues of innumerable other international agreements.

Ever since Secretary of State John Hay staged a political coup
in 1899 by summoning the supposedly wicked European powers
to sign up to the lofty principles of his Open Door notes (principles which neither they nor we had any awkward intention of observing), American statesmen have had a fondness for hurling
just such semantic challenges at their foreign counterparts, thereby placing themselves in a graceful posture before domestic
American opinion and reaping whatever political fruits are to be
derived from the somewhat grudging and embarrassed responses
these challenges evoke.

To say these things, I know, is to invite the question: how
about the Helsinki accords of 1975? These, of course, were numerous and varied. There is no disposition here to question the

value of many of them as refinements of the norms of international intercourse. But there were some, particularly those related to human rights, which it is hard to relegate to any category other than that of the high-minded but innocuous professions just referred to. These accords were declaratory in nature, not contractual. The very general terms in which they were drawn up, involving the use of words and phrases that had different meanings for different people, deprived them of the character of specific obligations to which signatory governments could usefully be held. The Western statesmen who pressed for Soviet adherence to these pronouncements must have been aware that some of them could not be implemented on the Soviet side, within the meanings we would normally attach to their workings, without fundamental changes in the Soviet system of power—changes we had no reason to expect would, or could, be introduced by the men then in power. Whether it is morally commendable to induce others to sign up to declarations, however high-minded in resonance, which one knows will not and cannot be implemented, is a reasonable question. The Western negotiators, in any case, had no reason to plead naiveté as their excuse for doing so.

When we talk about the application of moral standards to foreign policy, therefore, we are not talking about compliance with some clear and generally accepted international code of behavior. If the policies and actions of the U.S. government are to be made to conform to moral standards, those standards are going to have to be America's own, founded on traditional American principles of justice and propriety. When others fail to conform to those principles, and when their failure to conform has an adverse effect on American *interests*, as distinct from political tastes, we have every right to complain and, if necessary, to take retaliatory action. What we cannot do is to assume that our moral standards are theirs as well, and to appeal to those standards as the source of our grievances.

III

So much for basic principles. Let us now consider some categories of action that the U.S. government is frequently asked to take, and sometimes does take, in the name of moral principle.

These actions fall into two broad general categories: those that relate to the behavior of other governments that we find morally unacceptable, and those that relate to the behavior of our own government. Let us take them in that order.

There have been many instances, particularly in recent years, when the U.S. government has taken umbrage at the behavior of other governments on grounds that at least implied moral criteria for judgment, and in some of these instances the verbal protests have been reinforced by more tangible means of pressure. These various interventions have marched, so to speak, under a number of banners: democracy, human rights, majority rule, fidelity to treaties, fidelity to the U.N. Charter, and so on. Their targets have sometimes been the external policies and actions of the offending states, more often the internal practices. The interventions have served, in the eyes of their American inspirers, as demonstrations not only of the moral deficiencies of others but of the positive morality of ourselves; for it was seen as our moral duty to detect these lapses on the part of others, to denounce them before the world, and to assure—as far as we could with measures short of military action—that they were corrected.

Those who have inspired or initiated efforts of this nature would certainly have claimed to be acting in the name of moral principle, and in many instances they would no doubt have been sincere in doing so. But whether the results of this inspiration, like those of so many other good intentions, would justify this claim is questionable from a number of standpoints.

Let us take first those of our interventions that relate to internal practices of the offending governments. Let us reflect for a moment on how these interventions appear in the eyes of the governments in question and of many outsiders.

The situations that arouse our discontent are ones existing, as a rule, far from our own shores. Few of us can profess to be perfect judges of their rights and their wrongs. These are, for the governments in question, matters of internal affairs. It is customary for governments to resent interference by outside powers in affairs of this nature, and if our diplomatic history is any indication, we ourselves are not above resenting and resisting it when we find ourselves its object.

Interventions of this nature can be formally defensible only if the practices against which they are directed are seriously injurious to our interests, rather than just our sensibilities. There will, of course, be those readers who will argue that the encouragement and promotion of democracy elsewhere is always in the interests of the security, political integrity and prosperity of the United States. If this can be demonstrated in a given instance, well and good. But it is not invariably the case. Democracy is a loose term. Many varieties of folly and injustice contrive to masquerade under this designation. The mere fact that a country acquires the trappings of self-government does not automatically mean that the interests of the United States are thereby furthered. There are forms of plebiscitary "democracy" that may well prove less favorable to American interests than a wise and benevolent authoritarianism. There can be tyrannies of a majority as well as tyrannies of a minority, with the one hardly less odious than the other. Hitler came into power (albeit under highly unusual circumstances) with an electoral mandate, and there is scarcely a dictatorship of this age that would not claim the legitimacy of mass support.

There are parts of the world where the main requirement of American security is not an unnatural imitation of the American model but sheer stability, and this last is not always assured by a government of what appears to be popular acclaim. In approaching this question, Americans must overcome their tendency toward generalization and learn to examine each case on its own merits. The best measure of these merits is not the attractiveness of certain general semantic symbols but the effect of the given situation on the tangible and demonstrable interests of the United States.

Furthermore, while we are quick to allege that this or that practice in a foreign country is bad and deserves correction, seldom if ever do we seem to occupy ourselves seriously or realistically with the conceivable alternatives. It seems seldom to occur to us that even if a given situation is bad, the alternatives to it might be worse—even though history provides plenty of examples of just this phenomenon. In the eyes of many Americans it is enough for us to indicate the changes that ought, as we see it, to be made. We assume, of course, that the consequences will be benign and happy ones. But this is not always assured. It is, in any case, not we who are going to have to live with those consequences: it is the offending government and its people. We are demanding, in effect, a species of veto power over those of their practices that we dislike, while denying responsibility for whatever may flow from the acceptance of our demands.

Finally, we might note that our government, in raising such demands, is frequently responding not to its own moral impulses or to any wide general movements of American opinion but rather to pressures generated by politically influential minority elements among us that have some special interest—ethnic, racial, religious, ideological or several of these together—in the foreign situation in question. Sometimes it is the sympathies of these minorities that are most prominently aroused, sometimes their antipathies. But in view of this diversity of motive, the U.S. government, in responding to such pressures and making itself their spokesman, seldom acts consistently. Practices or policies that arouse our official displeasure in one country are cheerfully condoned or ignored in another. What is bad in the behavior of our opponents is good, or at least acceptable, in the case of our friends. What is unobjectionable to us at one period of our history is seen as offensive in another.

This is unfortunate, for a lack of consistency implies a lack of principle in the eyes of much of the world; whereas morality, if not principled, is not really morality. Foreigners, observing these anomalies, may be forgiven for suspecting that what passes as the product of moral inspiration in the rhetoric of our government is more likely to be a fair reflection of the mosaic of residual ethnic loyalties and passions that make themselves felt in the rough and tumble of our political life.

Similar things could be said when it is not the internal practices of the offending government but its actions on the international scene that are at issue. There is, here, the same reluctance to occupy one's self with the conceivable alternatives to the procedures one complains about or with the consequences likely to flow from the acceptance of one's demands. And there is frequently the same lack of consistency in the reaction. The Soviet action in Afghanistan, for example, is condemned, resented and responded to by sanctions. One recalls little of such reaction in the case of the somewhat similar, and apparently no less drastic, action taken by China in Tibet some years ago. The question inevitably arises: is it principle that determines our reaction? Or are there other motives?

Where measures taken by foreign governments affect adversely American interests rather than just American moral sensibilities, protests and retaliation are obviously in order; but then they should be carried forward frankly for what they are, and not allowed to masquerade under the mantle of moral principle.

There will be a tendency, I know, on the part of some readers to see in these observations an apology for the various situations, both domestic and international, against which we have protested and acted in the past. They are not meant to have any such connotations. These words are being written—for whatever this is worth—by one who regards the action in Afghanistan as a grievous and reprehensible mistake of Soviet policy, a mistake that could and should certainly have been avoided. Certain of the procedures of the South African police have been no less odious to me than to many others.

What is being said here does not relate to the reactions of individual Americans, of private organizations in this country, or of the media, to the situations in question. All these may think and say what they like. It relates to the reactions of the U.S. government, as a government among governments, and to the motivation cited for those reactions. Democracy, as Americans understand it, is not necessarily the future of all mankind, nor is it the duty of the U.S. government to assure that it becomes that. Despite frequent assertions to the contrary, not everyone in this world is responsible, after all, for the actions of everyone else, everywhere. Without the power to compel change, there is no responsibility for its absence. In the case of governments it is important for purely practical reasons that the lines of responsibility be kept straight, and that there be, in particular, a clear association of the power to act with the consequences of action or inaction.

IV

If, then, the criticism and reproof of perceived moral lapses in the conduct of others are at best a dubious way of expressing our moral commitment, how about our own policies and actions? Here, at least, the connection between power and responsibility—between the sowing and the reaping—is integral. Can it be true that here, too, there is no room for the application of moral principle and that all must be left to the workings of expediency, national egoism and cynicism?

The answer, of course, is no, but the possibilities that exist are only too often ones that run against the grain of powerful tendencies and reflexes in our political establishment.

In a less than perfect world, where the ideal so obviously lies beyond human reach, it is natural that the avoidance of the worst should often be a more practical undertaking than the achievement of the best, and that some of the strongest imperatives of moral conduct should be ones of a negative rather than a positive nature. The structures of the Ten Commandments are perhaps the best illustration of this state of affairs. This being the case, it is not surprising that some of the most significant possibilities for the observance of moral considerations in American foreign policy relate to the avoidance of actions that have a negative moral significance, rather than to those from which positive results are to be expected.

Many of these possibilities lie in the intuitive qualities of diplomacy—such things as the methodology, manners, style, restraint and elevation of diplomatic discourse—and they can be illustrated only on the basis of a multitude of minor practical examples, for which this article is not the place. There are, however, two negative considerations that deserve mention here.

The first of these relates to the avoidance of what might be called the histrionics of moralism at the expense of its substance. By that is meant the projection of attitudes, poses and rhetoric that cause us to appear noble and altruistic in the mirror of our own vanity but lack substance when related to the realities of international life. It is a sad feature of the human predicament, in personal as in public life, that whenever one has the agreeable sensation of being impressively moral, one probably is not. What one does without self-consciousness or self-admiration, as a matter of duty or common decency, is apt to be closer to the real thing.

The second of these negative considerations pertains to something commonly called secret operations—a branch of governmental activity closely connected with, but not to be confused with, secret intelligence.

Earlier in this century the great secular despotisms headed by Hitler and Stalin introduced into the pattern of their interaction with other governments clandestine methods of operation that can only be described as ones of unbridled cynicism, audacity and brutality. These were expressed not only by a total lack of scruple on their own part but also by a boundless contempt for the countries against which these efforts were directed (and, one feels, a certain contempt for themselves as well). This was in essence not new, of course; the relations among the nation-states of earlier centuries abounded in examples of clandestine iniquities of every conceivable variety. But these were usually moderated in practice by a greater underlying sense of humanity and a greater respect for at least the outward decencies of national power. Seldom was their intent so cynically destructive, and never was their scale remotely so great, as some of the efforts we have witnessed in this century.

In recent years these undertakings have been supplemented, in their effects on the Western public, by a wholly different phenomenon arising in a wholly different quarter: namely, the unrestrained personal terrorism that has been employed by certain governments or political movements on the fringes of Europe as well as by radical-criminal elements within Western society itself. These phenomena have represented, at different times, serious challenges to the security of nearly all Western countries. It is not surprising, therefore, that among the reactions evoked has been a demand that fire should be fought with fire, that the countries threatened by efforts of this nature should respond with similar efforts.

No one will deny that resistance to these attacks requires secret intelligence of a superior quality and a severe ruthlessness of punishment wherever they fall afoul of the judicial systems of the countries against which they are directed. It is not intended here to comment in any way on the means by which they might or should be opposed by countries other than the United States. Nor is it intended to suggest that any of these activities that carry into this country should not be met by anything less than the full rigor of the law. On the contrary, one could wish the laws were even more rigorous in this respect. But when it comes to governmental operations—or disguised operations—beyond our borders, we Americans have a problem.

In the years immediately following the Second World War the practices of the Stalin regime in this respect were so far-reaching, and presented so great an apparent danger to a Western Europe still weakened by the vicissitudes of war, that our government felt itself justified in setting up facilities for clandestine defensive operations of its own; all available evidence suggests that it has since conducted a number of activities under this heading. As one of those who, at the time, favored the decision to set up such facilities, I regret today, in light of the experience of the intervening years, that the decision was taken. Operations of this nature are not in character for this country. They do not accord with its traditions or with its established procedures of government. The effort to conduct them involves dilemmas and situations of moral ambiguity in which the American statesman is deprived of principled guidance and loses a sense of what is fitting and what is not. Excessive secrecy, duplicity and clandestine skulduggery are simply not our dish—not only because we are incapable of keeping a secret anyway (our commercial media of communication see to that) but, more importantly, because such operations conflict with our own traditional standards and compromise our diplomacy in other areas.

One must not be dogmatic about such matters, of course. Foreign policy is too intricate a topic to suffer any total taboos. There may be rare moments when a secret operation appears indispensable. A striking example of this was the action of the United States in apprehending the kidnappers of the *Achille Lauro*. But such operations should not be allowed to become a regular and routine feature of the governmental process, cast in the concrete of unquestioned habit and institutionalized bureaucracy. It is there that the dangers lie.

One may say that to deny ourselves this species of capability is to accept a serious limitation on our ability to contend with forces now directed against us. Perhaps; but if so, it is a limitation with which we shall have to live. The success of our diplomacy has always depended, and will continue to depend, on its inherent honesty and openness of purpose and on the forthrightness with which it is carried out. Deprive us of that and we are deprived of our strongest armor and our most effective weapon. If this is a limitation, it is one that reflects no discredit on us. We may accept it in good conscience, for in national as in personal affairs the acceptance of one's limitations is surely one of the first marks of a true morality.

V

So much, then, for the negative imperatives. When we turn to the positive ones there are, again, two that stand out.

The first of them is closely connected with what has just been observed about the acceptance of one's limitations. It relates to the duty of bringing one's commitments and undertakings into a reasonable relationship with one's real possibilities for acting upon the international environment. This is not by any means just a question of military strength, and particularly not of the purely destructive and ultimately self-destructive sort of strength to be found in the nuclear weapon. It is not entirely, or even mainly, a question of foreign policy. It is a duty that requires the shaping of one's society in such a manner that one has maximum control over one's own resources and maximum ability to employ them effectively when they are needed for the advancement of the national interest and the interests of world peace.

A country that has a budgetary deficit and an adverse trade balance both so fantastically high that it is rapidly changing from a major creditor to a major debtor on the world's exchanges, a country whose own enormous internal indebtedness has been permitted to double in less than six years, a country that has permitted its military expenditures to grow so badly out of relationship to the other needs of its economy and so extensively out of reach of political control that the annual spending of hundreds of billions of dollars on "defense" has developed into a national addiction—a country that, in short, has allowed its financial and material affairs to drift into such disorder, is so obviously living beyond its means, and confesses itself unable to live otherwise—is simply not in a position to make the most effective use of its own resources on the international scene, because they are so largely out of its control.

This situation must be understood in relationship to the exorbitant dreams and aspirations of world influence, if not world hegemony—the feeling that we must have the solution to everyone's problems and a finger in every pie—that continue to figure in the assumptions underlying so many American reactions in matters of foreign policy. It must also be understood that in world affairs, as in personal life, example exerts a greater power than precept. A first step along the path of morality would be the frank recognition of the immense gap between what we dream of doing and what we really have to offer, and a resolve, conceived in all humility, to take ourselves under control and to establish a better relationship between our undertakings and our real capabilities.

The second major positive imperative is one that also involves the husbanding and effective use of resources, but it is essentially one of purpose and policy.

Except perhaps in some sectors of American government and opinion, there are few thoughtful people who would not agree that our world is at present faced with two unprecedented and supreme dangers. One is the danger not just of nuclear war but of any major war at all among great industrial powers—an exercise which modern technology has now made suicidal all around. The other is the devastating effect of modern industrialization and overpopulation on the world's natural environment. The one threatens the destruction of civilization through the recklessness and selfishness of its military rivalries, the other through the massive abuse of its natural habitat. Both are relatively new problems, for the solution of which past experience affords little guidance. Both are urgent. The problems of political misgovernment, to which so much of our thinking about moral values has recently related, is as old as the human species itself. It is a problem that will not be solved in our time, and need not be. But the environmental and nuclear crises will brook no delay.

The need for giving priority to the averting of these two overriding dangers has a purely rational basis—a basis in national interest—quite aside from morality. For short of a nuclear war, the worst that our Soviet rivals could do to us, even in our wildest worst-case imaginings, would be a far smaller tragedy than that which would assuredly confront us (and if not us, then our children) if we failed to face up to these two apocalyptic dangers in good time. But is there not also a moral component to this necessity?

Of all the multitudinous celestial bodies of which we have knowledge, our own earth seems to be the only one even remotely so richly endowed with the resources that make possible human life—not only make it possible but surround it with so much natural beauty and healthfulness and magnificence. And to the degree that man has distanced himself from the other animals in such things as self-knowledge, historical awareness and the capacity for creating great beauty (along, alas, with great ugliness), we have to recognize a further mystery, similar to that of the unique endowment of the planet—a mystery that seems to surpass the possibilities of the purely accidental. Is there not, whatever the nature of one's particular God, an element of sacrilege involved in the placing of all this at stake just for the sake of the comforts, the fears and the national rivalries of a single generation? Is there not a moral obligation to recognize in this very uniqueness of the habitat and nature of man the greatest of our moral responsibilities, and to make of ourselves, in our national personification, its guardians and protectors rather than its destroyers?

This, it may be objected, is a religious question, not a moral-political one. True enough, if one will. But the objection invites the further question as to whether there is any such thing as morality that does not rest, consciously or otherwise, on some foundation of religious faith, for the renunciation of self-interest, which is what all morality implies, can never be rationalized by purely secular and materialistic considerations.

VI

The above are only a few random reflections on the great question to which this paper is addressed. But they would seem to suggest, in their entirety, the outlines of an American foreign policy to which moral standards could be more suitably and naturally applied than to that policy which we are conducting today. This would be a policy founded on recognition of the national interest, reasonably conceived, as the legitimate motivation for a large portion of the nation's behavior, and prepared to pursue that interest without either moral pretension or apology. It would be a policy that would seek the possibilities for service to morality primarily in our own behavior, not in our judgment of others. It would restrict our undertakings to the limits established by our own traditions and resources. It would see virtue in our minding our own business wherever there is not some overwhelming reason for minding the business of others. Priority would be given, here, not to the reforming of others but to the averting of the two apocalyptic catastrophes that now hover over the horizons of mankind.

But at the heart of this policy would lie the effort to distinguish at all times between the true substance and the mere appearance of moral behavior. In an age when a number of influences, including the limitations of the electronic media, the widespread substitution of pictorial representation for verbal communication, and the ubiquitous devices of "public relations" and electoral politics, all tend to exalt the image over the essential reality to which that image is taken to relate—in such an age there is a real danger that we may lose altogether our ability to distinguish between the real and the unreal, and, in doing so, lose both the credibility of true moral behavior and the great force such behavior is, admittedly, capable of exerting. To do this would be foolish, unnecessary and self-defeating. There may have been times when the United States could afford such frivolity. This present age, unfortunately, is not one of them.

EXORCISING WILSON'S GHOST:
MORALITY AND FOREIGN POLICY IN AMERICA'S THIRD CENTURY[2]

As the United States goes about the making of the president, 1988, it seems certain that issues of morality and foreign policy will be argued with much heat, if not commensurate light, during the campaign.

What ought the United States do in Central America? Is strategic defense a more morally acceptable means of security than deterrence maintained by the threat of mutual assured destruction? What responsibilities does America have for the cause of human rights in the world? What is a human right, for that matter? Do the world's democrats have a moral claim on America's support? And what happens when those claims abut other grave national security interests?

There is something quintessentially American about these arguments. It is hard to imagine their equivalents arising on the Quai d'Orsay [the French Foreign Office] or in Whitehall [the British Foreign Office]—much less, one hardly needs to add, in Eduard Shevardnadze's staff meetings. They crop up with impressive regularity in our public discourse for any number of reasons—among them, that Americans are an incorrigibly religious people who, since the days of John Winthrop and Roger William, have brought their religious convictions and the moral norms they derive therefrom into the public square. But the most important reason why the morality and foreign policy debate remains

[2]Reprint of an article by George Weigel, president of the James Madison Foundation in Washington, D.C. Reprinted from the Autumn 1987 issue of *The Washington Quarterly* (vol. 10, no. 4, pp. 31–40) by permission of the MIT Press, Cambridge, Massachusetts. Copyright © by the Center for Strategic and International Studies and the Massachusetts Institute of Technology.

a hardy perennial in the garden of American political controversy has to do with the very nature of the American experiment itself.

Unlike other nations, which are based on the realities of tribe, race, ethnicity, or language, the United States is a country whose casements rest on an idea. Thomas Jefferson expressed it succinctly in the Declaration of Independence: "All men are created equal." At Gettysburg, Abraham Lincoln described Jefferson's claim as a "proposition" that would always be tested by our public life. Here, argued the great Jesuit theologian John Courtney Murray, Lincoln was speaking with "conceptual propriety," for in philosophy a proposition is "the statement of a truth to be demonstrated." Jefferson's definition of the "American proposition" has had, and continues to have, a pronounced effect on the conduct of America's business with the world. In that sense, Murray's notion of a continually-tested proposition is validated by every morning's headlines.

Jefferson's claim was, of course, a moral claim. Its impact on U.S. foreign policy, for better and for worse and often for both, derives from its universality. The Founding Fathers did not pledge their "lives, fortunes, and sacred honor" to a narrow claim ("All English colonists living on the Eastern seaboard of North America between the Atlantic Ocean and the Mississippi River are created equal") but to a simple, flat, universal claim: All men are created equal. Moreover, the Declaration argued, this claim could be known by all men of good will. It did not derive from a sectarian religious tradition, but from human nature itself. "Nature, and Nature's God," had created all men equal.

Thus, from its inception, the American experiment was more than a matter of a new "is" in world affairs. The Founding Fathers asserted an "ought." Charles Krauthammer of *The New Republic* has made the connection between this "ought" and the distinctive character of American nationalism: "Our nationalism is unlike others, in that our very nationhood is bound up with and is meant to give expression to the idea of freedom." That this morally based nationalism would have its effect on U.S. foreign policy was as certain a speculation as one could have made, even in the days of America's hemispheric isolation. Given the right historical circumstances, Americans would have to deal with the world. And they would, inevitably, cast that encounter in terms that reflected their originating experience and continuing experiment.

No small part of our present difficulties with the morality and foreign policy debate derives from the historical circumstances in which that encounter happened in World War I. That it was Woodrow Wilson who first articulated the themes of America's entry as a great power onto the world stage has made an enormous difference. For Wilson embodied a specific form of American Protestant moral sensibility that has been the entry point for, as well as the chief defect of, the morality and foreign policy debate ever since April 1917.

Throughout the nineteenth century and well into the twentieth, the United States had a semi-established religion, what sociologist Peter Berger has described as *Kulturprotestantismus*. This generalized Protestant religiosity carried with it a particular understanding of morality, traces of which can be found in artifacts ranging from the McGuffey readers to the League of Nations Charter and the Kellogg-Briand Treaty.

It was a morality that found the good in the will of God, rather than in human reason. As Murray once described it, Kulturprotestantismus taught that " . . . the good is good because God commands it; the evil is evil because God forbids it." The notion that morality might have something to do with human reason and its capacity to discern moral norms from human nature and human history did not sit well.

The morality of Kulturprotestantismus likewise knew where one looked for the revelation of God's will: one looked to the Old and New Testaments. There was a fundamentalist current at play here. Scholarly biblical exegesis was not of much moment. One took the biblical texts as they stood, and applied them to the policy arena in a kind of one-to-one correspondence.

Wilson's morality also set great store by one's intentions. As Murray put it, "It set primary and controlling value on a sincerity of interior motives; what matters is not what you do but why you do it." This led rather easily to a form of extreme moral idealism, which taught that the motive of love which ought to inform one's dealings with one's fellows could be applied, forthwith, to relations between organized political communities. Thus individualism was a fourth distinctive element in the moral sensibility of Kulturprotestantismus: standards of Christian perfection applicable to the individual could also be applied to the behavior of states. Thus one could hope for, work for, and indeed expect the say when there would be no "moral problems" for domestic or international society, which blessed condition would automatically obtain if and when all men loved their neighbors.

This "older morality," as Murray was wont to call it, may have been marginally useful in providing rhetorical grease for America's sidestep into world politics. But it did little to illuminate those politics, and still less to provide moral standards for the formulation of policy. Its failure, though, should not be attributed to the fact that the world is an infinitely messy place, vastly plural in its religious, ethical, and ideological understandings and commitments, and thus constructed in a way that no moral norm could possibly be relevant to the design and conduct of U.S. foreign policy. Rather, the true fault lay in the concept of morality that was embedded in Kulturprotestantismus, and that can be aptly described as Wilsonian moralism. The deepest question to be addressed did not lie on the policy side of the morality and foreign policy dialectic. It lay on the first side of the equation. The priority question was, "What do we mean by 'morality'?"

A first and important cut at answering this question from outside boundaries of the liberal Protestant hegemony came in the work of Reinhold Niebuhr and other Christian realists. Niebuhr and colleagues such as John C. Bennett argued in the 1930s that Protestant moralism was utterly incapable of guiding the conduct of policy in the face of modern totalitarianism. Rather, the social ethicist had to recover a classic Christian understanding: that the Kingdom of God would not be a work of human hands. In this world as it is, Christian theology and social theory had to take account of the irreducible facts of tragedy, irony, and pathos in the human condition. To attempt blithely to transcend these facts of life in a fallen world, as Niebuhr believed Wilsonian moralism and Protestant liberalism did, was not only political folly; it was a corruption of Christian understandings of—in the classic images—the world, the flesh, and the devil. In the very first chapter of his seminal book, *Moral Man and Immoral Society*, Niebuhr stated flatly that "the dream of perpetual peace and brotherhood for human society will never be fully realized." That did not mean, as many have misinterpreted, that society and politics were somehow outside the boundaries within which moral reason could operate. It did mean that social ethics was a distinctive enterprise, which ought not be confused with the ethics of interpersonal relationships. One did not think morally about dealing with Hitler in precisely the same way that one reasoned morally about dealing with Aunt Mary.

Niebuhr's great accomplishment, which shaped and was shaped by his interaction with anti-Communist liberal internationalism of the early ADA sort, was to nail this point down for a generation: the voluntarism, fundamentalism, subjectivism, and individualism of the older morality made a chaos of both public policy and Christian doctrine. But Niebuhr did not venture very far beyond this essential contribution, and he never sketched a calculus by which moral reason could be applied, through the mediating virtue of prudence, to the design and conduct of foreign policy.

This was John Courtney Murray's critique of Niebuhr. Murray welcomed Niebuhr's insistence that complexity was the inescapable hallmark of policy choice; that historical circumstances had to be taken seriously; that the consequences of one's actions must be factored into the calculus of moral reason and policy choice; and that human tendencies toward evil were a built-in part of the human condition, not to be removed by therapy or baptism. In short, Niebuhr had dealt a serious blow to that sentimentalism which was a leitmotif of the older morality and a corrupting influence within it.

But Niebuhr had stopped too soon, Murray suggested. Niebuhr was correct to assert the distinctiveness of social ethics against the ethics of interpersonal relationships. But the problem posed by liberal Protestant individualism was, at bottom, a false problem, and Niebuhr's solution to it posed a new danger: to posit the distinction between social and interpersonal ethics without grounding both in the functions of human reason and its ability to apprehend moral norms through reflection on human nature and human history raised the prospect of social ethics simply dropping off the ledge of our public discourse.

Nor did the themes of irony, tragedy, and pathos, evocative as they were, provide much grist for a task that Murray deemed paramount: the creation of a public philosophy expressed in a mediating language that could cut across the pluralisms of Protestant/Catholic/Jewish and religious/secular in such a way that genuinely public moral argument, rather than public moral emoting, was made possible in American political culture.

What Reinhold Niebuhr offered, in short, was a sensibility that ought to furnish one corner of the intellect of anyone who dared to enter the minefield called morality-and-foreign-policy. But more than a Niebuhrian sensibility was needed, in Murray's judgment. One needed a natural law–based social ethic which recognized that society and the state had their own distinctive purposes, not to be confused with private purposes. One needed an ethic which acknowledged the centrality of national interest in the conduct of policy and was not embarrassed by it, but which related national interest to a larger scheme of national purpose by resolutely drawing the line at *raison d'etat* as a possible criterion for action. One needed a social ethic which knew that power—the ability to achieve a common purpose—was the central reality at the heart of any organized community. One needed a structure of moral reasoning which could distinguish, normatively, between power and sheer violence, and which could relate the proportionate and discriminate use of limited armed force to the pursuit of peace, security, and freedom. One needed, finally, a method of casuistry which could dialectically engage moral norms with messy human situations through the mediation of the central political virtue of prudence. One-to-one correspondences—between Scriptural texts or moral norms, and the exigencies of policy—should be held frankly suspect, and precisely on moral grounds. Moral reasoning was not a set of how-to-do-it instructions that might be followed by any dolt; it was a matter of endless argument, research, reflection, more argument, and empirical testing.

How does this question stand, as we enter America's third century, and, beyond the possible fascinations of intellectual history, why should those concerned with the day-to-day crises of power care anyway?

The second question is answered simply, if provocatively, by recognizing that the concept of value-free judgment in politics is an absurdity. There are no value-free judgments, no ethical free lunches. Every political judgment involves a calculus, usually inarticulate, involving questions of "ought" as well as "is." John F. Kennedy was simply in a rationalist Shangri-La when he told the graduates of Yale University in 1962 that the real problems of the modern world were not philosophical or ideological (and thus embroiled with issues of meaning and value) but technical and managerial. The central problem is not whether we shall apply what we understand to be moral norms and values to foreign policy, but how. The real issues have to do, as always, with the quality of moral reasoning that is brought to bear on a particular problem. And that must be of concern to anyone with a responsibility, in public or private life, for the business of America's encounter with the world.

As to the present quality of the argument, an exceedingly mixed picture presents itself, particularly as one surveys the American religious community, in which the morality and foreign policy debate is shaped to a considerable although not exclusive degree.

Intellectuals and activists in the great churches of mainline Protestantism—the various offshoots of Congregationalism, the Presbyterians, Methodists, and Episcopalians—seem to have reverted, in general, to a pre-Niebuhrian liberalism, now shaped by the personalist psychology of Carl Rogers, feminism, and the vulgarized Marxism that underlay some early forms of liberation theology. Mainline activist religious leaders show scant traces of a Niebuhrian sense of irony and ambiguity, and often seem more confident in their public policy judgments than in their theological convictions. The recent Methodist bishops' pastoral letter on nuclear weapons issues, "In Defense of Creation," was sharply criticized, for example by Duke Divinity School moral theologian Stanley Hauerwas, as one in which "the bishops feel more comfortable condemning SDI than they do in proclaiming God's soreveignty over our existence." (That Hauerwas is a principled pacifist added even more piquancy to his devastating critique of his bishops' work.) Then there is the Presbyterian Church–USA, which has produced a study guide asking whether it is not time for American Presbyterians to think of themselves as a resistance church, on the model of the "Confessing Church" of the Barmen Declaration in Nazi Germany. Such pronouncements have raised important countercurrents; one might note the formation of groups like Presbyterians for Democracy and Religious Freedom, in which former Undersecretary of the Navy R. James Woolsey has taken a leading role. But the mainline church bureaucracies, their principal ecumenical agencies, and the mainline Protestant peace movement remain firmly in the hands of those who would argue for some form or another of the confessing church model. This seems a rather unlikely position from which to broker a wide-ranging civic conversation on morality and foreign policy.

Resurgent Protestant evangelicalism might contribute to such a conversation. The National Association of Evangelicals, for example, has recently produced a "Guidelines" document for its new "Peace, Freedom, and Security Studies" program that challenges the mainline churches' theology and politics and calls on evangelical congregations and denominations to begin the kind of first-principles moral argument envisioned by Murray. That natural law forms of moral reasoning (even if identified by different terms, like "general revelation" or "two kingdoms") are not automatically ruled out of bounds in some evangelical intellectual circles suggests the possibility of an important new ecumenism.

This new ecumenism would engage, of course, Roman Catholic intellectuals, activists, and religious leaders. Here, one finds both good news and bad, from the point of view of the task identified by John Courtney Murray a generation ago. On the asset side of the ledger, there remains significant agreement among Catholic scholars in the United States that moralism remains an ever present danger, and that casuistry rooted in classic methods of moral reasoning is a moral imperative. Yet there is on the other hand a new Catholic moralism among activists and some bishops that occupies a considerable position in the American Catholic debate. Here, the traditional characteristics of Kulturprotestantismus—especially its fundamentalism and individualism—have been ecumenically transposed. Catholicism's rediscovery of its Scriptural heritage in the wake of the Second Vatican Council has been both a boon and a distraction on these questions. Murray used to tell of a distinguished journalist who was confused by the 1950s debate over morality and foreign policy because he could not understand what foreign policy had to do with the Sermon on the Mount; when asked by Murray why he deemed morality to be reducible to the Sermon on the Mount, he became even more confused and asked unhappily, "You mean it isn't?" That question is being regularly raised by Catholic activists today and suggests that one significant component of the American Catholic community will be of little help in constructing a public philosophy able to recreate public moral argument that is conducted without resort to biblical trump cards.

Some Jewish political intellectuals—one thinks immediately of Charles Krauthammer—are working hard at the problem of public moral argument on foreign policy issues. Other Jewish scholars, like Rabbi David Novak of Jewish Theological Seminary in New York, are deeply interested in the natural law tradition as it bears on issues of public policy.

Thus there is good reason to think that a new morality and foreign policy debate, exorcising Wilson's ghost and scounting out new intellectual terrain ahead of today's right- and left-wing moralisms, may be aborning. It will be an interestingly diverse argument, involving as it will Roman Catholics, evangelical Protestants, Jews, mainline Protestants who refuse to concede the field to the resistance enthusiasms of their brethren, and secular scholars who appreciate the imperative public need for a movement beyond the rock of moralism and the hard place of relativism and/or Realpolitik.

What would the argument focus on? In the first instance, it would have to address, in a publicly accessible way, the question of the very meaning of "moral reasoning." Themes for such an address have been sketched above. But what about the application of moral reason to the policy agenda? Where is there room for useful debate here? Two broad areas of concern suggest themselves to this observer.

First, assuming that the United States government is not filled with pacifists and/or radical neo-isolationists, there is inevitably going to be a military component to America's encounter with a persistently hostile world. This suggests that the intellectual and cultural health of just war theory—that is, our ability to think through the ways in which the proportionate and discriminate use of armed force can (and cannot) contribute to peace, security and freedom in the world—is of crucial importance.

Where is just war theory alive in American political culture? Where has it died? It is alive in our military manuals, in the Uniform Code of Military Justice, in the service academies and the officer corps. It is alive among political philosophers, even if, like Stanley Hoffman and Michael Walzer, they feel compelled to reinvent it. It is alive in international law, although in a truncated form. And it is alive among Roman Catholic, mainline and evangelical Protestant, and Jewish theologians, ethicists, and religious leaders. It is dead or dying among many religious peace activist intellectuals and ecclesiastical leaders, and among Realists like Robert Tucker who continue to insist that just war theory is a matter of squaring the circle.

A revivial of just war theory in the argument over morality and foreign policy would address, among other things, the new pressures that modern forms of political violence—terrorism, guerrilla warfare, low-intensity conflict—have put on the classic just war criteria. International law in its present form poses one set of problems, recognizing as it does that self-defense is the only legally legitimate reason to threaten or resort to force of arms. But what constitutes self-defense in a situation of chronic ideological and political conflict such as one finds in U.S.–Soviet relations? Can just war theory adequately ground the practice of deterrence, for example, and in what form? How does one discriminate between conbatants and noncombatants in guerrilla warfare? What is proportional use of armed force in Third World conflicts? How does one determine that the last resort has been reached, and armed force thus justified, in revolutionary situations? What does just war theory do to illuminate decisions faced by U.S. policymakers in a situation like Grenada, where the immediate threat to U.S. security is minimal but the possibilities for supporting democrats and displacing tyrants are great? And how, if at all, can just war theory's classic *ad bellum* criterion of "punishment for evil" as a legitimate moral reason for the resort to armed force help guide policy in the face of international terrorism, particularly if it is state sponsored? Absent persuasive answers to, or at least persuasive argument on, these pressing issues, one important resource for considering the relationship between moral norms and foreign policy practice may well continue to die the death of a thousand intellectual cuts in our political culture.

Such a death is also possible because just war theorists, in the main, have done a less than satisfactory job in relating their theory to the pursuit of peace. Classic just war theorists speak of the *ius ad bellum* (what William V. O'Brien has called "war-decision law") and the *ius in bello* ("war-conduct law," in O'Brien's terminology). But it can also be argued—and, in an American context, must be argued—that just war theory contains, in its interstices and its basic intellectual trajectory, an *ius ad pacem*, a concept of peace as rightly ordered political community. The resort to proportionate and discriminate armed force must be directed toward peace, which is to say toward the establishment of a minimum of public order in international affairs. How this can be done in a way that avoids the sentimentalities of much contemporary "world order" thinking is a large, although not impossible, task. But given the pressures put on the classic theory by modern forms of political violence and, perhaps above all, by the fact of nuclear weapons, a just war theory that does not address the nature and pursuit of peace is unlikely to play the significant role it should in American political discourse.

Second, liberation theologies have contributed what seems likely to be an enduring phrase to our morality and foreign policy vocabulary: there should be, they insist, a "preferential option for the poor" in devising policy affecting the world's underclass. Thanks to the work of Peter Berger, Michael Novak, and others, one can speculate and hope that the future debate on such questions of development economics will focus on means, rather than on whether such an option exists.

But there is another related issue remaining to be pressed here. Should there be a "preferential option for freedom" in U.S. foreign policy? Do the world's democrats, in other words, have a special moral claim on our attention and assistance?

Experienced theorists and policymakers are cautious, indeed even skeptical, about letting the American evangelical spirit loose in the world. There are surely cautions to be observed here, as the wreckage of the presidencies of Woodrow Wilson and, more recently, Jimmy Carter, attest. But one ought to draw and maintain a clear distinction between healthy realism and cynicism. The ghost of Woodrow Wilson is not going to be exorcised by the incantations of a Realpolitik that cuts straight across the grain of our national character.

Moreover, something that looks suspiciously like a democratic revolution is going on throughout the world. Fragile as the democratic achievements of recent Latin American and Philippine history may appear, they are genuine achievements. They reflect human aspirations that will not be ignored. Furthermore, there are strategic reasons supporting a "preferential option for freedom." Democratic ideology is the most persuasive answer the West can offer to the current Soviet public diplomacy barrage. Historically, democracies do not go to war with each other, and thus the democratic revolution serves the cause of peace. And, on Berger's and others' research, there would seem to be connections between democratic, or at least predemocratic, societies and economic development. Put the other way around, and as illustrated by the "four little dragons" of East Asia, economic achievement creates pressures for democratization which, if unaddressed, will eventually threaten economic achievement.

Therefore, one can make the case that a "preferential option for freedom" should occupy a central place in a post-Wilsonian consensus on morality and foreign policy. As Roman Catholic Archbishop J. Francis Stafford of Denver argued in a recent pastoral letter, America should "be a leader for ordered liberty, in and among nations." The world will not become Connecticut in the twinkling of an eye, and foreign policy realists rightly warn against the perennial temptations of American universalism. But there are sufficient numbers of people, in transitional Third World societies in particular, who wish, if not to be in Connecticut, then at least to be ruled by something better than *caudillos*—peoples whose aspirations we ignore at our peril in the great contest with Soviet Leninism throughout the Third World.

One can also find, in the work of dissident intellectuals such as Czechoslovakia's Vaclav Havel, Poland's Adam Michnik, and Hungary's George Konrad, claims that Western policy should support the rebuilding of "the civil society" in Soviet-dominated Central Europe. Havel, Michnik, and Konrad are not so naive as to think that democracy is about to break out in Stalin's empire; but they do argue that Western support for building some measure of predemocratic institutional and cultural distance between the individual and the Leninist state serves the causes of human freedom and, ultimately, peace. Aaron Wildavsky has made similar proposals for a U.S. policy of "containment plus pluralization" vis-à-vis the Soviet Union itself.

The broad and bipartisan congressional support now enjoyed by the National Endowment for Democracy (NED) suggests that the democratic revolution has, in its various forms, struck a deep chord in the American conscience. Yet there are moral quandaries that deserve more public argument. On one hand, how should the claims of a country's democrats be weighed against the dangers of instability in the face of an aggressive Leninist enemy which, in the case of South Korea, is as close to Seoul as Dulles airport is to Capitol Hill? On the other hand, how do we determine when and if frustrated pressures for democratization will themselves lead to instabilities that threaten freedom? Then there is the question of where this dimension of the morality and foreign policy debate will be "located" in American political culture. For example, as many religious activists continue to beat a retreat from the bourgeois reformism of Corazon Aquino in the Philippines, who will make the moral case for democracy as the Philippines are caught between traditional authoritarian pressures and the New People's Army? Finally, there is the general question, by no means settled, of whether America has any business forcing change in other societies. By what authority do we conduct interventions for democracy around the world? A publicly persuasive answer to that question—an answer that cuts across partisan, denominational, and ideological grounds—is essential for the long-term stability of initiatives such as NED.

Americans like problems that can be solved with some finality. We have a cultural predisposition to avoid debates, like that involving morality and foreign policy, which by nature are open ended and perennial. But perennial need not mean "circular." It can mean, simply, perennial—and one can hope that such arguments lead, in time, to wisdom in policy-making as well as to shelves of scholarly books. The path beyond circularity in the American morality and foreign policy debate will be open, to return to the beginning, when we recover (or, in some cases, discover) that the key issue is the nature of moral reasoning itself.

Those committed to such a recovery or discovery can find inspiration (and perhaps chagrined comfort) in Jacques Maritain's description of the plight of the social ethicist. In *Man and the State*, Maritain wrote:

Moralists are unhappy people. When they insist on the immutability of moral principles, they are reproached for imposing unlivable requirements on us. When they explain the way in which those immutable principles are to be put into force, they are reproached for making morality relative. In both cases, however, they are only upholding the claims of reason to direct life.

The Niebuhrian/realist rejection of moralism has been a necessary and cleansing exercise in this "nation with a soul of a church," as Chesterton once described the United States. But the realist tendency to identify morality exclusively with the moralism that characterized pre-Niebuhrian liberal Protestantism and that characterizes post-Niehbuhrian thinking on these issues in a depressingly large segment of the American religious community repeats the mistake it attempts to correct. There is another way to go at this, and that is to rediscover the tradition of moral reasoning as exemplified (but hardly exhausted) by the natural law tradition of Murray and Maritain. If, with Maritain, we believe that reason rather than unbridled passion ought to direct life (and even public policy), there is considerable work to be done in nailing down that claim by reconstructing the way in which we conduct public moral argument over America's right role in world affairs.

MORALITY AND THE REAGAN DOCTRINE[3]

As heir to the European colonial powers, the United States is a status quo power. The United States, particularly under FDR, did favor decolonization (much to the displeasure of Britain and France) but took upon itself the task of preserving the Western orientation of the new states (e.g., in the Persian Gulf, Vietnam) and of weak, dependent old states (Greece, Turkey) against the threats and ambitions of the new have-not power, the Soviet Union.

Next March marks the 40th anniversary of the formal declaration of this American role: "It must be the policy of the United States to support free peoples who are resisting attempted subjugation by armed minorities or by outside pressures." The Truman Doctrine set the United States on the side of legitimate governments against insurgencies. Starting with Greece, and extending later to the postcolonial successor governments of the Third World, the United States has resisted guerrilla insurgencies, occasionally with men, often with matériel, always with rhetoric. "The world is not static, and the status quo is not sacred," said Truman in his Joint Address to Congress, "But we cannot allow changes in the status quo in violation of the Charter of the United Nations by such methods as coercion, or by such subterfuges as political infiltration."

Forty years later, the Soviet Union is a full-fledged superpower with an impressive array of colonies. Although not yet a status quo power, it has much to defend. Today in several crucial regions, the United States and the Soviet Union find themselves in historically reversed roles. Soviets and their clients act as the status quo power, learning everything from counterinsurgency to the proper uses of international law and the World Court. And the United States finds itself supporting guerrilla insurgencies in four corners of the earth, Afghanistan, Angola, Cambodia, and Nicaragua. The American policy that declares the legitimacy of American support for these wars is known as the Reagan Doctrine.

[3]Reprint of an article by Charles Krauthammer, senior editor and columnist for *The New Republic. The New Republic*, S. 8, 1986, pp. 17–24. Reprinted by permission of Charles Krauthammer © 1986.

The Reagan Doctrine is not a one-man or one-party show. Support for each of these guerrilla armies has been approved by Congress. True, there is no great popular support for these enterprises. But then there never is for intervention (except following a direct attack on the United States), and only rarely for any foreign policy initiative in the absence of a crisis. Public opinion polls taken after the declaration of the Truman Doctrine showed a majority favoring economic aid, but 60 percent opposed military aid, either in the form of supplies or of military advisers. By a 2-to-1 margin, Americans thought that military aid to Greece would increase the likelihood of war with Russia, and that the problem should be turned over to the U.N., yesterday's Contadora. Indeed, were there a referendum today on, say, keeping American troops in Korea, or on spending $150 billion a year to defend our European allies and Japan, popular support would hardly be greater that it is for the Reagan Doctrine.

In any case, the Reagan Doctrine of active, military support for guerrilla war is current American policy, initiated by the president and supported by Congress. It has an obvious strategic logic as a post-Vietnam (i.e., only indirectly interventionist) strategy for challenging the most recent and most vulnerable acquisitions of the Soviet empire. But for a democracy, and particularly one founded on a political idea, strategy cannot be enough. Any foreign policy must meet a second test. That test is ideological—moral, if you will. The Reagan Doctrine may be strategically compelling. But is it wrong?

The objections fall into three categories. The first objection is to intervention generally, on the grounds that whatever fine values (e.g., freedom) we think motivate our interventions, what we are really engaged in is the pursuit of American power and interests.

The second objection concerns only a specific form of intervention: intervention on the side of insurgency. Trying to overthrow governments is both illegal and immoral. Indeed, our engagement in this enterprise represents the Sovietization of American strategy. The inviolability of sovereignty is one of the oldest international principles. Its violation is Soviet practice, declared by Khrushchev at the World Communist Party Congress of 1960 as the doctrine of "national liberation" and practiced by every Soviet leader before and since. Now, after 40 years of cold war, we have finally succumbed to the tactics of our enemies. And, by sinking to their moral level, we have forfeited a large part of the war.

The third objection has to do not with ends but with means, guerrilla means. Guerrilla war is morally problematic because it is, by nature, a form of warfare that deliberately blurs the line between civilian and military. It thus challenges the conventional and consensual standards of ethical combat. If we support guerrilla war, does that not mean that we, like the Soviets, put in with terrorism, torture, and assassination?

I. The Critique of Interventionism

Anti-interventionism, the polite word for isolationism, is a popular and highly pedigreed American foreign policy. For some, such as George Kennan, anti-interventionism has nothing to do with moral questions. Indeed, they profess to be anti-moralists. They merely believe it is hopelessly imprudent, an example of the triumph of American innocence over American intelligence, for the United States to involve itself in conflicts that have no direct effect on its survival.

But Kennan's bloodless amoralism is unattractive to most Americans. The more powerful strain of American anti-interventionism is moral. And it comes in two versions. One is to say that the United States goes abroad in search not of freedom but of markets. The more modern, less crudely Marxist (or more precisely: Leninist) version goes now by the name of "moral equivalence": whatever we may tell ourselves, the United States intervenes abroad for the same reason any great power does—power.

One must not, and cannot, deny that considerations of power or economic advantage motivate American intervention. Considerations of interest motivate all intervention, current and historical, American and otherwise. And they should. Diplomacy is not philanthropy. Foreign policy is necessarily mostly about interests. But that does not mean that we cannot then distinguish between policies that are moral and those that are not. The fact that one may have strategic interests does not mean that one's intervention does not also have a genuinely moral purpose and does not produce a morally defensible result. True, the American imperium is about power, but power in the service of certain values.

These values we hold, domestically, to be not only good but self-evidently good. And as we have gone abroad, we have spread them. In Europe, the line where American armies stopped at the end of World War II marks the limits of free, self-governing societies. Every inch of soil that lies behind American lines is now a liberal democracy. And elsewhere, where liberal democracy has not been achieved, American-made or American-supported frontiers—the DMZ in Korea, the Strait of Formosa, the Thai-Cambodian border—divide better from worse.

To be sure, liberty has not always been the American purpose. Guatemala 1954 exemplifies American banana diplomacy, undertaken under the assumptions that democracy is not a real option in the Third World, and that interest is the only relevant consideration. But history is not destiny, and today's America is not Teddy Roosevelt's or Eisenhower's or even that imagined by Ronald Reagan, the candidate. Because of many factors—our experience in Vietnam, the decline of race stereotypes in American consciousness and culture, the recent startling success of democracy in Latin America and elsewhere, and, most importantly, the disastrous consequences of our long-term postwar support for dictators like Batista and Somoza—democracy in the Third World has become, for the right as well as the left, a principal goal of American foreign policy. The last of the unconverted, Jesse Helms, has done his best to make the point. His bitter quarrel with the Reagan administration is precisely over the State Department's advancement of democracy, rather than blind anti-communism, as a guiding foreign policy principle.

Today's anti-imperialist case is an echo of the belief, fashionable at the height of the Vietnam War, that American power was, perhaps despite itself, a force for evil in the world. That echo is heard today only on the extreme left of the Democratic Party, and even there in muted form. Jesse Jackson carries the idea that American foreign policy is necessarily intervening on the wrong side of history. Five years ago that sentiment could emanate from mainstream Democrats, such as Senator Christopher Dodd of Connecticut who, at the time, characterized our choice in El Salvador as either "to move with the tide of history" or "stand against it." Fewer and fewer Democrats say that today.

It is an argument that has suffered much from history, the history that followed American failures in Vietnam and elsewhere, where the successor regimes have proven far more tyrannous, ruthless, and, in some cases, barbaric than the regimes we were supporting. Cuba, Vietnam, Cambodia, Iran, and now Nicaragua. The sweeping anti-interventionist argument, based on moral—i.e., anti-imperial—grounds, is a slogan in search of an applicable history.

II. The Critique of Insurgency

One need not be a pan-isolationist (though it helps) to oppose the Reagan Doctrine and its enthusiasm for insurgency. Indeed, the mainstream position of the Democratic Party approves American intervention in support of counterinsurgency in, for example, El Salvador and the Philippines, and opposes American intervention in support of insurgency in Nicaragua and Angola. It is opposed, then, not to intervention in general, but to a particular kind, the kind that tries to topple legitimate governments. It can live quite comfortably with the Truman Doctrine. But it questions the morality of going around trying to change governments we do not like. On three related grounds: world order, international law, and popular will.

Order. When we speak of order in the international arena, we mean two things. One is peace, the other is rules. The first is concrete: you start a war, you destroy the peace of a region, of a country, of families. The other is abstract. You start a war and, it is said, you injure the structure of international relations, including international law. World order enthusiasts speak of a "web of international relations," the implication of the metaphor being that if it is weakened here, it threatens to unravel there.

Consider first, order as peace. There must always be a moral presumption for peace. War means death. You must therefore have a good reason to start one, particularly one in which you seek to overthrow the government of another country. One such good reason is rescue, freeing a subjugated people from particularly oppressive rule. George McGovern proposed American intervention against the Cambodian regime of Pol Pot. Tanzania invaded Uganda in 1979 and ousted Idi Amin. And in 1983, the United States invaded Grenada and rid the island of its Marxist-Leninist rulers, much to the relief of its people.

Reagan Doctrine opponents would say that the degree of malignity of Pol Pot or Amin or Coard might justify unilateral intervention, but that in Reagan Doctrine countries today that is not the case. Rescue can justify invasion. Unfreedom cannot.

But to grant that is merely to say that the United States may not unilaterally invade other countries in the name of liberation, that it may not arrogate to itself the decision of whether freedom is a higher value than peace in these countries. But the Reagan Doctrine is not about invasion. It is about helping one side in a civil war. In Reagan Doctrine conflicts, the question of breaching the peace has been pre-empted. There already is civil war. A large number of people in a country have concluded—at the risk of their own lives and the suffering of their countrymen—that freedom is more precious to them than peace. The question then is not whether to give peace a chance but whether to give one side (generally, the weaker side) a chance.

Now, we may not agree exactly where the threshold that justifies an indigenous insurrection lies, but we can agree that it is lower than that for a foreign (even if benevolent) invasion. The former need not prove, say, genocide. Oppression will do. For Jonas Savimbi or Adolfo Calero to justify leading a rebellion requires less of a provocation than for Ronald Reagan to launch a liberating invasion.

Yet a Calero still needs reasons. Order (as peace) has its claims. It requires those who propose to breach the peace to produce reasons: a history of oppression, the call of freedom, and the like. Jefferson compiled an impressive list of grievances the redress of which are morally superior to order. (And leaving aside the question of whether Calero is Jefferson, one is hard-pressed to argue that the oppression suffered by the American colonists was worse than that experienced now by Nicaraguans, Angolans, Afghans, or Cambodians.)

We believe in freedom. That may not be enough reason to disturb the peace in places where there is no freedom. But if indigenous rebels, claiming their right to freedom, meet the (lesser) requirements to justify revolution and call for American support, it is hard to see what morally proscribes us from responding.

But by responding are we not jeopardizing order in another sense, order as rules? By showing disrespect for the rules against non-intervention and particularly against overthrowing a legitimate government, do we not weaken the fabric of international society?

The case for world order is this: the international arena is not quite a state of nature. There is a fragile structure. That structure depends on all states adhering to certain rules. The most basic of these is respect for sovereignty. The West (and the United States, in particular) is the great inventor and upholder of this order. If it goes around breaking it to suit other ends, what will be left of it?

This is a familiar argument generally made by pragmatists. But is it a moral argument? Is order—the predictable, non-threatening conduct of international affairs according to rules—a moral value? Even the great anti-moralist, Hans Morgenthau, felt compelled to answer yes. True, he says, in the international arena there is no morality; it is only within states that a moral order can exist. "There is a profound and neglected truth hidden in Hobbes's extreme dictum that the state creates morality as well as law and that there is neither morality nor law outside the state." Vis-à-vis each other, states are not moral agents; vis-à-vis their own citizens, they are. However, since world order is the necessary condition for the stability of individual states, world order becomes the indispensable condition for the existence of any moral order.

Thus order achieves moral dignity (Morgenthau's phrase), instrumentally. Though not itself a moral value, it permits the survival of moral values. But it is one thing to say that order is thus, in a backhanded way, a moral good. It is quite another to elevate it to the status of supreme good, which is what those who oppose the Reagan Doctrine on the grounds that it is wrong to overthrow legitimate governments must argue.

There are other goods more important than order. There are wrongs worth righting even at the cost of injuring order. To demonstrate this, one does not have to resort to the obvious and all-purpose example of a war against Hitler. Consider the supreme principle of the Organization of African Unity: in order to minimize conflict, colonial boundaries, however wrongly drawn, are to be the basis of the new sovereignties of Africa. This is the perfect example of an otherwise arbitrary rule that, because of its contribution to order, acquires moral status. Yet: Biafra rejected that principle when it declared its independence. In pressing its anti-secessionist war, Nigeria was upholding that principle. Whether that declaration was a good idea is not the point. The

point is that the "order" principle does not tell you on which side
of this war morality lay.

There is one exception: nuclear order. If disorder takes the
form of a third world war, then the defenders of the status quo
have a winning case. Liberating, say, Czechoslovakia does not
warrant the risks it entails. But the brushfire conflicts of the Reagan Doctrine are not wars over which the superpowers are themselves going to go to war. Thus when critics of the Reagan
Doctrine argue in the name of order, they mean not nuclear
peace but the status quo. It is a profoundly reactionary position.
There are things worse than disorder. A major premise of the
Reagan Doctrine is that living under a Leninist dictatorship is one
of them.

But there is something even more wrong with the order-as-
rules argument: the assumption that, on the question of subverting and overthrowing existing regimes, there is a world order to
be violated in the first place. In fact, there is not. At best there
is only half an order. The Soviet system proclaimed rejection
of the idea with its policy of support for "wars of national
liberation."

Those taken with the "web" metaphor sometimes argue that
if we start supporting guerrillas where we want, they will support
guerrillas where they want. The fact is, they already support
guerrillas where they want, and have been doing so wherever it
suits their interests going back to Greece. The Soviet bloc does
not have to learn its internationalism from the West. Quite the
contrary.

In some spheres of international life there is an order. All
states adhere to the postal code because they recognize that adhering to this set of rules brings long-term advantages that out-
weigh the short-term gain that would come from breaking them.
But that is simply not the case with the entirely different sphere
of international order having to do with military action and violations of sovereignty. In this case, the existence of some order is
a convenient Western fiction. It admits to Soviet "violations," as
if these were not systematic and intentional. The word
"violations" implies that a pre-existing norm is abused. In fact,
systematic violations of a norm by one of the two major parties
pledged to it renders it nonexistent. It does not enjoy a platonic
life outside of history.

International Law. But should we not respect the rules because they are law? The unsentimental case against assisting insurgency is the need for order. The sentimental case is the imperative of international law: that we are contractually bound, treaty bound, morally bound to obey it, just as individuals are enjoined to obey domestic law; that, whatever the theory underlying international law, it has a moral claim on us; and that therefore "illegal" violations of sovereignty are immoral. In the case of Nicaragua, the World Court has just ruled that American actions in Nicaragua violate international law on not one but ten counts.

The Nicaragua case is a particularly elegant example of the absurdity of such rulings. Elegant, because Nicaragua at first openly, and then, for prudential reasons, covertly, has been the principal supplier and sanctuary for the Salvadoran insurgency. A regime that at one point publicly declared its support for "liberation movements" to be not simply policy but an internationalist obligation then proceeds to the World Court (and now— the ultimate homage of vice to virtue—to American courts) to declare illegal precisely such actions by the United States.

Why should the democratic world then adhere to such a law? Either because (*a*) the underlying basis of the law—the need for rules of order in international life—is morally compelling (which I have considered above); or (*b*) the promise to do so is morally compelling. Consider b. We solemnly promised. But surely, if the moral obligation is sanctity of contract, and the other major party to the contract is given to repeated, systematic, and open "violations," then the obligation, like the contract, is rendered void. The point is not that Nicaragua violated the law and therefore it is not binding. The point is that Nicaragua (and Cuba and the Soviet Union) don't consider the law binding—on them—in principle. That is why it is no longer binding on other parties.

Does that mean that all contracts are void, that all of international law is useless? Do we, for example, throw out the Geneva conventions? No. The fallacy again is to see "international law" as a seamless whole. There are distinctions to be made.

International law encompasses a variety of norms with very different moral valences. Conventions (like the 200-mile fishing limit) require reciprocity to be useful. Moral imperatives (like proscriptions against the maltreatment of prisoners of war) do not. If one side begins torturing its prisoners of war, it does not follow that the other side may do the same. Similarly, if one side in a war uses terror (e.g., deliberate attacks on innocent civilians), that does not excuse the use of that tactic by the other side. Moral imperatives command no matter what happens on the other side. Conventions have no meaning unless adhered to by both sides.

The rule prohibiting intervention against existing governments, like the OAU rule against secession, is an order-contributing convention. Respect for sovereignty in itself is not a moral imperative. It cannot be. The sanctity of sovereignty enshrines a radical moral asymmetry. It grants legitimacy and thus protection to whoever has guns and powder enough to be in control of a government. Those challenging that government, the Salvadoran no less than the Nicaraguan guerrillas, have no standing before the World Court. They cannot get a ruling, for whatever it's worth, against their government. Unlike domestic courts, it is an arena for the haves only.

Popular Will. But is there not a third reason why intervening to overthrow other governments is wrong? Not because it threatens order, nor because we promised not to do so, but because it is wrong for one people to impose its will upon another? Yes, but that assumes that overthrowing a government is necessarily to oppose the will of the people, which, in turn, assumes that governments reflect the will of the people. This is true of democracies. It is not true of dictatorships. It cannot be true that if, say, Aquino had requested outside intervention last February, giving it would have been wrong because it was one people imposing its will on another. Dictators are in the business of imposing their will on unwilling people. Deposing them may be wrong for other reasons (order, promises), but not on the grounds of violating a people's autonomy.

For some ctitics, popular will is a crucial determinant of the morality of intervention. Michael Walzer opposes American support to the Nicaraguan *contras* on moral grounds but says, "I would feel differently about a genuinely popular struggle."

I would accept Walzer's popular will condition. So does Arturo Cruz. In Cruz's first, somewhat anguished, declarations of support for the *contras*, he said that he was prepared to join and to lead because (among other reasons) the *contras* had become an authentic national resistance. The difference, then, between Walzer and Cruz becomes an empirical one: Is the current resistance truly popular?

One does not have to believe that Cruz or Robelo or Calero are national heroes to believe that the resistance itself, decentralized and fought on many fronts, represents an authentic "revolt of Nicaraguans against oppression by other Nicaraguans" (Cruz's phrase). Are they a majority? No one knows. Despotisms don't permit such facts to be ascertained. How does one prove, or know, whether the NLF commanded a majority of South Vietnamese opinion? What counts is whether large sectors of the nation are engaged in resistance. In Nicaragua, I would argue, they are. Some of it is armed, some is unarmed, though it gives obvious, if veiled, support to the armed resistance. (For example, the writings in the *Washington Post* of *La Prensa* editor Roberto Cardenal Chamorro and Cardinal Obando y Bravo are both clearly in support of the resistance.) True, there is, as yet, no action in the cities. That is difficult against an efficient secret police, such as that at the disposal of Tomás Borge. But is the Nicaraguan resistance any less popular than that in El Salvador? Or than the Sandinista resistance in its fifth year (1966)? Or than the Sandinista dictatorship today?

The case against assisting rebels is weak enough. Ironically, it is fairly well undermined by a remarkable detail in the World Court's recent long and otherwise unremarkable decision on Nicaragua. It seems, according to a majority of the Court, that intervention is against international law, unless it involves "the process of decolonization," an exception with which "the Court is not here concerned." This detail is remarkable not because it shows the anti-Western bias of the majority of the Court— "colonialism," in UNese, is an exclusively Western practice—but because of what it says about the principles that underlie the nonintervention rule.

Popular will? Presumably, intervening against colonialism cannot violate a people's autonomy because no people can conceivably prefer colonial status to freedom. The Reagan Doctrine assumes (with good historical reason) that no people willingly bear a communist dictatorship.

Order? The Court's exception also establishes that there are values higher than order, and decolonization is one of them. The Reagan Doctrine does not really challenge that premise. It merely says that any definition of colonialism that excludes Soviet colonialism and any definition of wars of national liberation that

excludes anti-communist insurgencies makes for moral nonsense.
(To hold that Western colonialism is the only evil that justifies intervention leads to other interesting moral nonsense. Foreign
support for the insurgencies in British East Africa—i.e., before
independence—would be justified. The Tanzanian invasion of
Uganda that toppled Idi Amin 17 years after decolonization
would not.)

To say that the rules against intervention or against supporting insurgencies are unconvincing is not to say that all guerrilla
wars are morally worthy of support. How to decide? I suggest
three tests.

One, already discussed, is evidence of popular support.

A second is ends. Ultimately we decide which insurgencies are
worthy of support and which are not in the same way we decide
about other causes: we ask what they are trying to achieve. I accept the World Court's view that there are higher principles than
non-intervention and higher values than order. The real moral
question is: What are those higher values? I would accept decolonization as one, but would generalize it to read freedom,
meaning a regime of democratic rule and individual rights, or,
where that is not possible (Afghanistan, for example), of national
independence and the relative freedom of living under a traditional govenment rather than under communism.

Because ends are so important, I make an exception for the
administration's (and Congress's) position on the Cambodian insurgency. The forces of Son Sann and Sihanouk are worthy of
support. However, the Khmer Rouge, whose aims for Cambodia
are not a mystery, so dominate the insurgency that it is they who
are likely to rule in a post-revolutionary Cambodia. Although it
might serve Western interests, that is not an outcome that the
West can in good conscience promote.

The same three tests would apply in, say, South Africa. I see
no moral objection to supporting those trying to overthrow the
apartheid regime, even if by force of arms. The usual question—
are they for or against violence?—is not the relevant moral
one. Oppression justifies violent resistance in South Africa just as
it does in Nicaragua or Aghanistan. The question of whether one
should support one opposition group or another should hinge on
other considerations: popular support, ends (what kind of South
Africa is this group likely to produce should it prevail), and
means.

III. The Critique of Guerrilla War

Which brings us to the last, and, in my view, most serious moral objection to the Reagan Doctrine, or, for that matter, any policy or theory that proposes support for insurgent guerrillas. The problem is not the ethics of intervention or even of insurgency. It is with the way irregular war is fought.

Guerrilla war is the most morally troubling type of war because its technique is to subvert one of the most fundamental rules of war, the distinction between soldier and civilian. That does not mean that there are no rules in guerrilla war. The conventional code of distinguishing between uniformed soldier and ordinary civilian gives way in guerrilla war to a "political code" in which the crucial distinction is between those who are and are not agents of a (perceived) oppressive political structure (even—perhaps especially—if they are not soldiers, since soldiers are often conscripts just carrying out orders).

The current American anti-war movement reached a peak of indignation two years ago with the publication of a CIA manual that talked about "neutralizing," i.e., assassinating, Sandinista officials. One does not recall the Vietnam anti-war movement being similarly disturbed over the massive NLF assassination campaign of the early '60s, which killed 7,500 South Vietnamese government officials. But hypocrisy is not the issue. The issue is whether assassination of officials is a war crime. In a closely argued analysis of the NLF assassination campaign, in *Just and Unjust Wars*, Walzer shows—convincingly, I believe—why not. Since guerrilla war is by nature a political ("hearts and minds") struggle, and village officials are agents of the enemy political structure, they have a role somewhat analogous to that of military officials in a conventional war. With political power comes responsibility, and danger. "I do not mean to defend assassination . . . and yet 'just assassinations' are at least possible, and men and women who aim at that kind of killing and renounce every other kind need to be marked off from those who kill at random—not as doers of justice, necessarily, for one can disagree about that, but as revolutionaries with honor."

There are limits, however. Walzer rightly finds "disturbing" the NLF's expansion of the category of official (and, thus, of assassination target) to include even low-level, non-political functionaries and private notables who were pro-government. The line of where real political power ends is, he argues, an indistinct one, but in principle it exists. "Assuming that the regime is in fact oppressive, one should look for agents of oppression and not simply for government agents."

A good line. It implies immediately that one should not look for ordinary civilians, who are agents of humanity only. The practice of deliberately targeting random innocents has another name: terrorism. The exigencies of guerrilla war are no excuse for terrorism. Assassination of (perceived) agents of oppression, problematic as it is, is one thing; the murder of innocents is another. Even guerrilla war has rules.

One, therefore, is the impermissibility of terrorism. Simple enough. But guerrilla war has a subtler dynamic. Guerrillas classically try to make *the government* resort to terror. They try to provoke increased repression—"heightening the contradictions" —in order to build the insurgency and undermine popular support for the government. As the contradictions heighten and the war gets dirtier, then, who is to blame?

Walzer argues that at a certain point when an insurgency has grown sufficiently large and has acquired sufficient popular support, it becomes truly a "people's war." The distinction between soldier and civilian has then indeed been erased, and the government finds itself at war with a people. "It is no longer an anti-guerrilla but an anti-social war. . . . " Counterinsurgency becomes a form of genocide. At that point, no matter what the aims of either side, the means that the government must use to fight become so evil as to make any end morally insupportable.

Did the Vietnam War ever reach this critical point of popular support, where it was the United States and its client army against the people? It is difficult to argue that now, particularly given what we have learned from the testimony of former NLF officials. In fact, the NLF was largely sacrificed in the Tet offensive of 1968. Thereafter the armed forces of Hanoi bore the brunt of the war and were the agents of victory. But if Saigon's war was not then truly a "war against the people," that gravely weakens the argument that the means the Saigon side had to use were necessarily morally impermissible.

Hence an updated, slightly modified version of this argument. It says not that the communist side of the war was "the people" but that it was implacable and relentless. It was the utter tenacity of the guerrillas–North Vietnamese that made the war, for our side, morally unfightable. The communists would not relent whatever the suffering, most of which was incurred on their side. Because of that, we really did have to destroy too much of Vietnam in order to save it. Thus, however just the aim—and in retrospect it is more just now than it had appeared at the time—the means of conducting that war were too awful to sustain *any* purpose.

At least that was said when the United States was in the counterinsurgency business. Now the United States finds itself in several places around the world in the insurgency business. If guerrillas now are deemed the ones morally obliged to cease and desist, a simple rule emerges regarding guerrilla war and just means: if you are fighting communists, dedicated relentless communists, you are morally obliged to quit; it does not matter whether they are the government or the guerrillas; they will escalate whatever the civilian toll; therefore the injustice of war's means outweighs the value of any possible end. I am not prepared to say this. It is a perverse political reflex that takes a moral stance against the suffering of guerrilla war but manages to assign blame for bringing it on to whatever side, insurgent or counterinsurgent, happens to be fighting communists (and thus is aligned with the United States).

On the contrary. Each side is responsible for its own actions only. Now that the Soviets and their clients find themselves in the counterinsurgency business, they, like the United States in Vietnam, are to be held accountable for means they use to suppress revolt. Reagan Doctrine guerrilla forces are entitled to the same moral standard that was extended to the NLF in Vietnam.

Each side accounts for its own actions. And, we agree, those actions, even in guerrilla war, must exclude terrorist means. What, then, of the atrocities (euphemistically called "human rights violations") committed by the anti-communist guerrillas supported by the Reagan Doctrine? This is not a minor problem. Indeed, it is such a crucial moral challenge to the Reagan Doctrine that, in the case of Nicaragua, supporters have pushed very hard for ways (structures, procedures, increased direct American control) to reduce the abuses.

By abuses I do not mean blowing up power lines, burning crops, and mining harbors, tactics that have aroused much protest in the United States. The moral indignation here seems to me misplaced. Attacks on property seem a far more humane way to conduct a war than attacks on even military targets, since this often means soldiers, who are apt to die as a result.

By abuses I mean terror and torture. If these are committed by members of an armed force, its cause is not necessarily delegitimized. These abuses always occur. The important question is whether or not the use of such means is deliberate policy, and whether the army, guerrilla or otherwise, establishes rules prohibiting such conduct and takes steps to enforce the rules.

It seems to me that the guerrilla army that least meets these criteria is in Afghanistan. Its guerrilla force, for example, rarely takes prisoners, except a few for purposes of propaganda or exchange. Yet the Afghan rebels enjoy unflinching liberal support. On Capitol Hill, Afghanistan is perhaps the holiest cause, even among critics of the Reagan Doctrine in Nicaragua and Angola. On October 4, 1984, the House passed, without dissent, the Ritter resolution "to encourage and support the people of Afghanistan in their struggle to be free from domination" and "to provide the people, if they so request, with material assistance . . . to help them fight effectively." March 21, 1985, was "Afghanistan Day" in the United States, so declared by a joint resolution of Congress, also passed by unanimous consent. Receptions are held and toasts given to Afghan guerrilla commanders.

Why do Afghan atrocities not de-legitimize their struggle, and require us to cease support? Again the issue is not hypocrisy. It must be morally self-evident to both critics and supporters of the Reagan Doctrine that the Afghan guerrillas still deserve support. Some other principles must be involved here.

It has, I think, to do with control. The sensibilities of the West and its idea of rules of engagement will not change the Afghans. They can be counted on to carry on regardless. If we were fighting Soviet forces in the United States (or even Afghanistan) we should not permit ourselves to fight this way. But the Afghans will anyway. We have only one choice: to decide between the lesser of two evils. And we decide that, taking into account both the means and ends of the guerrillas and of their enemy, the lesser evil is to support the rebels.

I am not pretending that strategic considerations do not dwarf these moral considerations and that these considerations are not why even liberals embrace the Afghan guerrillas. But, as in all such decisions, strategic considerations are insufficient if the policy is morally unacceptable. There must always be two tests. I have never gotten an adequate accounting from those who indignantly protest Savimbi and the *contras* as to how the Afghan war passes a moral test. My reasoning above is the best I can do, for them and for myself.

It is, I believe, fair reasoning, with important historical precedent. This is not the first time we make such choices. We could not dictate Stalin's tactics either. And yet we chose to ally ourselves with the second greatest monster of the century in order to defeat the first. The decision to do so was not even a close call. Or consider the Spanish Civil War. The atrocities committed by the Loyalist forces are the equal of those attributed to any of the Reagan Doctrine forces. That does not prevent Walzer from terming "shameful" (I agree) the democracies' refusal to intervene (as legitimate counterintervention against German and Italian efforts to "turn the balance") on the Loyalist side. My point is not that this is hypocrisy. Not at all. It is merely an example of making a necessary moral calculus when faced with two sides, the behavior of neither of which we are likely to alter substantially. There are no moral foxholes.

The same lesser-of-two-evils case can be made for the other Reagan Doctrine conflicts. But it would be insufficient. Afghan atrocities do expose hypocrisy, but they do not provide moral cover, because in Nicaragua (and, to a minor extent, in Angola) the United States had more control over the insurgency. (One need not accept the Sandinista fantasy that the resistance is a CIA puppet to maintain this.) And with control comes responsibility. One responsibility is to see to it that the guerrilla war is fought within certain moral boundaries. No more use of pressure-sensitive land mines. A human rights office to investigate reported atrocities. This is the standard to which we would hold ourselves were we conducting a guerrilla war of our own. We are morally obliged to try to impose it in support of guerrilla wars where possible, i.e., where we exercise a sufficient degree of control. We are obliged to try to prevent abuses and to ensure that resort to such tactics does not become guerrilla policy. But that is different from saying that we are obliged to wash our hands of the war because, in this war as in others, such abuses occur.

There is one final critique of the use of guerrilla means. Not that they violate the rules of war, but they violate another standard, the Vince Lombardi standard: the rebels cannot win. The immorality lies in using foreign peasants as cannon fodder for a cynical American policy of bleeding the Soviets and their allies.

What is not explained is why so many people are willing to go to their deaths (they are not, by and large, drafted) in order to serve the marginal interest of an alien power. I offer a better explanation. These guerrillas must believe either that they can win, or that their fight will force some solution short of victory that is better than the status quo, so much better that it is worth dying for. These guerrillas ask for our help. It seems a form of moral hauteur to deny them the help (and, incidentally, expose them to more danger, since in most cases they will carry on regardless) because we know better whether they can achieve what they are prepared to risk their lives to achieve.

Moreover, how do Reagan Doctrine critics know that these wars are unwinnable? The Vietnamese communists, starting with a very small number of cadres, took 30 years to expel the French and Americans and ultimately subdue all of their Indochinese neighbors. It took three decades, too, for Chinese communists to achieve victory. In less than half a decade the Reagan Doctrine has produced no success. That is not proof that these wars are unwinnable. Unless one adds: these wars must fail because our enemies will always match us and escalate to meet any challenge by our side. But just because that was true in Vietnam does not mean it will be true everywhere else. It was not, for example, true of Malaysia or Thailand, where the communist side was defeated. Moreover, this critique degenerates into the earlier argument that because they will fight to win at all cost, our contesting their will (or more precisely: our assisting others who choose to contest their will) becomes morally untenable. We return to the proposition that fighting determined communists who refuse to quit is in itself a moral offense.

Americans might be more humble about deciding which wars are winnable and which are not. Our track record in this department is not good. It was once thought that a fifth-rate military power in Southeast Asia could not possibly defeat the premier power of the world. War is mostly a matter of will. People are not going out into the field and being shot in unwinnable wars because they are being forced to or bribed by the United States.

They are doing so because they think their struggle is worth fighting for. Some people fight to the death for honor, but not many.

The Reagan Doctrine is a strategic response of the United States to the needs of a containment policy and to a change in the correlation of forces in the world in the 1970s. But it cannot be defended purely on strategic grounds. It must be morally defensible. An analysis of the principles underlying intervention, insurgency, and guerrilla war yields, in my view, the conclusion that it is. It also yields certain conditions for this to remain so—conditions of popular support, ends, and means. (For example, it is my view that the Cambodian insurgency fails a crucial test of ends.)

But what of the real suffering that war necessarily brings to real people? There is no denying the suffering. Nevertheless, the cry of the bereaved mother is not an argument against war. It is an argument against unjust war. It is an argument for careful thinking about principles that justify war and for doing what one can to prevent wanton destruction. In any war, we owe that to both sides and to ourselves.

EXECUTIVE SUMMARY OF THE REPORT OF THE CONGRESSIONAL COMMITTEES INVESTIGATING THE IRAN-CONTRA AFFAIR[4]

Findings and Conclusions

The common ingredients of the Iran and Contra policies were secrecy, deception, and disdain for the law. A small group of senior officials believed that they alone knew what was right. They viewed knowledge of their actions by others in the Government as a threat to their objectives. They told neither the Secretary of State, the Congress nor the American people of their

[4]100th Congress, 1st Session, 1987. H. Rept. No. 100–433, S. Rept. No. 100–216, pp. 3–22.

actions. When exposure was threatened, they destroyed official documents and lied to Cabinet officials, to the public, and to elected representatives in Congress. They testified that they even withheld key facts from the President.

The United States Constitution specifies the process by which laws and policy are to be made and executed. Constitutional process is the essence of our democracy and our democratic form of Government is the basis of our strength. Time and again we have learned that a flawed process leads to bad results, and that a lawless process leads to worse.

POLICY CONTRADICTIONS AND FAILURES

The Administration's departure from democratic processes created the conditions for policy failure, and led to contradictions which undermined the credibility of the United States.

The United States simultaneously pursued two contradictory foreign policies—a public one and a secret one:

—The public policy was not to make any concessions for the release of hostages lest such concessions encourage more hostage-taking. At the same time, the United States was secretly trading weapons to get the hostages back.

—The public policy was to ban arms shipments to Iran and to exhort other Governments to observe this embargo. At the same time, the United States was secretly selling sophisticated missiles to Iran and promising more.

—The public policy was to improve relations with Iraq. At the same time, the United States secretly shared military intelligence on Iraq with Iran and North told the Iranians in contradiction to United States policy that the United States would help promote the overthrow of the Iraqi head of government.

—The public policy was to urge all Governments to punish terrorism and to support, indeed encourage, the refusal of Kuwait to free the Da'wa prisoners who were convicted of terrorist acts. At the same time, senior officials secretly endorsed a Secord-Hakim plan to permit Iran to obtain the release of the Da'wa prisoners.

—The public policy was to observe the "letter and spirit" of the Boland Amendment's proscriptions against military or paramilitary assistance to the Contras. At the same time, the NSC [National Security Council] staff was secretly assuming direction and funding of the Contras' military effort.

—The public policy, embodied in agreements signed by Director Casey, was for the Administration to consult with the Congressional oversight committees about covert activities in a "new spirit of frankness and cooperation." At the same time, the CIA [Central Intelligence Agency] and the White House were secretly withholding from those Committees all information concerning the Iran initiative and the Contra support network.

—The public policy, embodied in Executive Order 12333, was to conduct covert operations solely through the CIA or other organs of the intelligence community specifically authorized by the President. At the same time, although the NSC [National Security Council] was not so authorized, the NSC staff secretly became operational and used private, non-accountable agents to engage in covert activities.

These contradictions in policy inevitably resulted in policy failure:

—The United States armed Iran, including its most radical elements, but attained neither a new relationship with that hostile regime nor a reduction in the number of American hostages.

—The arms sales did not lead to a moderation of Iranian policies. Moderates did not come forward, and Iran to this day sponsors actions directed against the United States in the Persian Gulf and elsewhere.

—The United States opened itself to blackmail by adversaries who might reveal the secret arms sales and who, according to North, threatened to kill the hostages if the sales stopped.

—The United States undermined its credibility with friends and allies, including moderate Arab states, by its public stance of opposing arms sales to Iran while undertaking such arms sales in secret.

—The United States lost a $10 million contribution to the Contras from the Sultan of Brunei by directing it to the wrong bank account—the result of an improper effort to channel that humanitarian aid contribution into an account used for lethal assistance.

—The United States sought illicit funding for the Contras through profits from the secret arms sales, but a substantial portion of those profits ended up in the personal bank accounts of the private individuals executing the sales—while the exorbitant amounts charged for the weapons inflamed the Iranians with whom the United States was seeking a new relationship.

FLAWED POLICY PROCESS

The record of the Iran-Contra Affair also shows a seriously flawed policymaking process.

CONFUSION

There was confusion and disarray at the highest levels of Government.

—McFarlane embarked on a dangerous trip to Tehran under a complete misapprehension. He thought the Iranians had promised to secure the release of all hostages before he delivered arms, when in fact they had promised only to seek the hostages' release, and then only after one planeload of arms had arrived.

—The President first told the Tower Board that he had approved the initial Israeli shipments. Then, he told the Tower Board that he had not. Finally, he told the Tower Board that he does not know whether he approved the initial Israeli arms shipments, and his top advisers disagree on the question.

—The President claims he does not recall signing a Finding approving the November 1985 HAWK shipment to Iran. But Poindexter testified that the President did sign a Finding on December 5, 1985, approving the shipment retroactively. Poindexter later destroyed the Finding to save the President from embarrassment.

—That Finding was prepared without adequate discussion and stuck in Poindexter's safe for a year; Poindexter claimed he forgot about it; White House asserts the President never signed it; and when events began to unravel, Poindexter ripped it up.

—The President and the Attorney General told the public that the President did not know about the November 1985 Israeli HAWK shipment until February 1986—an error the White House Chief of Staff explained by saying that the preparation for the press conference "sort of confused the Presidential mind."

—Poindexter says the President would have approved the diversion, if he had been asked; and the President says he would not have.

—One National Security Adviser understood that the Boland Amendment applied to the NSC; another thought it did not. Neither sought a legal opinion on the question.

—The President incorrectly assured the American people that the NSC staff was adhering to the law and that the Government was not connected to the Hasenfus airplane. His staff was in fact conducting a "full service" covert operation to support the Contras which they believed he had authorized.

—North says he sent five or six completed memorandums to Poindexter seeking the President's approval for the diversion. Poindexter does not remember receiving any. Only one has been found.

DISHONESTY AND SECRECY

The Iran-Contra Affair was characterized by pervasive dishonesty and inordinate secrecy.

North admitted that he and other officials lied repeatedly to Congress and to the American people about the Contra covert action and Iran arms sales, and that he altered and destroyed official documents. North's testimony demonstrates that he also lied to members of the Executive branch, including the Attorney General, and officials of the State Department, CIA and NSC.

Secrecy became an obsession. Congress was never informed of the Iran or the Contra covert actions, notwithstanding the requirement in the law that Congress be notified of all covert actions in a "timely fashion."

Poindexter said that Donald Regan, the President's Chief of Staff, was not told of the NSC staff's fundraising activities because he might reveal it to the press. Secretary Shultz objected to third-country solicitation in 1984 shortly before the Boland Amendment was adopted; accordingly, he was not told that, in the same time period, the National Security Adviser had accepted an $8 million contribution from Country 2 even though the State Department had prime responsibility for dealings with that country. Nor was the Secretary of State told by the President in February 1985 that the same country had pledged another $24 million—even though the President briefed the Secretary of State on his meeting with the head of state at which the pledge was made. Poindexter asked North to keep secrets from Casey; Casey, North, and Poindexter agreed to keep secrets from Shultz.

Poindexter and North cited fear of leaks as a justification for these practices. But the need to prevent public disclosure cannot justify the deception practiced upon Members of Congress and

Executive branch officials by those who knew of the arms sales to Iran and of the Contra support network. The State and Defense Departments deal each day with the most sensitive matters affecting millions of lives here and abroad. The Congressional Intelligence Committees receive the most highly classified information, including information on covert activities. Yet, according to North and Poindexter, even the senior officials of these bodies could not be entrusted with the NSC staff's secrets because they might leak.

While Congress's record in maintaining the confidentiality of classified information is not unblemished, it is not nearly as poor or perforated as some members of the NSC staff maintained. If the Executive branch has any basis to suspect that any member of the Intelligence Committees breached security, it has the obligation to bring that breach to the attention of the House and Senate Leaders—not to make blanket accusations. Congress has the capability and responsibility of protecting secrets entrusted to it. Congress cannot fulfill its legislative responsibilities if it is denied information because members of the Executive branch, who place their faith in a band of international arms merchants and financiers, unilaterally declare Congress unworthy of trust.

In the case of the "secret" Iran arms-for-hostages deal, although the NSC staff did not inform the Secretary of State, the Chairman of the Joint Chiefs of Staff, or the leadership of the United States Congress, it was content to let the following persons know:

—Manucher Ghorbanifar, who flunked every polygraph test administered by the U.S. Government;

—Iranian officials, who daily denounced the United States but received an inscribed Bible from the President;

—Officials of Iran's Revolutionary Guard, who received the U.S. weapons;

—Secord and Hakim, whose personal interests could conflict with the interests of the United States;

—Israeli officials, international arms merchants, pilots and air crews, whose interests did not always coincide with ours; and

—An unknown number of shadowy intermediaries and financiers who assisted with both the First and Second Iranian Channels.

While sharing the secret with this disparate group, North ordered the intelligence agencies not to disseminate intelligence on the Iran initiative to the Secretaries of State and Defense. Poindexter told the Secretary of State in May 1986 that the Iran initiative was over, at the very time the McFarlane mission to Tehran was being launched. Poindexter also concealed from Cabinet officials the remarkable nine-point agreement negotiated by Hakim with the Second Channel. North assured the FBI liaison to the NSC as late as November 1986 that the United States was not bargaining for the release of hostages but seizing terrorists to exchange for hostages—a complete fabrication. The lies, omissions, shredding, attempts to rewrite history—all continued, even after the President authorized the Attorney General to find out the facts.

It was not operational security that motivated such conduct— not when our own Government was the victim. Rather, the NSC staff feared, correctly, that any disclosure to Congress or the Cabinet of the arms-for-hostages and arms-for-profit activities would produce a storm of outrage.

As with Iran, Congress was misled about the NSC staff's support for the Contras during the period of the Boland Amendment, although the role of the NSC staff was no secret to others. North testified that his operation was well-known to the press in the Soviet Union, Cuba, and Nicaragua. It was not a secret from Nicaragua's neighbors, with whom the NSC staff communicated throughout the period. It was not a secret from the third countries—including a totalitarian state—from whom the NSC staff sought arms or funds. It was not a secret from the private resupply network which North recruited and supervised. According to North, even Ghorbanifar knew.

The Administration never sought to hide its desire to assist the Contras so long as such aid was authorized by statute. On the contrary, it wanted the Sandinistas to know that the United States supported the Contras. After enactment of the Boland Amendment, the Administration repeatedly and publicly called upon Congress to resume U.S. assistance. Only the NSC staff's Contra support activities were kept under wraps. The Committees believe these actions were concealed in order to prevent Congress from learning that the Boland Amendment was being circumvented.

It was stated on several occasions that the confusion, secrecy and deception surrounding the aid program for the Nicaraguan freedom fighters was produced in part by Congress' shifting positions on Contra aid.

But Congress' inconsistency mirrored the chameleon-like nature of the rationale offered for granting assistance in the first instance. Initially, Congress was told that our purpose was simply to interdict the flow of weapons from Nicaragua into El Salvador. Then Congress was told that our purpose was to harrass the Sandinistas to prevent them from consolidating their power and exporting their revolution. Eventually, Congress was told that our purpose was to eliminate all foreign forces from Nicaragua, to reduce the size of the Sandinista armed forces, and to restore the democratic reforms pledged by the Sandinistas during the overthrow of the Somoza regime.

Congress had cast a skeptical eye upon each rationale proffered by the Administration. It suspected that the Administration's true purpose was identical to that of the Contras—the overthrow of the Sandinista regime itself. Ultimately Congress yielded to domestic political pressure to discontinue assistance to the Contras, but Congress was unwilling to bear responsibility for the loss of Central America to communist military and political forces. So Congress compromised, providing in 1985 humanitarian aid to the Contras; and the NSC staff provided what Congress prohibited: lethal support for the Contras.

Compromise is no excuse for violation of law and deceiving Congress. A law is no less a law because it is passed by a slender majority, or because Congress is open-minded about its reconsideration in the future.

Privatization

The NSC staff turned to private parties and third countries to do the Government's business. Funds denied by Congress were obtained by the Administration from third countries and private citizens. Activities normally conducted by the professional intelligence services—which are accountable to Congress—were turned over to Secord and Hakim.

The solicitation of foreign funds by an Administration to pursue foreign policy goals rejected by Congress is dangerous and improper. Such solicitations, when done secretly and without Congressional authorization, create a risk that the foreign country will expect and demand something in return. McFarlane testified that "any responsible official has an obligation to acknowledge that every country in the world will see benefit to itself by ingratiating itself to the United States." North, in fact, proposed rewarding a Central American country with foreign assistance funds for facilitating arms shipments to the Contras. And Secord, who had once been in charge of the U.S. Air Force's foreign military sales, said "where there is a quid, there is a quo."

Moreover, under the Constitution only Congress can provide funds for the Executive branch. The Framers intended Congress's "power of the purse" to be one of the principal checks on Executive action. It was designed, among other things, to prevent the Executive from involving this country unilaterally in a foreign conflict. The Constitutional plan does not prohibit a President from asking a foreign state, or anyone else, to contribute funds to a third party. But it does prohibit such solicitation where the United States exercises control over their receipt and expenditure. By circumventing Congress' power of the purse through third-country and private contributions to the Contras, the Administration undermined a cardinal principle of the Constitution.

Further, by turning to private citizens, the NSC staff jeopardized its own objectives. Sensitive negotiations were conducted by parties with little experience in diplomacy, and financial interests of their own. The diplomatic aspect of the mission failed— the United States today has no long-term relationship with Iran and no fewer hostages in captivity. But the private financial aspect succeeded—Secord and Hakim took $4.4 million in commissions and used $2.2 million more for their personal benefit; in addition, they set aside reserves of over $4 million in Swiss bank accounts of the Enterprise.

Covert operations of this Government should only be directed and conducted by the trained professional services that are accountable to the President and Congress. Such operations should never be delegated, as they were here, to private citizens in order to evade Governmental restrictions.

LACK OF ACCOUNTABILITY

The confusion, deception, and privatization which marked the Iran-Contra Affair were the inevitable products of an attempt to avoid accountability. Congress, the Cabinet, and the Joint Chiefs of Staff were denied information and excluded from the decision-making process. Democratic procedures were disregarded.

Officials who make public policy must be accountable to the public. But the public cannot hold officials accountable for policies of which the public is unaware. Policies that are known can be subjected to the test of reason, and mistakes can be corrected after consultation with the Congress and deliberation within the Executive branch itself. Policies that are secret become the private preserve of the few, mistakes are inevitably perpetuated, and the public loses control over Government. That is what happened in the Iran-Contra Affair:

—The President's NSC staff carried out a covert action in furtherance of his policy to sustain the Contras, but the President said he did not know about it.

—The President's NSC staff secretly diverted millions of dollars in profits from the Iran arms sales to the Contras, but the President said he did not know about it and Poindexter claimed he did not tell him.

—The Chairman of the Joint Chiefs of Staff was not informed of the Iran arms sales, nor was he ever consulted regarding the impact of such sales on the Iran-Iraq war or on U.S. military readiness.

—The Secretary of State was not informed of the millions of dollars in Contra contributions solicited by the NSC staff from foreign governments with which the State Department deals each day.

—Congress was told almost nothing—and what it was told was false.

Deniability replaced accountability. Thus, Poindexter justified his decision not to inform the President of the diversion on the ground that he wanted to give the President "deniability." Poindexter said he wanted to shield the President from political embarrassment if the diversion became public.

This kind of thinking is inconsistent with democratic governance. "Plausible denial," an accepted concept in intelligence activities, means structuring an authorized covert operation so that, if discovered by the party against whom it is directed, United States involvement may plausibly be denied. That is a legitimate feature of authorized covert operations. In no circumstance, however, does "plausible denial" mean structuring an operation so that it may be concealed from—or denied to—the highest elected officials of the United States Government itself.

The very premise of democracy is that "we the people" are entitled to make our own choices on fundamental policies. But freedom of choice is illusory if policies are kept, not only from the public, but from its elected representatives.

INTELLIGENCE ABUSES

COVERT OPERATIONS

As former National Security Adviser Robert McFarlane testified, "it is clearly unwise to rely on covert action as the core of our policy." The Government cannot keep a policy secret and still secure the public support necessary to sustain it. Yet it was precisely because the public would not support the Contra policy, and was unlikely to favor arms deals with Iran, that the NSC staff went underground. This was a perversion of the proper concept of covert operations:

—Covert operations should be conducted in accordance with strict rules of accountability and oversight. In the mid-1970s, in response to disclosures of abuses within the intelligence community, the Government enacted a series of safeguards. Each covert action was to be approved personally by the President, funded by Congressional appropriations, and Congress was to be informed.

In the Iran-Contra Affair, these rules were violated. The President, according to Poindexter, was never informed of the diversion. The President says he knew nothing of the covert action to support the Contras, or the companies funded by non-appropriated monies set up by North to carry out that support. Congress was not notified of either the Iran or the Contra operations.

—Covert actions should be consistent with publicly defined U.S. foreign policy goals. Because covert operations are secret by definition, they are of course not openly debated or publicly approved. So long as the policies which they further are known, and so long as they are conducted in accordance with law, covert operations are acceptable. Here, however, the Contra covert operation was carried out in violation of the country's public policy as expressed in the Boland Amendment; and the Iran covert operation was carried out in violation of the country's stated policy against selling arms to Iran or making concessions to terrorists. These were not covert actions, they were covert policies; and covert policies are incompatible with democracy.

—Finally, covert operations are intended to be kept from foreign powers, not from the Congress and responsible Executive agencies within the United States Government itself. As Clair George, CIA Director of Operations, testified: "to think that because we deal in lies, and overseas we may lie and we may do other such things, that therefore that gives you some permission, some right or some particular reason to operate that way with your fellow employees, I would not only disagree with that I would say it would be the destruction of a secret service in a democracy." In the Iran-Contra Affair, secrecy was used to justify lies to Congress, the Attorney General, other Cabinet officers, and the CIA. It was used not as a shield against our adversaries, but as a weapon against our own democratic institutions.

The NSC Staff

The NSC staff was created to give the President policy advice on major national security and foreign policy issues. Here, however, it was used to gather intelligence and conduct covert operations. This departure from its proper functions contributed to policy failure.

During the Iran initiative, the NSC staff became the principal body both for gathering and coordinating intelligence on Iran and for recommending policy to the President. The staff relied on Iranians who were interested only in buying arms, including Ghorbanifar, whom CIA officials regarded as a fabricator. Poindexter, in recommending to the President the sale of weapons to Iran, gave as one of his reasons that Iraq was winning the Gulf war. That assessment was contrary to the views of intelligence professionals at the State Department, the Department of Defense, and the CIA, who had concluded as early as 1983 that Iran was winning the war. Casey, who collaborated with North and Poindexter on the Iran and Contra programs, also tailored intelligence reports to the positions he advocated. The record shows that the President believed and acted on these erroneous reports.

Secretary Shultz pointed out that the intelligence and policy functions do not mix, because "it is too tempting to have your analysis on the selection of information that is presented favor the policy that you are advocating." The Committees agree on the need to separate the intelligence and policy functions. Otherwise, there is too great a risk that the interpretation of intelligence will be skewed to fit predetermined policy choices.

In the Iran-Contra Affair, the NSC staff not only combined intelligence and policy functions, but it became operational and conducted covert operations. As the CIA was subjected to greater Congressional scrutiny and regulation, a few Administration officials—including even Director Casey—came to believe that the CIA could no longer be utilized for daring covert operations. So the NSC staff was enlisted to provide assistance in covert operations that the CIA could not or would not furnish.

This was a dangerous misuse of the NSC staff. When covert operations are conducted by those on whom the President relies to present policy options, there is no agency in government to objectively scrutinize, challenge and evaluate plans and activities. Checks and balances are lost. The high policy decisions confronting a President can rarely be resolved by the methods and techniques used by experts in the conduct of covert operations. Problems of public policy must be dealt with through consultation, not Poindexter's "compartmentation"; with honesty and confidentiality, not deceit.

The NSC was created to provide candid and comprehensive advice to the President. It is the judgment of these Committees that the NSC staff should never again engage in covert operations.

Disdain for Law

In the Iran-Contra Affair, officials viewed the law not as setting boundaries for their actions, but raising impediments to their goals. When the goals and the law collided, the law gave way:

—The covert program of support for the Contras evaded the Constitution's most significant check on Executive power: the President can spend funds on a program only if he can convince Congress to appropriate the money.

When Congress enacted the Boland Amendment, cutting off funds for the war in Nicaragua, Administration officials raised funds for the Contras from other sources—foreign Governments, the Iran arms sales, and private individuals; and the NSC staff controlled the expenditures of these funds through power over the Enterprise. Conducting the covert program in Nicaragua with funding from the sale of U.S. Government property and contributions raised by Government officials was a flagrant violation of the Appropriations Clause of the Constitution.

—In addition, the covert program of support for the Contras was an evasion of the letter and spirit of the Boland Amendment. The President made it clear that while he opposed restrictions on military or paramilitary assistance to the Contras, he recognized that compliance with the law was not optional. "[W]hat I might personally wish or what our Government might wish still would not justify us violating the law of the land," he said in 1983.

A year later, members of the NSC staff were devising ways to continue support and direction of Contra activities during the period of the Boland Amendment. What was previously done by the CIA—and now prohibited by the Boland Amendment—would be done instead by the NSC staff.

The President set the stage by welcoming a huge donation for the Contras from a foreign Government—a contribution clearly intended to keep the Contras in the field while U.S. aid was barred. The NSC staff thereafter solicited other foreign Governments for military aid, facilitated the efforts of U.S. fundraisers to provide lethal assistance to the Contras, and ultimately developed and directed a private network that conducted, in North's words, a "full service covert operation" in support of the Contras.

This could not have been more contrary to the intent of the Boland legislation.

Numerous other laws were disregarded:

—North's full-service covert operation was a "significant anticipated intelligence activity" required to be disclosed to the Intelligence Committees of Congress under Section 501 of the National Security Act. No such disclosure was made.

—By Executive order, a covert operation requires a personal determination by the President before it can be conducted by an agency other than the CIA. It requires a written Finding before any agency can carry it out. In the case of North's full-service covert operation in support of the Contras, there was no such personal determination and no such Finding. In fact, the President disclaims any knowledge of this covert action.

—False statements to Congress are felonies if made with knowledge and intent. Several Administration officials gave statements denying NSC staff activities in support of the Contras which North later described in his testimony as "false," and "misleading, evasive, and wrong."

—The application of proceeds from U.S. arms sales for the benefit of the Contra war effort violated the Boland Amendment's ban on U.S. military aid to the Contras, and constituted a misappropriation of Government funds derived from the transfer of U.S. property.

—The U.S. Government's approval of the pre-Finding 1985 sales by Israel of arms to the Government of Iran was inconsistent with the Government's obligations under the Arms Export Control Act.

—The testimony to Congress in November 1986 that the U.S. Government had no contemporaneous knowledge of the Israeli shipments, and the shredding of documents relating to the shipments while a Congressional inquiry into those shipments was pending, obstructed Congressional investigations.

—The Administration did not make, and clearly intended never to make, disclosure to the Intelligence Committees of the Finding—later destroyed—approving the November 1985 HAWK shipment, nor did it disclose the covert action to which the Finding related.

The Committees make no determination as to whether any particular individual involved in the Iran-Contra Affair acted with criminal intent or was guilty of any crime. That is a matter for the Independent Counsel and the courts. But the Committees reject any notion that worthy ends justify violations of law by Government officials; and the Committees condemn without reservation the making of false statements to Congress and the withholding, shredding, and alteration of documents relevant to a pending inquiry.

Administration officials have, if anything, an even greater responsibility than private citizens to comply with the law. There is no place in Government for law breakers.

CONGRESS AND THE PRESIDENT

The Constitution of the United States gives important powers to both the President and the Congress in the making of foreign policy. The President is the principal architect of foreign policy in consultation with the Congress. The policies of the United States cannot succeed unless the President and the Congress work together.

Yet, in the Iran-Contra Affair, Administration officials holding no elected office repeatedly evidenced disrespect for Congress' efforts to perform its Constitutional oversight role in foreign policy:

—Poindexter testified, referring to his efforts to keep the covert action in support of the Contras from Congress: "I simply did not want any outside interference."

—North testified: "I didn't want to tell Congress anything" about this covert action.

—Abrams acknowledged in his testimony that, unless Members of Congressional Committees asked "exactly the right question, using exactly the right words, they weren't going to get the right answers," regarding solicitation of third-countries for Contra support.

—And numerous other officials made false statements to, and misled, the Congress.

Several witnesses at the hearings stated or implied that foreign policy should be left solely to the President to do as he chooses, arguing that shared powers have no place in a dangerous world. But the theory of our Constitution is the opposite: policies formed through consultation and the democratic process are better and wiser than those formed without it. Circumvention of Congress is self-defeating, for no foreign policy can succeed without the bipartisan support of Congress.

In a system of shared powers, decision-making requires mutual respect between the branches of government.

The Committees were reminded by Secretary Shultz during the hearings that "trust is the coin of the realm." Democratic government is not possible without trust between the branches of government and between the government and the people. Sometimes that trust is misplaced and the system falters. But for officials to work outside the system because it does not produce the results they seek is a prescription for failure.

Who Was Responsible

Who was responsible for the Iran-Contra Affair? Part of our mandate was to answer that question, not in a legal sense (which is the responsibility of the Independent Counsel), but in order to reaffirm that those who serve the Government are accountable for their actions. Based on our investigation, we reach the following conclusions.

At the operational level, the central figure in the Iran-Contra Affair was Lt. Col. North, who coordinated all of the activities and was involved in all aspects of the secret operations. North, however, did not act alone.

North's conduct had the express approval of Admiral John Poindexter, first as Deputy National Security Adviser, and then as National Security Adviser. North also had at least the tacit support of Robert McFarlane, who served as National Security Adviser until December 1985.

In addition, for reasons cited earlier, we believe that the late Director of Central Intelligence, William Casey, encouraged North, gave him direction, and promoted the concept of an extra-legal covert organization. Casey, for the most part, insulated CIA career employees from knowledge of what he and the NSC staff were doing. Casey's passion for covert operations— dating back to his World War II intelligence days—was well known. His close relationship with North was attested to by several witnesses. Further, it was Casey who brought Richard Secord into the secret operation, and it was Secord who, with Albert Hakim, organized the Enterprise. These facts provide strong reasons to believe that Casey was involved both with the diversion and with the plans for an "off-the-shelf" covert capacity.

The Committees are mindful, however, of the fact that the evidence concerning Casey's role comes almost solely from North; that this evidence, albeit under oath, was used by North to exculpate himself; and that Casey could not respond. Although North told the Committees that Casey knew of the diversion from the start, he told a different story to the Attorney General in November 1986, as did Casey himself. Only one other witness, Lt. Col. Robert Earl, testified that he had been told by North during Casey's lifetime that Casey knew of the diversion.

The Attorney General recognized on November 21, 1986 the need for an inquiry. His staff was responsible for finding the diversion memorandum, which the Attorney General promptly made public. But as described earlier, his fact-finding inquiry departed from standard investigative techniques. The Attorney General saw Director Casey hours after the Attorney General learned of the diversion memorandum, yet he testified that he never asked Casey about the diversion. He waited two days to speak to Poindexter, North's superior, and then did not ask him what the President knew. He waited too long to seal North's offices. These lapses placed a cloud over the Attorney General's investigation.

There is no evidence that the Vice President was aware of the diversion. The Vice President attended several meetings on the Iran initiative, but none of the participants could recall his views.

The Vice President said he did not know of the Contra resupply operation. His National Security Adviser, Donald Gregg, was told in early August 1986 by a former colleague that North was running the Contra resupply operation, and that ex-associates of Edwin Wilson—a well known ex-CIA official convicted of selling arms to Libya and plotting the murder of his prosecutors—were involved in the operation. Gregg testified that he did not consider these facts worthy of the Vice President's attention and did not report them to him, even after the Hasenfus airplane was shot down and the Administration had denied any connection with it.

The central remaining question is the role of the President in the Iran-Contra Affair. On this critical point, the shredding of documents by Poindexter, North, and others, and the death of Casey, leave the record incomplete.

As it stands, the President has publicly stated that he did not know of the diversion. Poindexter testified that he shielded the President from knowledge of the diversion. North said that he never told the President, but assumed that the President knew. Poindexter told North on November 21, 1986 that he had not informed the President of the diversion. Secord testified that North told him he had talked with the President about the diversion, but North testified that he had fabricated this story to bolster Secord's morale.

Nevertheless, the ultimate responsibility for the events in the Iran-Contra Affair must rest with the President. If the President did not know what his National Security Advisers were doing, he should have. It is his responsibility to communicate unambiguously to his subordinates that they must keep him advised of important actions they take for the Administration. The Constitution requires the President to "take care that the laws be faithfully executed." This charge encompasses a responsibility to leave the members of his Administration in no doubt that the rule of law governs.

Members of the NSC staff appeared to believe that their actions were consistent with the President's desires. It was the President's policy—not an isolated decision by North or Poindexter—to sell arms secretly to Iran and to maintain the Contras "body and soul," the Boland Amendment notwithstanding. To the NSC staff, implementation of these policies became the overriding concern.

Several of the President's advisers pursued a covert action to support the Contras in disregard of the Boland Amendment and of several statutes and Executive orders requiring Congressional notification. Several of these same advisers lied, shredded documents, and covered up their actions. These facts have been on the public record for months. The actions of those individuals do not comport with the notion of a country guided by the rule of law. But the President has yet to condemn their conduct.

The President himself told the public that the U.S. Government had no connection to the Hasenfus airplane. He told the public that early reports of arms sales for hostages had "no foundation." He told the public that the United States had not traded arms for hostages. He told the public that the United States had not condoned the arms sales by Israel to Iran, when in fact he had approved them and signed a Finding, later destroyed by Poindexter, recording his approval. All of these statements by the President were wrong.

Thus, the question whether the President knew of the diversion is not conclusive on the issue of his responsibility. The President created or at least tolerated an environment where those who did know of the diversion believed with certainty that they were carrying out the President's policies.

This same environment enabled a secretary who shredded, smuggled, and altered documents to tell the Committees that "sometimes you have to go above the written law;" and it enabled Admiral Poindexter to testify that "frankly, we were willing to take some risks with the law." It was in such an environment that former officials of the NSC staff and their private agents could lecture the Committees that a "rightful cause" justifies any means, that lying to Congress and other officials in the executive branch itself is acceptable when the ends are just, and that Congress is to blame for passing laws that run counter to Administration policy. What may aptly be called the "cabal of the zealots" was in charge.

In a Constitutional democracy, it is not true, as one official maintained, that "when you take the King's shilling, you do the King's bidding." The idea of monarchy was rejected here 200 years ago and since then, the law—not any official or ideology—had been paramount. For not instilling this precept in his staff, for failing to take care that the law reigned supreme, the President bears the responsibility.

Fifty years ago Supreme Court Justice Louis Brandeis observed: "Our Government is the potent, the omnipresent teacher. For good or for ill, it teaches the whole people by its example. Crime is contagious. If the Government becomes a law-breaker, it breeds contempt for law, it invites every man to become a law unto himself, it invites anarchy."

The Iran-Contra Affair resulted from a failure to heed this message.

II. ETHICS AND THE EXECUTIVE BRANCH

EDITOR'S INTRODUCTION

Laws prohibiting the use of public office for private gain have been on the books since the nation was founded. Until the early 19th century, however, the federal government suffered few major scandals, and no formal system of regulating conflict-of-interest in the executive branch was established until the time of the Civil War. After that war, however, corruption came to be seen as a serious problem as government expanded to control the burgeoning private sector, which generated enormous wealth and powerful interest groups. Scandals and allegations involving preferential treatment for business interests added impetus to calls for more stringent measures to prevent private economic interests from exerting excessive influence over government officials. The demand for tighter conflict-of-interest laws intensified in the first half of this century, when the government expanded further to cope with two world wars and the problems of the Depression. In the postwar period, executive-branch officials have been subjected to increasingly tough laws designed to prevent the use of public office for private gain.

As a result of the Watergate scandal, concern over preventing even the *appearance* of conflict-of-interest culminated in the passage of the Ethics in Government Act of 1978. In an excerpt from his book, *Ethics-in-Government Laws: Are They Too Ethical?*, University of Missouri Law School professor Alfred S. Neeley IV outlines the provisions of the ethics act and other laws that apply to the executive branch, many of which, he maintains, have undermined excellence in government by deterring qualified and honorable people from entering public service.

After finding that conflict-of-interest laws had impeded recruitment efforts and slowed the appointment process, the Reagan administration pressed Congress to ease financial disclosure requirements. Its efforts to amend the ethics act proved increasingly difficult as allegations of misconduct on the part of high-level appointees began to mount. By the end of Reagan's second term, more than a hundred executive-branch officials had been in the news for alleged malfeasance. The second piece, an article entitled "The Office of Government Ethics: Vigilant Watchdog or Toothless Terrier?," by W. John Moore, appeared in *Government Executive* and assesses the effectiveness of the Office of Government Ethics in preventing conflict-of-interest by federal employees. In the third selection, reprinted from *The Nation*, Frank Donner and James Ledbetter describe malfeasance in five federal agencies and suggest that corruption and willful incompetence on the part of agency officials have been used as tools to weaken regulation. The final piece, an excerpt from Robert N. Roberts' book, *White House Ethics: The History of the Politics of Conflict of Interest Legislation,* proposes ways to improve ethics laws to avert future violations and restore public confidence in the executive branch of government.

ETHICS IN GOVERNMENT LAWS[1]

No American public official has a uniform, but all receive salaries. This . . . is the result of democratic principles. A democracy could surround its magistrates with pomp, covering them in silk and gold, without making any direct attack on the principle of its existence. Such privileges are ephemeral, going with the place rather than with the man. But to establish unpaid official positions is to create a class of rich and independent functionaries and to shape the core of an aristocracy. Even if the people still retain the right of choice, the exercise of that right comes to have inevitable limitations.

When a democratic republic converts salaried appointments into unpaid ones, I think one may conclude that it is steering toward monarchy. And when a monarchy begins paying its unsalaried officials, that is a sure sign that it is working either toward a despotic or toward a republican condition.

I therefore think that the change from salaried to unpaid appointments by itself constitutes a real revolution.

I regard the complete absence of unpaid duties as one of the clearest indications of democracy's absolute sway in America. The public pays for all services of whatever sort performed in its interest; hence any man has the chance as well as the right to perform them.

TOCQUEVILLE, *Democracy in America*

[1]Excerpted from Ethics-in-Government Laws: Are They Too Ethical? by Alfred S. Neely IV, Edward H. Hinton Professor of Law at University of Missouri Law School. Reprinted by permission of the American Enterprise Institute for Public Policy Research. Copyright © 1984.

These observations by Alexis de Tocqueville concerned America in the first half of the nineteenth century. Yet, as is so often the case, his insights travel well. Today compensation in return for public service continues to be a trait of public life in America, and presumably the likelihood of Tocqueville's "real revolution" remains remote. Nevertheless, there are persistent reports of persons who decline public positions or leave them prematurely because of inadequate compensation. To the extent that this is or becomes a major phenomenon, inadequate compensation may have the same effect as none at all on the character and quality of public life.

The purpose here is not to analyze and debate the adequacy of compensation in public life. Tocqueville's commentary serves, however, to highlight a point of obvious and fundamental importance: economics may play as important a role as devotion to the public good in a decision to accept or reject a public position. Indeed, this led Tocqueville to the conclusion that "in the United States it is men of moderate pretensions who engage in the twists and turns of politics. Men of . . . vaulting ambition generally avoid power to pursue wealth; the frequent result is that men undertake to direct the fortunes of the state only when they doubt their capacity to manage their private affairs." One need not be so harsh to accept the view that the economics of public service may often prove a deterrent to persons who are otherwise able and willing to serve.

There may be barriers to public service other than direct remuneration that are less obvious and dramatic but are still essentially economic. Ethics-in-government laws are one possible source of such barriers.

In general it would seem that there can never be a surplus of ethics in the conduct of governmental affairs. This perception may arise especially where there is real or potential competition between the personal inclinations and interests of a public servant and notions of the public interest. In such cases the high value placed on ethics in government dictates subordination of personal interests to the public interest. This is understandable inasmuch as it is both philosophically and politically expedient to equate the highest standards of ethical conduct with the highest standards of good government.

During the 1970s, particularly in the post-Watergate era, there arose an intense and resurgent interest in ethics in government. This was reflected in the passage of the Ethics in Government Act of 1978, which, among other things, created a new Office of Government Ethics. The interest was not confined to the public sector. Bar associations, for example, devoted considerable time and effort to ethical standards for attorneys with past or present government service.

The purpose of this study is to examine various facets and implications of federal ethics-in-government laws. The premise is not and should not be that ethical conduct in governmental affairs is not a worthy and desirable objective. A premise that does merit examination, however, is that ethics-in-government laws are not without costs, which must be identified and weighed in the balance against their benefits. It may well be that the marginal costs of additional limits on those in or considering government service are such that those limits are difficult to justify in light of their overall effect on the nature and quality of government. If so, greater ethical constraints in government may not necessarily produce better government in the long run.

There is reason to believe that ethics-in-government laws create potential barriers to entry into, exit from, and consequently excellence in the federal public service. If this is so, it may be time for reexamination and refinement of those laws to make certain that their costs are fully understood and appreciated when measured against their benefits. The ultimate objective should be to ensure that whatever balance is struck between these interests is reflected accurately in the ethics-in-government laws.

The varieties of ostensibly ethical constraints on government service are numerous. Here, however, the focus is not on the propriety of entertainment of government officials while in office or of a gift of a turkey at Thanksgiving. Nor is it on blatant bribery of public officials, although these are important as background and contrast and are examined to some extent. Rather, the concern here is with the ethical constraints of less obvious and compelling force that may have the effect of inhibiting entry into or exit from government service. . . .

The Modesty of Direct Costs
and the Immodesty of Indirect Costs

The direct costs of present ethics-in-government laws are relatively modest. Certainly various persons while in government service and after leaving it find that they are unable to do various things they might otherwise do, but these limits tend to be recognized, if not always accepted, as simply one more aspect of the restrictions on personal freedom that accompany most forms of employment. Compliance with these requirements is rather straightforward, though on occasion painful. For most they are another thing to consider and for some another report to file. The mere act of compliance is not especially burdensome, and the uncertainty accompanying compliance usually is not great. When in doubt, avoid it, divest it, or resign.

From the government's perspective also the direct costs are not significant. Added costs for enforcement and administration are not particularly high in the grand scheme of things, although they may be somewhat greater since the creation in 1978 of the Office of Government Ethics.

Indirect costs, however, though less conspicuous, may tend toward the immodest. . . .

This, of course, does not mean that the government will be left untended. Other persons have comparable background and experience may be willing to make the adjustments necessary under present laws. . . . As former Treasury Secretary William Simon once observed in objecting to the implications of the 1978 act: "It is just ridiculous. We're going to end up with nothing but academics and neuters." Yet even if this statement is too strong, the government has suffered a loss; its options have been limited, as some persons who presumably were its first choice have been excluded from consideration.

The assertion that the ethics-in-government laws hinder the ability of the government to attract some of the persons it desires for public service has met with skepticism. One editorial commentator noted, for example: "Now that President-elect Reagan has chosen almost all of his Cabinet, some preliminary answers emerge to a question raised by the transition workers: Does the 1978 Ethics in Government Act now make top-level recruitment too hard? To oversimplify a bit, the answer is no." Others have suggested, however, that the problem is even more pronounced at "the sub-Cabinet level—where public service largely lacks the incentive of a title that 'your grandchildren will remember.'"

It is on this point that empirical research would be most beneficial. To know who was lost to the government and under what circumstances would add much to the debate. But that is beyond the scope of this study, and a few examples from the popular press will have to suffice. In the future, congressional hearings on the issue would be a useful substitute for empirical research.

During the transition from the Carter to the Reagan administration there were reports of various losses. A banker declined the job of deputy energy secretary because of family oil interests. A senior vice-president of a major corporation turned down the position of under secretary of the interior because he concluded that the restrictions on the activities of a former government employee would have precluded his becoming president of his company when he returned. Another person refused the position of secretary of the interior because of conflicts with family grazing rights on federal lands. The reader can decide whether these cases reflect a problem and constitute a loss to the government.

Naturally, if a person is monastic in his inclinations, has few personal needs outside his work, takes a self-imposed vow of poverty, renounces his worldly possessions, and has no family or an extremely supportive one, these matters should be of little more than academic interest. The same may be true of very wealthy persons. A few years ago the extremely wealthy son of a famous family observed during a gubernatorial race that he, unlike his opponent, had sufficient money that the public need not be concerned that he would dip into the public fisc. Both are extreme cases.

The experience of one state with ethics in government is more typical. The legislature passed a law requiring extensive disclosure of personal financial interests. A psychiatrist, facing the problem of identifying his patients by name, decided not to stand for reelection. Lawyers had the same problem concerning clients, and the number of lawyers in the legislature decreased dramatically. Some would see that as undeniably beneficial, but the indirect cost was the unavailability of such persons for public office. Federal ethics-in-government laws create the same indirect costs. Only their magnitude is unknown.

Ethics-in-Government Laws
and the Quality of Government:
Can Government Ever Be Too "Ethical"?

The ethics-in-government laws reflect one set of significant and worthwhile values. In great measure they serve to develop and protect public confidence in the integrity of government. It is important to note that present ethics-in-government laws do not attempt to achieve the highest conceivable standards. They are not unbending but reveal a degree of pragmatism and compromise in response to the exigencies as well as the aspirations of good government. Thus, in asking whether government can ever be too ethical, we must bear in mind that present laws are not as demanding as they might be.

To follow the implications of many of the present ethics-in-government laws, however, is to glimpse the underlying ideal of absolute ethical conduct in government service. This ideal might be reached by removing the temptations and circumstances that have led to the present legal restrictions, which afford a picture of the ideal public servant.

The ideal public servant should have no personal financial needs that the rewards he receives in return for his service cannot satisfy. There should be no need for part-time jobs to supplement his public income. And he should have no financial interests that might present conflicts. His personal finances should be simple. What he brings to government or accumulates while there should be invested in nothing more flamboyant than U.S. savings bonds.

Naturally the ideal public servant must come from somewhere, but it is preferable if he comes to the government directly after graduation from the educational system. He will then not carry with him any baggage of potential conflicts arising from prior employment and experience. Moreover, the ideal public servant should have no desire or opportunity to move out of government service for any reason other than retirement or death.

This ideal obviously does not exist. Present ethics-in-government laws fall far short of pursuing this barren absolute. Is that to be taken as an indication that present laws are inadequate or that they are, at least to a degree, "unethical"? The clear and correct answer is that it is not. Present laws merely reflect and accommodate other equally important values. Legislators may value a public service cadre that is a mixture of career employees and those who come to government for a relatively short period of time. If realization of this goal requires some relaxation in the ideal of the public servant, that does not constitute a slide toward less ethical or unethical standards. Rather it constitutes a rejection of the notion of a permanent bureaucracy and a recognition of the reality that if we value the influx of new people and ideas into government, we cannot extract a promise that they stay for life in the name of ethics and expect most of them to come.

It is thus quite possible for ethics-in-government laws to be too ethical. One may conclude, for example, that avoidance of all appearances of conflict of interest is to be valued above all else. The laws that follow will be too ethical to the extent that they sacrifice other important values. There is nothing improper in this if a consensus is reached that one value is higher than all others and is to be pursued at their expense. But if there is no single-minded commitment to a single value, something less can be expected, understood, and valued as the outcome of a competition among different and competing values. That is why present ethics-in-government laws are not in any sense "unethical" and why slightly less stringent laws would be no more so.

The importance of this cannot be overstated. The temptation in discussing ethics in government is to view any relaxation from some ideal of conduct as a subversion of the ideal and a fortiori less ethical. That view is unduly superficial; what may seem less is more accurately only different—a different value. If the other value is worthy and prevails to some extent when weighed in competition with the ideal, it is not unethical.

The danger that must be recognized and avoided is the assumption that there can never be a harmful surplus of ethics in government. In reality ethics in government are susceptible to the adverse consequences of oversupply. It is like purity in foods; as one approaches the absolute of purity in foods, the costs of each additional increment of purity rise exponentially.

A Time for Reexamination and Refinement

Obviously the goal of ethical conduct in the performance of public duties should not be abandoned. But periodic reexamination and refinement of the ethics-in-government laws are reasonable and worthwhile undertakings. Today is not too soon. Ample time has passed to permit a degree of detachment from the atmosphere of Watergate without losing sight of its most important lessons. In addition, the government has had over five years and a transition in administrations to gain experience in the workings of the Ethics in Government Act of 1978.

If a reexamination does occur, a number of refinements deserve consideration. Assessment of their merits depends in great measure on certain basic assumptions, the most important of which is that a career bureaucracy, especially at the higher levels in the executive branch, is undesirable and therefore to be rejected. From this it follows that public service for less than a lifetime is to be encouraged.

In this context it is easier to recognize that federal public service is but one among many alternatives open to persons capable of serving at the higher levels of government and making substantial contributions to the quality of government. Government service competes in a wider marketplace for the services of these persons, and in the absence of a system of conscription for nonmilitary public officers and employees, their decisions to accept or reject public positions are voluntary. Consequently, ethics-in-government laws are part of a bargain; if they are unduly restrictive, no bargain will be struck, and the government will lose the services of persons it wants and needs.

With these points and principles in mind, we can consider without guilt the following areas in which the ethics-in-government laws merit reexamination and perhaps refinement. Modification of the laws need not be viewed as a sacrifice of the public interest to the cause of private gain. The ultimate interest of the government in modification of these laws may be just as great as that of private persons or even greater.

The adequacy of federal compensation is beyond the scope of this study, but it is common knowledge that compensation for those in the higher reaches of government is not fully competitive with that in the private sector. Apparently political realities make direct resolution of this problem impossible. But some change in the ethics-in-government laws could ameliorate the effects of otherwise inadequate compensation. Under the government's supervision and with its consent, the ban on other compensation for government services should be lifted. This would open the way for private sector supplementation of government wages and remove the specter of a loss in necessary income from the list of considerations of many prospective government employees.

Similarly, the 15 percent ceiling on outside earned income for high-level officers and employees should be raised or entirely eliminated. For a person with a $50,000 federal salary, the 15 percent limit is unrealistic. Such persons are likely to have the capacity for greater earnings without significant expenditures of time and effort. A government employee who has outside employment as a consultant at a rate of $100 an hour will spend little time on the outside before encountering the ceiling. The opportunity to earn more may be essential if he is to join the government and remain for a reasonable time. The only limiting factors should be that the outside activities must not jeopardize the employee's capacity to perform his government duties and must not create conflicts of interest with those duties. With these restrictions, lifting or removing the ceiling might delay the day when the employee leaves government service to put his children through college.

The financial disclosure laws should also be altered. The information that must be disclosed seems reasonable. The government has an interest in making an independent determination of the existence or appearance of improprieties and conflicts. What is less clear is the necessity for public dissemination of this information. If independent public officials review the information and take whatever action they believe necessary, the fundamental interests of the government should be protected. Admittedly, the interests of the media and some of the public would not be served, but to satisfy these interests as well is to accept certain costs.

In the last transition of administrations, it was reported that one perspective appointee for a high position withdrew upon learning of the disclosure requirements and observed: "Nobody knows how wealthy I am. I don't even want my children to know." A desire to preserve privacy concerning personal affairs is not difficult to understand, and if this interest and the interests of the government can be accommodated, they should be. Public reporting without public disclosure would be an alternative middle ground. This was the approach taken before the Ethics in Government Act under Executive Order No. 11222, and a return to it has merit. Otherwise we may lose the public services of persons who have nothing to hide but do have something they value— their privacy. Recalling that the Constitutional Convention managed to produce commendable results while conducting its proceedings in secrecy, we can recognize secrecy as not inevitably untoward or undesirable.

Another area for inquiry is the role of professional organizations such as bar associations in the development of standards that become de facto federal ethics-in-government laws. As others have suggested:

Problems arise . . . when the bar attempts to develop special rules that are applicable only to government attorneys. Insofar as conflict-of-interest rules for government lawyers are based on judgments about public policy and effective government rather than professional regulation alone, such choices are more appropriately made within the government as a part of the normal policymaking process. Thus, while professional standards that apply to all attorneys are the proper province of the bar associations, rules applicable to government attorneys alone are more appropriately formulated by the government entity.

This reasoning is sound and justifies the conclusion that some federal preemption of the activities of professional organizations is in order to the extent that those activities purport to control the ethical conduct of government attorneys. Furthermore, there is reason to extend this approach to matters relating to the activities of former government attorneys. What is permissible after leaving government service may affect government interests as much as what is permissible while in it.

Another area of the law that warrants closer scrutiny concerns the personal interests of government officers and employees. Some thought should be given to the possibility of allowing separation of control over personal assets through a trust without insisting on divestiture. Although a trust that retains assets originally placed in it is not a blind trust, it may be too much to expect some persons to dispose of their assets to eliminate questions of conflicts of interest.

The alternative may be especially undesirable to the government. An extensive disqualification agreement may reduce the effectiveness of the employee and make divestiture the only alternative. . . . The problem is the appearance of impropriety. If disqualification were limited to actual conflicts and such persons were allowed to place their assets in trust beyond their control but without an effective mandate to divest, an accommodation might be reached that would permit government service.

The need for such accommodations is particularly acute for some. Self-made persons are likely to have assets that are concentrated in a single area or company rather than diversified; questions of the need for divestiture will be more common among them. Presumably the traits exhibited by the self-made person would be of some use to the government.

These are a few illustrative areas for reexamination and refinement. They suggest the kind of government interests that might be given greater weight than in the past in devising ethics-in-government laws. To do so might improve the quality of government. A greater pool of willing and capable talent would be available for federal public service. The disproportionate effects of the ethics-in-government laws, especially on the middle class and the private sector, would be reduced. If there are fewer barriers to entry and exit, there should be greater opportunities for excellence.

THE OFFICE OF GOVERNMENT ETHICS:
VIGILANT WATCHDOG OR TOOTHLESS TERRIER?[2]

Attorney General Edwin Meese III has made the U.S. Office of Government Ethics (OGE) famous. Obscurity may never have looked so good.

Since 1985, controversy over Meese's byzantine financial dealings has twice thrust the federal government's guardian of public virtue into the limelight. That year, OGE's staff drafted a memorandum stating that Meese had violated a prohibition against creating the appearance of a conflict of interest in his financial arrangements. But David H. Martin, OGE's former director, created an uproar on Capitol Hill when he said the admonition to avoid the appearance of impropriety was only a goal, not a rigid rule of conduct. In July, OGE again was in hot water on Capitol Hill because of Meese. Congressional critics like Rep. Gerry Sikorski, D-Minn., chairman of the House panel that oversees government ethics, chastized Martin for ignoring the alleged conflict of interest revealed by the attorney general's financial disclosure records. A special prosecutor in investigating the Attorney General's finances.

The two episodes raised troubling questions about OGE's willingness to tackle tough ethics issues involving prominent political appointees. To a growing number of critics, OGE's track record in the Meese case symbolizes the agency's reluctance to follow through on allegations of misconduct by high-level execu-

[2]Reprint of an article by W. John Moore, staff correspondent for *National Journal. Government Executive*, O. 1987, pp. 22–25. Reprinted by permission of National Journal Inc. Copyright © National Journal Inc.

tive branch employees. "OGE has failed to exercise this crucial authority," Sikorski said at a hearing held by his Post Office and Civil Service Subcommittee on Investigations last year. "Some have suggested that this supposed watchdog is more a toothless terrier on valium."

But lawyers and some former OGE ethics officials question the critics' focus on enforcement issues. They maintain that potential examples of criminal wrongdoing are referred to the Justice Department and that the federal agencies' own ethics officials are supposed to have the primary responsibility for criticizing any misconduct on the part of public officials. For example, the Veterans Administration's ethics office earlier this year conducted a major investigation into agency employees' relationship with the pharmaceutical industry. The VA has taken action ranging from proposed removal to ethics counseling against almost 100 agency employees.

Acting OGE director Donald E. Campbell says that while OGE may take a variety of "corrective actions" toward agencies or individuals to prevent a conflict of interest or other unethical situation, the agency is not empowered to dismiss employees or initiate criminal proceedings; where these kinds of punitive actions are concerned, OGE's capacity is purely advisory.

Established nine years ago in response to the ethical lapses uncovered during the Watergate period, OGE is the branch of the Office of Personnel Management charged with ensuring a high standard of conduct among executive branch officials. A House ethics committee and the Senate counsel perform similar functions for the legislative branch. Judges and other judicial officers are covered by the financial reporting requirements of the Ethics in Government Act, and the Judicial Conference of the United States has established its own Judicial Ethics Committee.

OGE has an annual budget of $1.25 million and a staff of 23, including nine management analysts, seven attorneys and a support staff. Martin, who left OGE in August to join a law practice, says the office is supposed to add seven to 12 more people to its staff this year and perhaps another five officials next year. The most important addition to the staff will be Martin's replacement. The White House announced in mid-September that President Reagan would ask the Senate to approve Frank Q. Nebeker, a federal appeals judge, as the new OGE director.

OGE's size reflects the design of the federal government's ethics program. "It has been structured as a very decentralized program," Campbell says. "The responsibility for ethics remains in each executive-branch agency. That is where the real heart of the ethics program is."

Designated ethics officials at each department or agency review financial disclosure statements, counsel employees on ethics standards and provide training and counseling on ethical issues. The inspectors general in the agencies usually investigate allegations of misconduct, while overall direction of executive-branch ethics issues is left to OGE.

Conflicts of Interest

Under the 1978 Ethics in Government Act, which was amended in 1983, OGE seeks to prevent conflicts of interest by federal employees. To accomplish that goal, the office implements financial disclosure requirements, enforces ethical standards of conduct, monitors the agencies' ethics programs and implements revolving-door regulations, which govern the post-employment activities of former government employees.

"The heart of the act was the first-ever requirement of high-ranking officials to file a public financial disclosure form," Martin says. Under the financial disclosure requirements, approximately 1,000 political appointees subject to Senate approval must annually file a comprehensive public report directly with OGE. Another 9,000 government employees whose salaries are equivalent to the GS-17 level or above must do the same within their agencies. Also, approximately 100,000 employees below that level who hold sensitive jobs in bank auditing, government contracting and defense procurement must file confidential financial reports with designated agency ethics officials.

Federal employees are prohibited under the ethics laws from having a financial interest that conflicts with their government duties and from engaging in business transactions that rely on information obtained through government employment. Few financial disclosure filings are cause for concern. Designated agency ethics officials can usually detect problems early in the process by comparing the candidate's investment portfolio with the job description. "Most are easy calls that are screened out at the agency before they get here," Campbell says.

In more complicated cases, OGE may ask employees to disqualify themselves from regulating companies in which they have a financial interest or working relationship. Divestiture of a financial stake in a company may be required in some instances. Blind trusts, an arrangement by which people are kept unaware of their own investments, have been used to avoid potential conflict-of-interest problems by approximately 40 appointees, including Meese and Alan Greenspan, the new chairman of the Federal Reserve Board.

In addition to ensuring adequate financial disclosure, the OGE must also protect against conflicts of interest in the activities of federal employees after they leave public service. All former executive branch employees are prohibited for life from representing another person before a U.S. agency, department or court in connection with a matter in which they participated "personally and substantially" while in government. Senior employees face two additional, temporary bans: For two years after leaving an agency, they may not *assist* in representing another person in connection with any matter in which they participated "personally and substantially," and for one year, they are prohibited from representing anyone which intent to influence actions of the agency from which they retired. Accountants, lawyers, lobbyists and any other "representatives" are covered by the law.

In at least one controversial decision, OGE has interpreted these conflict-of-interest rules somewhat broadly. High-ranking White House aides may lobby their former colleagues as soon as they leave government despite the apparent ban on such influence-peddling. At the request of then–White House counsel Fred Fielding in 1983, the ethics office ruled that for lobbying purposes, at least, the 1,500 member Executive Office of the President consists of nine separate compartments. The heads of each compartment would have to wait a year before they could lobby other White House officials. But staff members could immediately lobby officials in any part of the White House except those in their individual unit. At a congressional hearing in June, General Accounting Office witnesses said they found no support for OGE's decision to split up the Executive Office of the President, but the decision stands for now.

The Enforcement Problem

The most controversial part of OGE's job is enforcement. Under the ethics law, OGE can review allegations of wrongdoing and order "corrective action" for agencies and employees. Such action includes monitoring agency ethics programs, issuing public statements on highly publicized ethics cases, ordering public officials to comply with ethics laws and, in the most serious cases, referring ethics violations to the Justice Department for criminal prosecution.

OGE's performance as enforcer of the ethics laws has come under fire from many quarters. Critics of the government ethics office under former Reagan-Administration appointee Martin believe he ducked most of the tough enforcement decisions. "He is supposed to be an ethics cop but too often he failed to blow the whistle," says, Sen. Carl Levin, D-Mich., chairman of the Governmental Affairs Subcommittee on Oversight of Government Management.

"OGE under David Martin has been a farce," added Ann McBride, senior vice president of Common Cause, the citizen's lobbying group that was instrumental in getting ethics legislation passed on Capitol Hill.

But Martin and others argue that criticism of his regime at OGE is based on a misreading of the ethics statute. "We're not investigators," Martin stressed in an interview. "If we were viewed as prosecutors and cops, we really could not do our job in terms of training, ethics counseling, consulting and bringing people into compliance" with the law, he added.

Some government ethics officials agree with Martin's analysis. Former ethics chief J. Jackson Walter, now president of the National Trust for Historic Preservation, believes the primary mission of the ethics office is to bring government employees into compliance with disclosure and other standards rather than to punish them for failing to do so. "OGE is not a prosecutorial agency," he stressed. Gary Edwards, executive director of the Ethics Resource Center, a non-profit Washington group working to strengthen public trust in business and government, thinks OGE's mission may need to be redefined to include stronger enforcement provisions. "Whether the office was adequately conceived or not is something that Congress perhaps ought to reconsider," he says.

In some instances, says acting director Campbell, the agency may seem to be slow in its response to alleged ethics infractions only because the case has been sent to the Justice Department. Once a matter has been referred to the Justice Department for criminal action, OGE won't take any corrective action until the matter is resolved. OGE doesn't want to prejudice the ongoing criminal proceeding, Campbell says.

Double Standard?

There are long-standing allegations that OGE has a double standard when it comes to government employees. The ethics agency, its critics say, tends to be soft on political appointees with obvious conflicts of interest and tough on career civil servants who may have committed minor transgressions. "If you are powerful, politically connected, an appointee of a popular president, and your conduct is questionable, OGE acts like a St. Bernard and comes to your rescue. If you aren't big, aren't connected, aren't wealthy, the Feds come on like Doberman pinschers," Rep. Sikorski said at a September 1986 hearing on the Ethics in Government Act held by the House Post Office and Civil Service Subcommittee on Investigations.

Ethics experts contrast the strict punishment meted out to career employees who violate the "appearance of impropriety" prohibition with OGE's argument during Meese's confirmation hearing that such appearances are not a violation of conflict-of-interest laws.

Careerists who violated the appearance rules include a Housing and Urban Development appraiser who was fired in 1979 because of his involvement with a housing project owned by his wife. In another case, an Interior Department coal-mine inspector was suspended in 1984 for writing a letter to a coal company alleging that it had denied his son a job because of a citation the government had issued against the firm.

"The perception [of a double standard] is there," Campbell acknowledged, adding that he knows of no instances in which career employees were treated more harshly than political appointees.

Martin discounted those charges in an interview. He claimed career employees are unhappy with the less stringent ethical standards imposed on legislative branch. "Whenever I lecture to career people they agree that there is a double standard but they say it exists between the legislative branch and the executive branch," Martin says.

Some believe OGE's problems derive from the difficult balancing act facing any OGE director. "You are a political appointee, and yet you are often asked to make judgments on other political appointees who may be closer to the President than you are," says David R. Scott, former acting director of OGE and now a lawyer for Rutgers University in New Jersey.

But others dispute this analysis of OGE's intrinsic weakness. "The tools needed to be an effective watchdog are there. OGE needs a strong director willing to exercise those powers," countered Common Cause's McBride.

DEREGULATION BY SLEAZE[3]

Scandals in the Reagan Administration have become as regular as press releases. The House Subcommittee on Civil Service has issued a list of more than 200 Administration appointees accused of legal violations and ethical lapses. The rogues range from the President's California buddies—Attorney General Edwin Meese 3d, Lyn Nofziger, Michael Deaver—to the Board of Governors of the U.S. Postal Service.

A press that seems to avert its eyes, and a numbed Congress, have prevented the public from perceiving the systemic nature of the scandals, but the facts are clear: Ronald Reagan has presided over a wider range of official misdeeds than any other President in our history.

Some of this corruption stems from the doctrines of the Reagan revolution: If you believe that government is part of the problem and that regulation is illegitimate, then it's not wrong to help your friends in big business or to lie to Congress. But a closer examination of the ethical lapses reveals another pattern: The

[3]Reprinted from an article by Frank Donner, who has written two other books about current political issues, and James Ledbetter, research director of The Democracy Project, a public-policy institute in New York City. *The Nation.* F. 6, 1988. pp. 163–65. Reprinted by permission of The Nation Company, Inc. Copyright © 1988.

more opposed the Reagan Administration is to the goals of a given government agency, the more vulnerable the agency's officials are to corruption. This can be as simple as regulators allying with the regulated, or involve more complicated schemes of rule breaking, even graft. If it's politically impossible to shut down a regulatory agency, the Administration reasons, staff it with right-wingers who would rather stall and steal than enforce the law. The coincidence of ideology with malfeasance suggests that willful incompetence and corruption can be effective deregulatory tactics. Following are case studies of five Federal agencies that have been brought to a halt by greedy and derelict appointees.

The Occupational Safety and Health Administration

Ronald Reagan's hostility to OSHA preceded his presidency; in 1978, he termed OSHA "one of the most pernicious of the watchdog agencies," and in 1979 he warmly endorsed a bill calling for its abolition. Reagan also claimed that "through things such as OSHA, the government is trying to minimize the ownership of private property in this country."

While Reagan hasn't quite killed OSHA, he has managed to maim it. OSHA's staff has been slashed, and inspections of manufacturing concerns have declined by some 30 percent; OSHA finds far fewer violations than it did under previous Administrations, and it assesses lower fines—$13 million less in 1986 than in 1980, a drop of nearly 50 percent. This newfound leniency doesn't reflect an outbreak of safety, only the Reagan doctrine of industrial self-regulation.

This is not to say that there has been no activity at OSHA. Chair switching, for example, is popular: OSHA has had three official administrators under Reagan, and all have been accused of ethical violations and conflicts of interest. Thorne Auchter was the OSHA head in 1981, an ardent deregulator. He resigned in 1984 after allegations that he approved the dismissal of $12,080 in penalties and twelve proposed safety citations against a Kansas company owned by a firm of which he was president. Auchter also owned almost $22,000 in Du Pont stock during the time he refused to establish a formaldehyde standard, which Du Pont opposed. In addition, the U.S. government paid for trips that Auchter and his aides took to resort hotels in Palm Springs, California; Las Vegas; and St. Thomas, the Virgin Islands. Government-paid junkets are so widespread under Reagan that they merit the title "Billingsgate."

Auchter was replaced by Robert Rowland, a successful fund-raiser in Ronald Reagan's 1980 campaign, who continued his predecessor's inaction as well as his conflicts of interest. Rowland refused to set standards for formaldehyde, ethylene oxide and agricultural field sanitation despite his investments of several hundred thousand dollars in chemical and agricultural companies directly affected by his official decisions.

Top OSHA officials have also shared the President's view that their agency is fundamentally illegitimate and un-American. During Congressional testimony, Rowland admitted that he had said there were "Commies" at OSHA. OSHA health standards director Leonard Vance told one woman on his staff that she sounded as if she'd been "trained in Moscow." OSHA deputy director Jim Meadows told the staff that the way to deal with employees who criticize agency policy was to "kick asses and take names."

OSHA officials have also taken a hard line against Congressional oversight. Vance told a Congressional committee that he couldn't turn over his records because his "dog had barfed all over them."

The Nuclear Regulatory Commission

Like OSHA, the N.R.C. has been handed over to ideologues whose motto seems to be, "Industry, regulate thyself." The Institute of Nuclear Power Operations (INPO), a utility consortium founded after the Three Mile Island accident, has taken over many traditional N.R.C. responsibilities, such as setting safety standards and conducting inspections. "It's not just that policy is being made for the nuclear industry; in many cases it's being made by it," says Michael Mariotte, executive director of the Nuclear Information and Resource Service.

INPO-inspired deregulation has been ratified by the five N.R.C. commissioners, all Reagan appointees. Certain regulators have especially cozy relations with the nuclear industry. N.R.C. Commissioner Thomas Roberts has been under Congressional fire since last April, when he was charged with leaking a confidential memorandum to a nuclear utility that was under investigation for safety problems. Roberts, a former fund-raiser for Vice President George Bush, first suggested that a janitor might have taken the document from his office, then told Congress he had destroyed the memo for fear that someone was setting him up; finally he found a copy in his desk. Roberts later tried to interfere with an Office of Government Ethics investigation of his conflicts of interest. Seven Congressional leaders called for his resignation, to no avail.

While coddling the nuclear industry, top N.R.C. officials have turned against their own employees. N.R.C. executive director of operations Victor Stello has been accused of repeated harassment of employees. In one instance, Stello is said to have tipped off a Tennessee Valley Authority nuclear official on how to sidestep an N.R.C. stop-work order at a plant under construction. When the N.R.C.'s director of investigations suggested that N.R.C.-T.V.A. relations be monitored more closely, Stello shook his fist in the man's face and said, "I'm going to get you!" Stello also tried to force a regional official to undergo psychiatric "retraining" after the official submitted a report criticizing safety at a Texas nuclear plant.

The N.R.C.'s assorted derelictions were documented in a year-end Congressional report. A former Justice Department official in charge of N.R.C. cases told Congress, "I know of no other agency where senior officials have taken as many bizarre and seemingly deliberate actions intended to hamper the investigation and prosecution of individuals and companies [whom] the agency regulates."

The Legal Services Corporation

The right has always opposed publicly financed legal services for the poor. In *Mandate for Leadership*, the Heritage Foundation's blueprint for the Reagan Administration, Alfred Regnery wrote that L.S.C.'s work is designed to "erode the free enterprise system" and concluded that "the only real option is [L.S.C.'s] demise." (Regnery later became the Justice Department's director of juvenile justice but resigned in the wake of allegations stemming from a cache of pornography that was found in his house.)

The call for L.S.C.'s abolition was made as recently as last February by no less than the corporation's president, William Clark Durant 3d. Although every White House budget for the past seven years has allocated no money for L.S.C., Congress has kept it alive, only to see it staffed by a series of greedy ideologues:

• Michael Wallace was confirmed to the L.S.C. board in 1985, despite the fact that his legal experience included vigorous opposition to the extension of the Voting Rights Act and orchestrating the Administration's infamous "Bob Jones" decision to grant tax exemptions to segregated schools.

• One Reagan appointee who never got a chance to direct legal aid to the poor was George Paras, who allegedly attacked a Hispanic judge as a "professional Mexican," explaining that there were also "professional blacks, professional Greeks, professional Dagos and professional Jews" who "put their ethnic origin ahead of everything else." His appointment was withdrawn.

• William Harvey, chair of the L.S.C. board from 1981 to 1982, submitted highly inflated expense reports to the government, including $442 a day for driving expenses between Washington and his home in Indianapolis. Former L.S.C. president Donald Bogard's contract, negotiated with Harvey, his friend, included government payment for a private club membership, twenty-four trips home per year and a year's severance pay if fired. William Olsen, L.S.C. director, collected hefty consulting fees from the government.

Commenting on the Harvey and Olsen scandals, Representative M. Caldwell Butler said, "I'm a Republican, and we bring in these Republicans to take charge of this corporation . . . and it sounds an awful lot like the first thing they do was to go and put all four feet and a snout into the trough."

The Consumer Product Safety Commission

This agency, a relic of the Ralph Nader–influenced 1970s, was another target of *Mandate for Leadership*, which noted that since C.P.S.C.'s abolition "could prove politically unfeasible, the Administration [should] continue the agency but was drastic cutbacks in funding, permitting CPSC to operate only as an educational and informational agency."

Accordingly, after C.P.S.C. lost nearly a quarter of its already tiny budget, it announced that it could not study or correct products that cause 130,000 deaths and injuries each year, including rider lawn mowers, snow blowers and kerosene heaters. C.P.S.C. has not issued a final safety regulation since 1984.

C.P.S.C. officials have not been especially absorbed with public safety. Nancy Harvey Steorts, C.P.S.C. chair from 1981 to 1984, spent $10,000 in government funds to redecorate her office. She also requested that her chauffeur wear a uniform and hat and, advised that this was improper, told him to wear a suit instead. When he claimed that he could not afford one, two C.P.S.C. officials made the purchase for him. Apparently, the chauffeur had to look sharp when he drove Steorts' daughter to see her friends.

C.P.S.C. chair Terrence Scanlon had more serious extraregulatory interests. During his 1985–86 confirmation hearings (he had been acting chair for nearly a year), Scanlon was grilled about using government staff to handle his real estate investments, church duties and work on behalf of the anti-abortion movement. Scanlon denied the charges, prompting a C.P.S.C. staff member to document fifty-two cases of such abuse. Despite his apparent perjury and a Justice Department investigation, Scanlon was confirmed.

Recently the C.P.S.C. made headlines by banning "all-terrain vehicles." But its critics point out that the commission's years of delay contributed to nearly 700 deaths and 300,000 injuries and that C.P.S.C. let the industry off by not forcing a recall.

Last year Scanlon reassigned a longtime C.P.S.C. compliance chief to a field position. A fellow C.P.S.C. commissioner wrote to Scanlon bluntly: "If your objective is to paralyze the commission, you have succeeded."

The U.S. Civil Rights Commission

Nowhere has the Reagan Administration shown its mean spirit more than in its hostility to civil rights and racial minorities. Commissioner Clarence Pendleton Jr.'s war on civil rights has been so effective that even a fellow Reagan appointee to the commission has called for his resignation.

While the C.R.C.'s decline has been well documented [see Mary Frances Berry, "Taming the Civil Rights Commission," *The Nation*, February 2, 1985], the gross mismanagement and individual misdeeds at the agency are less known. Pendleton was sued by his former employer, the San Diego Urban League, for fraud, breach of contract, intent to deceive and defraud, and misuse of funds for personal use. He also misled the Senate during his confirmation hearings about $50,000 in expense reimbursements he had received without paying taxes on them.

Pendleton's personal assistant, Sydney Novell, was reportedly the target of a Small Business Administration investigation for self-dealing, conflicts of interest and breaches of trust, caused by the relationship between a consulting firm run by her and one owned by Pendleton. Former C.R.C. staff director Linda Chavez was accused of abusing Civil Service rules, mismanaging Federal employees and mishandling travel payments and financial records during her days at the commission.

A recent audit by the General Accounting Office could not account for $175,000 in Civil Rights Commission funds earmarked for a fair-housing hearing and noted a sharp drop in commission productivity. Pendleton, however, has not suffered; although chairing is a part-time job, he billed the government for 240 workdays in 1985, yielding a salary of $67,344, plus $29,300 in expenses. Last year, he was restricted to working 125 days.

Reagan has said that he hopes his historical imprint "will be one of high morality." Perhaps he was referring to his futile efforts to restore prayer in the public schools or to the "Just Say No" campaign. But the more likely legacy is sleaze. Intentional incompetence is part of a strategy to subvert Congress's wishes. Unless Congress can muster a stronger response than it has yet showed, the regulatory sabotage may endure well beyond our current age of scandal.

WHITE HOUSE ETHICS[4]

As in earlier administrations, during the Reagan Administration, the issue of public service ethics has become the focus of the news media, political candidates, and a concerned citizenry. A perjury case involving Michael Deaver, President Reagan's former chief of staff; a criminal lobbying case involving Lyn Nof-

[4]Excerpted from *White House Ethics: The History of the Politics of Conflict of Interest Legislation,* by Robert N. Roberts, Assistant Professor of Political Science of James Madison University. (Contributions in Political Science, No. 204, Greenwood Press, Inc., Westport, Ct., 1988), pp. 191–201. Copyright © 1988 by Robert N. Roberts. Reprinted with permission of author and publisher.

ziger, a former top political aide; questions about financial compliance by Attorney General Edwin Meese; and the whole business of the Iran-Contra affair, where profits from sales of arms to the Iranians were used to support Nicaraguan rebels, have fueled a debate over ethics that began before the Civil War.

Because Americans are more comfortable ignoring history, we respond to the scandals of each administration with a sense of outrage and a demand for action. However, before we begin agitating for quick remedies for deep-seated ills, it might be wiser to look at the present in the broader context of the past. . . .

The issue of ethics in government today is not drastically different from what it was in earlier administrations. However, the picture of former high-level federal officials turning to lobbying for a ready source of income, and other questionable forms of official conduct, have increased public cynicism over the ability of American society to keep government clean.

Without the risk of making a premature historical judgment, I can make these generalizations. First, during the Reagan Administration, political polarization over the issue of integrity in government has sharpened. Liberals continue to attack the president for letting private-interest groups set government policy and dictate the operation of key programs. On the other hand, conservatives continue to denounce provisions of the ethics law as intentionally designed to embarrass presidential appointees who came into government to implement the Reagan revolution. Such polarization will make it difficult to build a consensus on how to maintain integrity in the public service.

Second, extended media exposure and private-life muckraking have cooled the enthusiasm of many prospective government servants. The sleaze factor will make it more difficult to recruit top-flight executive talent for policy-making positions in presidential administrations. The cost of national public service in the fishbowl atmosphere of Washington, D.C., may be too high for sought-after candidates and their families.

Third, the integrity problems of the Reagan years will surely promote a prolonged debate over where we go from here in the management of government ethics.

The Politics of Integrity

The May 25, 1987, edition of *Time Magazine* pointed to the misconduct allegations leveled against more than one hundred high-level Reagan officials as evidence that the administration had apparently "suffered a breakdown of the immune system [and opened] the way to all kinds of ethical and moral infections." The article made the point that almost every one of the Reagan officials implicated in wrongdoing maintained that they had done nothing illegal or unethical.

On December 17, 1987, a federal grand jury found Michael Deaver guilty of three counts of perjury regarding his lobbying activities after leaving the Reagan White House. A day after the verdict, independent counsel Whitney North Seymour publicly lashed out against "too much 'loose money'" in Washington and about too little concern about ethics in government." Seymour declared that the Ethics in Government Act had done little to limit behind-the-scenes lobbying by former high-level officials because it contained too many loopholes. Almost eight years after the passage of the 1978 Ethics Act, the Deaver conviction is the first jury conviction obtained by an independent counsel appointed to investigate allegations of criminal conduct by senior government officials.

Still, confusion over ethics regulations persists. On December 15, 1987, Ronald Reagan signed the independent counsel reauthorization into law despite his "very strong doubts about its constitutionality." President Reagan argued that his veto of the law would have eroded public confidence in government. As the Reagan presidency draws to a close, the country seems no closer to solving the problems of conflicts of interest in government than it was when Congress enacted the Ethics in Government Act.

From the beginning of the Reagan Administration, the White House and Reagan nominees and appointees have taken a legalistic view of conflict of interest regulation and public service ethics. Despite the fact that Executive Order 11222 directed both political appointees and career officials to avoid even the appearance of impropriety, the Reagan White House has refused to publicly criticize a presidential appointee for violating the order. Since the media and most members of Congress know very little about the scope of the order, the strategy of simply ignoring it has worked throughout most of the Reagan Administration. Only possible violations of criminal law have warranted close administration attention.

The Reagan Administration has viewed the Ethics in Government Act of 1978 as liberal legislation designed to make it difficult for a conservative Republican president to recruit and retain supporters to lobby for and implement his programs. However, the Reagan White House soon realized that Congress would not repeal any provisions of the Ethics Act and that a significant watering down of Executive Order 11222 could reinforce the charge that the administration did not care about integrity in government. The sleaze factor, the administration maintains, is a political issue, and has nothing to do with the types of individuals recruited or the quality of leadership by the president. The Reagan White House has taken a position remarkably similar to that of the Eisenhower White House when it was confronted with charges of impropriety which had been leveled against many of its officials.

Critics of the Reagan Administration typically explain this attitude toward public service ethics as the result of overconfidence brought about by two landslide election victories and the recruitment of key officials with a disdain for government. However, this explanation is too simplistic when one looks at the evolution of conflict of interest regulation. The debate centers on sharp differences of opinion on how to keep both elected and nonelected officials accountable to the electorate as discretionary government increases. It reflects wide differences on the legislative and administrative steps Congress and a president should take to safeguard against even the appearance of financial interest in decision making.

Since the end of the Second World War, liberals have generally argued that, with the emphasis on the accumulation of wealth in our society, Congress and the president must take a strong stand to let appointed and career officials and employees know that personal financial interests must not play a role in any official action. Conservatives, on the other hand, argue that ethical rules and regulations can go only so far before they deter those individuals needed to make government run efficiently and effectively. Liberals, the conservatives argue, have pushed morality for political purposes rather than for better ethics in government.

In early 1985, during Senate confirmation proceedings, attorney general designate Edwin Meese pledged "to avoid any circumstance that could be misunderstood or misconstrued in any way," including taking "extraordinary steps in terms of [his] financial affairs." By the spring of 1987, the attorney general came under strong criticism for apparently failing to live up to his promise.

On April 30, 1987, Senator Carl Levin, Democrat from Michigan, asked David Martin, the director of the Office of Government Ethics, to investigate the failure of the attorney general to list on his annual financial disclosure statements transactions related to the management of a "limited blind partnership" Meese and his wife had entered into in May of 1985. The partnership drew national attention because it was managed by San Francisco businessman and former Wedtech Corp. official W. Franklin Chinn. On an initial investment of $50,662, Meese and his wife earned $35,000 over a two-year period.

The attorney general's financial disclosure statement reported the investment as managed by Financial Management, Inc. (a limited blind partnership) and also accurately reported income from the partnership. The Office of Government Ethics had not approved the partnership as a blind trust, however. Without approval of the Ethics Office, the financial interests acquired by the partnership were the financial interests of the attorney general even though he had no knowledge of the investments made by Mr. Chinn. This meant that federal law prohibited Meese from taking action with respect to any matter involving any of the investments made by the blind partnership. Although a subsequent disclosure by the attorney general revealed that none of the transactions involved a matter dealt with him personally, critics of Meese maintained that he had violated the Ethics Act.

On May 11, 1987, David H. Martin, the director of the Office of Government Ethics, informed Senator Levin that the Ethics Office had not approved the limited blind partnership as a blind trust, and that the law prohibited such an arrangement from obtaining approval. In early July 1987, when Senator Levin released this letter, the attorney general placed the blame for the confusion on the Office of Government Ethics because of its failure to notify him that the partnership did not qualify as a blind trust. Fred Wertheimer, president of Common Cause, laid the blame on the attorney general on the grounds that the attorney general, if anyone, should know what the law regulates. Wertheimer also urged appropriate government officials "to determine what sanctions should be imposed for Mr. Meese's violations."

A persistent critic of the Reagan Administration's record on integrity and the management of the Office of Government Ethics, Senator Levin held a hearing on July 9, 1987 to investigate the attorney general's blind partnership arrangement. Senator Levin sharply criticized the Office of Government Ethics for not questioning the blind partnership arrangement, and criticized Mr. Meese for not realizing that the Ethics Act did not permit the "blinding" of such an arrangement without Ethics Office approval. The attorney general continued to maintain that he had not realized his error. After the hearing, Meese accused Senator Levin of engaging in partisan politics by attempting to portray the blind partnership arrangement as an effort to conceal dealings with a former Wedtech official.

David Martin resigned his position as director of the Office of Government Ethics in late August 1987, to go into private law practice.

PUBLIC SERVICE AND LIFE BEYOND THE BELTWAY

Following the Second World War, debate over conflict of interest and other integrity issues has complicated recruitment for high-level political and career government positions. Publicity surrounding the problems of Reagan Administration officials will make it more difficult for future presidents to convince the country's executive talent to make the sacrifices associated with high-level federal service. Future presidents may then have to rely heavily on the increasing ranks of policy experts and consultants already living and working in the Washington, D.C., metropolitan area. These professionals typically have few relocation costs and tend to have a higher tolerance for the restrictions placed on their public and private conduct. However, increased reliance on the bureaucracy-in-waiting would have significant drawbacks: It would lessen the input of individuals who are not part of the Washington establishment and who might have a better understanding of the problems of the country as a whole. Significantly, the relationship between conflict of interest regulation and executive recruitment involves the problem of diversity of appointments rather than the problem of unfilled positions.

During the early 1950s, Senator Paul Douglas came to recognize that the modern administrative state multiplied opportunities for conflicts of interest on the part of nonelected government officials. More important, he also recognized that in an era of increased discretionary government, the success or failure of a policy or program often hinged on whether the legislative branch, the media, and the American public trusted the individual official responsible for advocating or implementing the policy. A major consequence of discretionary government had to be greater concern with the ethical behavior of public officials.

The importance of trust in public officials, as Senator Douglas observed, was illustrated during the recent Iran-Contra hearings. Before the majority of the American public accepted the explanation of Oliver North for his participation in the arm sales to Iran and in the diversion of profits to the Nicaraguan Contras, Colonel North had to explain why he had used travelers checks purchased with Contra funds for personal purposes and why he had accepted a security system from a private source when regulations prohibited the acceptance of gifts from individuals having dealings with the United States Government. North explained that he had used the travelers checks to reimburse himself for out-of-pocket expenses related to aiding the Contras, and that he had accepted the security because of the government's refusal to protect his family after terrorist threats. Oliver North, in other words, had to convince Americans that he had not gained personally from his activities.

High-level presidential appointments often underestimate the effect of minor appearance problems on the credibility of an official. Moreover, it is often even more difficult for these officials to understand the need to avoid appearance problems in order to protect the credibility of discretionary decision making. When the Bureau of Internal Revenue scandal erupted during the final years of the Truman Administration, Congress and key Truman advisers realized that, without quick action to clean up the mess, large numbers of taxpayers might write off the tax system as corrupt and further increase the already serious tax evasion problem.

Most government agencies rely on voluntary compliance with the rules and regulations essential to operating government programs. If the public loses trust in its nonelected or elected officials, voluntary compliance with these rules on the part of thousands of federal workers will suffer. To this extent, conflict of interest regulations serves a vital symbolic role: it demonstrates to the public that public service requires officials to remain beyond reproach, not just within the letter of the law.

However, conflict of interest regulation should not be used to exclude competent people from entering government on the claim of bias or predisposition. As explained by J. Jackson Walter, the director of the Office of Government Ethics from 1979 to 1983, "Whether [one's] previous career will permit objective and impartial performance in government office is a decision to be made in the first instance by the president, who is the appointing authority, and subsequently by the Senate, which is the confirming body."

MOVING INTO THE GLASS HOUSE

Since the early 1960s, the White House counsel's office has spent increasingly large amounts of time reviewing the backgrounds of nominees and appointees for conflict of interest problems and negotiating solutions. With the passage of the Ethics in Government Act in 1978, the Office of Government Ethics assumed an important clearance responsibility, but for reasons of time and policy, the emphasis on public trust and decision making has varied from one administration to the next. Many officials come to view the complex conflict of interest regulations as potential land mines hindering their ability to do their jobs, and work under the constant fear that they might unintentionally violate some regulation and find themselves on the front page of the *Washington Post* for an alleged violation.

While not stating it publicly, many political appointees believe that the appearance standard creates too much pressure and opens them to unjustified partisan attacks. To avoid an appearance of a conflict of interest, they are forced to examine and possibly alter all types of relationships they have developed over a lifetime. In brief, conflict of interest regulation lacks the institutional support of many officials responsible for setting the ethical tone of their government organizations.

During the Kennedy and Johnson administrations, John Macy worked to build the administrative ethics program in the belief that it would eliminate much of the confusion surrounding conflict of interest rules and regulations. Over time, he hoped, both career and political officials would come to rely on their designated agency ethics officials to guide them around potential problems. With detailed agency standards of conduct, he believed, employees and officials would know what was permitted and what was not. Clarifying the rules would remove one of the objections to entering government service. However, Macy greatly underestimated the organizational resistance to making ethics management a high-priority item.

BIPARTISANSHIP AND PUBLIC SERVICE ETHICS

Republican Administrations, the record shows, have regarded conflict of interest regulations as more burdensome on Republican appointees than on their Democratic counterparts. The Eisenhower, Nixon, and Reagan administrations actively recruited large numbers of individuals from business and industry on the theory that only executives who had to meet a payroll would have a good grasp of running an organization efficiently. In contrast, Democratic presidents Truman, Kennedy, Johnson, and Carter relied much more heavily on federal career officials, state and local officials, and university faculty to fill key positions. The media thus judge a new Republican administration in terms of how many successful private-sector supporters accept top positions. A Democratic president is not expected to recruit many corporate leaders to direct federal programs.

Republican administrations, consequently, expect liberals to challenge their appointees on the grounds that private-sector businessmen will use their positions to help their former employers or industries to gain special treatment. Democratic administrations, in contrast, expect conservatives to challenge Democratic appointees on the grounds that they will use their positions to impose stronger government regulation of business and industry. These opposing methods of staffing executive federal positions are reflected in attitudes about conflict of interest regulation. With the exception of Harry Truman, every post-Second World War Democratic president has strongly endorsed tighter conflict of interest regulations. In contrast, few Republican administrations have taken any conflict of interest initiatives.

Throughout most of this century, Democrats have campaigned on the platform that Republicans use their economic power to get candidates elected and later to tempt nonelected decision makers. Throughout most of this century, Republicans have campaigned on the platform that Democrats can run a government only by taxing and spending, whereas in fact government can be run efficiently only by those with practical business experience. Consequently, the morality-in-government issue, so often used by the Democrats, is to the Republicans a red herring to divert attention from the real issue—efficiency in government.

If conflict of interest regulation is ever going to be effective, it must be divorced from partisan politics. Until a consensus on conflict of interest policy is reached, these disputes will continue to hamper presidential administrations and to further polarize views on the usefulness of conflict of interest regulations. Until that consensus includes both criminal and noncriminal regulations and makes a legitimate effort to reduce the burden of conflict of interest regulations on executive recruitment, the issue of ethics in government will remain unresolved.

A National Commission on Public Integrity

Congress and President Carter believed that the Ethics in Government Act would restore public confidence in the objectivity of investigations involving allegations of wrongdoing on the part of high-level government officials. It has not done so. Because of lack of trust in the impartiality of the Department of Justice, the Office of Government Ethics, and investigations by individual agencies and departments, almost every allegation of impropriety results in a call for the appointment of an independent counsel. The Ethics Act, however, prohibits the attorney general from asking a special federal court to appoint an independent counsel unless there is reason to believe that an official has violated a criminal law. As noted, however, many abuses of public office do not involve criminal wrongdoing. The Ethics Act did not solve the credibility crisis because noncriminal conduct damages public trust as much as criminal conduct.

What steps can be taken? The suggestion made in December of 1960 by Professor Abram Chayes is worth reconsidering. Professor Chayes urged President-elect Kennedy to appoint a "panel of well-known legal figures outside the government" to review the financial affairs of appointees and nominees for potential conflict of interest problems. Chayes believed that an outside panel would have a great deal more credibility than an internal White House review. However, the Kennedy White House decided to keep conflict of interest reviews within the walls of the White House.

After almost thirty years, perhaps the time has come to build on the recommendations of Professor Chayes by considering the establishment of an entirely independent National Commission on Public Integrity to take over authority for conflict of interest clearance activities and to take responsibility for investigating all forms of alleged misconduct by high-level executive-branch officials. This commission could take over the public integrity responsibilities of the Department of Justice, the Office of Government Ethics, and the White House Counsel's Office with respect to high-level officials. If a preliminary investigation by the commission revealed possible criminal wrongdoing, the law could require the commission to request the appointment of an independent counsel. At the same time, the law could require the commission to issue public reports on whether the official had violated any other rule or regulation, or acted in any inappropriate manner.

Under the law, the commission could have the authority to pursue disciplinary action against any official found to have violated a law, rule, or regulation. This action might include fines, restitution, demotion, or removal from the federal government.

The Commission and the Presidential Transition

Besides giving this commission broad investigatory and prosecutorial powers, Congress could give it broad authority to help resolve potential conflict of interest problems and case recruitment. First, to speed up the clearance and confirmation process, Congress could permit the nominees for president to submit the names of possible appointments for preliminary background checks. At the request of the nominee, the commission could have the authority to work with possible nominees on transition-related problems.

After the election, and prior to sending the name of a nominee to Congress, federal law could require the nominee to enter into a contract with the commission detailing steps taken or steps that the nominee will take to deal with actual or apparent conflict of interest problems. In return for a candidate taking these steps, the commission could have the authority to provide supplemental transition assistance. For instance, because of the extremely high cost of housing in the metropolitan Washington, D.C., area the commission could have the authority to grant very low-interest mortgage loans up to a specified amount. Officials would have to repay the loan when they left the designated position or the federal government.

Current federal law, as noted, does not generally require the divestiture of financial interests. It does require the official not to take action on a matter that might affect a financial interest of the official or the official's family. Congress should amend federal law to sharply limit the use of disqualification agreements as a remedy for potential conflict of interest problems. In return, Congress should give the commission the authority to grant capital-gains tax exemptions for individuals directed to divest themselves of certain financial interests.

To assure that each designated nominee or appointee avoids conflict of interest and other misconduct problems during his or her period of service, the commission could assign a staff member to act as the official's designated ethics officer. On a periodic basis, the commission ethics officers could hold orientation sessions with nominees and appointees to assure that no confusion existed regarding the application of appropriate rules and regulations. Federal law could also require nominees or appointees to contact their ethics officers prior to negotiating for employment with any entire outside the federal government.

Finally, the commission could have the authority to grant severance payments, not to exceed one year's salary, to those officials who agreed not to lobby any federal agency or department regarding any matter for a period of four years after leaving government service.

To guarantee the independence of the commission, the president could nominate five individuals to lifetime terms. Confirmed by the Senate, commission members could have the authority to hire and fire all staff necessary to accomplish its mission. Moreover, the law could appropriate funds for the operation of the commission on a ten-year basis.

A National Commission on Public Integrity is one approach to a problem of long concern. Unfortunately, the likelihood of Congress and a president approving such a commission is slight. Few presidents want to place in the hands of an independent commission the power to review the qualifications of high-level appointees. The Department of Justice would vigorously oppose the concept of placing criminal conduct issues under the jurisdiction of the commission, just as it historically has opposed the appointment of an independent counsel as reflecting badly on the objectivity of the Justice Department. Other groups would strongly oppose any move to supplement the salaries of high-level officials or grant them tax exemptions on the grounds that they already receive high enough salaries and should be willing to sacrifice to serve their country.

Since such a commission would certainly grow to have tremendous power and influence, there is always the risk of centralizing this type of authority. If anything has been learned from the history of the evolution of conflict of interest regulation, no way has yet been found to resolve controversies over the integrity of high-level national officials without automatically making the controversies part of much larger partisan political battles.

Whether such a commission is feasible or desirable may be as arguable today as it was in the 1960s, yet the solution raises a point that needs to be heard. It might put an end to the constant debate over imposing newer and tighter regulations and turn our attention to making existing laws work. In the Deaver lobbying case, for example, Morton Halperin argued in a *New York Times* interview, that "strengthening the law" was not the answer. Unless the government can identify some pattern of harm, he argued, then longer-term and broader restrictions will abridge the First Amendment rights of former officials. They in effect make a condition for government employment a surrendering of First Amendment rights. The point here is that we need a workable mechanism to enforce the law.

Throughout American history, public integrity issues have had major political overtones. But the focus on conflicts of interest since the end of the Second World War has profoundly changed the public integrity landscape. While the Reagan revolution slowed the growth of the non-military side of federal government, it did not reduce the power of elected and nonelected federal officials to shape the development and implementation of public policy.

It is the exercise of discretion that creates the opportunity for officials to use their public positions to further their own financial interests. Because so many decisions with national implications are made behind closed doors, the appearance of self-interest can effectively destroy public confidence in the fairness and impartiality of government decision making.

The American public wants to believe that there are individuals who still view public service as a public trust rather than as a road to personal fortune. Sometimes the public expects its public servants to adhere to standards of conduct not demanded of anyone else. Regardless, a significant number of public officials will not be able to live up to the expectations of the American public. When it occurs, this failure to respect the theory of public trust must be dealt with. As yet, no one has come up with a fool-proof method of predicting which public servants will put self interest ahead of public interest.

The challenge is to find a way to enforce high standards and to make our public servants accountable without making every violation of the public trust a partisan issue. An even greater challenge will be to attract to public service qualified individuals, regardless of their positions on the issues of the day and regardless of their backgrounds, who understand the trust that must go with public service.

At a time when America is celebrating the Constitution and honoring its writers, it is fitting to recall the words of James Madison:

It may be a reflection on human nature, that such devices should be necessary to control the abuse of government. But what is government itself, but the greatest of all reflections on human nature? If men were angels, no government would be necessary. If angels were to govern men, neither external nor internal controls on government would be necessary. In framing a government which is to be administered by men over men, the great difficulty lies in this: you must first enable the government to control the governed; and in the next place oblige it to control itself. (*The Federalist, No. 51*)

III. INTEGRITY AND COMPROMISE IN CONGRESS

EDITOR'S INTRODUCTION

Congress did not exempt itself entirely from the ethics reforms it enacted in the wake of Watergate. In 1977, while preparing to subject executive-branch officials to tougher conflict-of-interest laws, Congress adopted new ethics codes and established permanent ethics committees. Although other reforms have been enacted since then, the laws that apply to members of Congress are still less stringent than those imposed on high-level executive-branch officials.

While some observers decry the double standard, others maintain that stricter ethics rules might impair the legislative process, which moves forward only through compromise. Those who believe that constraints on legislators should be kept to a minimum maintain that strict, black-letter codes are unsuited to a system that requires legislators to promote the interests of their constituents as well as those of the nation while simultaneously working to raise the vast sums needed to win reelection.

In the first piece presented here, excerpted from his book, *The Glass House: Politics and Morality in the Nation's Capital,* Senator Paul Simon reflects on the difficulty of reconciling conscience and political effectiveness. Next, Jay Hedlund's "Lobbying and Legislative Ethics," reprinted from *Representation and Responsibility: Exploring Legislative Ethics,* argues that legislators' reliance on funds provided by political action committees is undermining the integrity of Congress.

If the outcomes of elections are any indication, the integrity of those they wish to elect to Congress is not foremost in the minds of many Americans when they cast their ballots, as "Tainted Saint," Brooks Jackson's article in *Common Cause,* relates. Rhode Island representative Fernand St Germain managed to win his 1986 reelection bid even after his questionable financial dealings had become front-page news. He was subsequently defeated, however, in the 1988 contest. In the final article, reprinted from *Ethics: Easier Said Than Done,* Daniel Callahan and

Bruce Jennings, co-directors of The Hastings Center Legislative and Representative Ethics Project, call for a more constructive and comprehensive approach to the promotion of ethics in Congress.

THE GLASS HOUSE[1]

Politics affects all citizens. Literally everyone is involved, either actively or passively; but it is the leaders or nominal leaders who can, through the power of their vote or the power of their decisions, create a world with more hope or less hope, more justice or less justice, and literally have the power to destroy civilization. Legislators are leaders by definition, and few get to their position without a willingness to take some risks. We are people with strong convictions, strong opinions, strong ambitions, strong passions, and more power than most. We have volunteered to take more pressure than most citizens do, as well as more criticism and more praise. Each member of Congress has the opportunity to display strengths and weaknesses, and those who follow the congressional scene closely see both in each of us. Because of the spotlight on House and Senate membership, our virtues and vices are magnified. We are in one of the few professions in which a person is required to stand up and publicly say, "I can do a better job than my opponent." That takes a special kind of ego.

The public image of those on the Washington scene is much like a TV crime show or an old-fashioned western, with "good guys" and "bad guys"—clearly defined. That simplistic view is not accurate in your community, and it is also far from accurate in Washington.

There is *some* truth to Lord Acton's famous quote: "Power tends to corrupt, and absolute power corrupts absolutely." All government power needs checks. No individual and no government should be given unrestrained authority. But Acton's state-

---

[1]Excerpted from *The Glass House: Politics and Morality in the Nation's Capital,* by Illinois Senator Paul Simon. Reprinted by permission of the Continuum Publishing Co.: New York. Copyright 1984.

ment can easily get distorted into two falsehoods. The first is that it is possible and in the public interest to have an absence of power. Generally, a power vacuum cannot be created, and where free systems have had drifting, ineffective government, the result has not been ennobling. Poland's often unhappy history includes such a period, when there was no concentration of power and all members of the Polish Diet were required to give their approval before any action could be taken. The resulting chaos helped to bring down the government. Second, Acton's maxim has been interpreted by some to suggest that those who avoid power are somehow more virtuous. Although this may comfort those without power, an unwillingness to use power, and the opportunities for good that come with it, is not a moral stance. The consciences of those unwilling to assume responsibility should not be so easily salved. The souls of those with leadership potential who avoid power are as tainted as those who abuse it. That is the lesson of the biblical story of the man who entrusted responsibility to his servants while he went on a journey. Those who used their talents were rewarded. The man who failed to use his talent was punished.

Lord Acton's statement appears in a variety of forms. Poet William Blake wrote:

> The strongest poison ever known
> Came from Caesar's laurel crown.

Poison it sometimes is. But the public should know who the modern Caesars are and what the real nature of the struggle is.

Richard Neuhaus made an observation more astute than Lord Acton's: "Politics is concerned with the distribution and exercise of power. The goal is not to get beyond . . . the use of power but to make [it] as apparent, as accessible and as just as possible."

The difficulties faced in the exercise of power are apparent daily in Congress.

A small, informal meeting had just ended. It involved House and Senate members who gather once a month to discuss the food and overpopulation problems facing poor countries. As I left and walked down the corridor of that graceless hulk called the Rayburn Building, I talked with Representative Millicent Fenwick, a pipe-smoking Republican, who in 1982 lost a race for the Senate.

The citizens of the Fifth Congressional District of New Jersey elected her to the House at the age of sixty-four. "You know," she said as we walked along, "I come away from a meeting like this tremendously impressed by the quality of the membership of Congress. But somehow the end product does not seem to reflect that quality."

Both of her observations are valid. New Jersey Senator Nicholas Brady, a businessman appointed to fill the seat left vacant by the resignation of Senator Harrison Williams in the wake of the Abscam scandal, noted the same: "The people here are of a higher caliber than I imagined in my fondest dreams. But the place doesn't work very well. It's very frustrating."

It would not make news—or sell books—to describe the membership of Congress as much above the quality the public perceives, and some would add, deserves. The truly great champion of high ethical standards, Senator Paul Douglas, told me a few months before his death that the Senate "today is a much finer body than when I served in it." He referred not to ability but to ethical standards. In 1977, ninety-two-year old historian Will Durant said that the intellectual level of Congress is "as high as at any time in our history, except the first generation of the Founding Fathers, and really we were ruled by an aristocracy then." Although we now revere the Founding Fathers (a phrase given us by Warren G. Harding), a critic of one of the first congresses said it was "a prostitution of the name of Government to apply it to such a vagabond, strolling, contemptible crew as Congress." One of the harshest critics of politicians in U.S. history, muckraking journalist Lincoln Steffens, wrote in his autobiography: "The ethics and morals of politics are higher than those of business." The evolving change in ethical standards can be seen in the newspapers almost daily and in examples through the years.

In 1956 the courts convicted Representative Thomas J. Lane of Massachusetts of evading $38,542 in income taxes. During his fifteenth year in Congress he served five months in a federal penitentiary. After his release, his colleagues welcomed him back to the halls of Congress. Two months later the voters of his Massachusetts constituency reelected him. Today he would not be able to return to Congress and he probably would not be reelected.

Daniel Webster often has been held up as a heroic example of a great nineteenth-century senator. But if a United States senator today openly demanded money from the railroads for support of legislation, as Webster did, that solon would quickly lose his or her seat.

Representative James Garfield accepted a gift of stock from a company seeking legislative favors, and he neither found his career ruined (he later became president) nor faced censure in the House.

Members of the House and Senate share responsibility for the bad public image because it is politically popular to denounce Congress, to say by implication, "I am a good guy, but watch out for these other rascals." Robert Cornell, a Roman Catholic priest who served in the House from Wisconsin, recalls:

Some members are responsible for the low esteem in which Congress is held by the public because [they] campaign against Congress. I recall that during my reelection campaign in 1976 I defended Congress at a fundraiser and my campaign manager, a Capitol Hill veteran . . . remarked: "That was a good speech, but I wouldn't have given it. That won't win you votes."
The first speech I gave after leaving office was at a weekly breakfast of a retired businessmen's club. . . . I emphasized that miscreant members of Congress get the news coverage, not the many fine, dedicated, hardworking people I came to know. I observed that most of them compared very well with the members of the religious order to which I belong. Nevertheless the first questioner remarked: "I don't care what you say; they're all crooks."

There are some in Congress who are venal, but my guess is that they are few. Venality is markedly rarer in Congress than it was in the General Assembly of Illinois during my days there. That body and most state legislatures have improved in the last twenty years. Others can speak more knowledgeably than I about local government, though one Massachusetts legislator once noted that Diogenes went through the Boston City Council seeking an honest man and came out without his lantern. Nevertheless, it is my impression that the level of integrity in local government has risen, just as it has in the state and federal governments. The few members of Congress who may be corrupt don't advertise who they are. I have a few suspicions, as do other members, as do reporters, but all of us could be wrong in our guesses. What is certain is that the outright corrupt—those who accept direct bribes—are a small minority.

Before being elected to Congress in 1974, I had visited Washington often. But I did not expect the overall quality that I found when I became a member. Although I had been in public life before coming to Congress, I had absorbed enough of the bad news to believe that Capitol Hill lawmakers would not be appreciably more able than those I had observed in state legislative bodies. I misjudged. For every old and crotchety member there are several who are old and wise. For every young and arrogant member there are several who are young and eager to learn. For every ethically devious member there are many who take their responsibilities seriously.

Sometimes the collective performance of 435 House members or 100 senators is enough to send you home at night discouraged. But the problems are not going to be solved by simplistic images. The moral dilemmas House and Senate members face are not as clear-cut as, for example, the proper response to a bribe, but rather relate to a host of issues and problems far more subtle, far more complex.

A few years ago a casual conversation about former Representative Wilbur Mills of Arkansas would not have reflected well on him. When he publicly squired striptease artist Fannie Fox around the country, headline writers and comedians had a field day. One of the most respected members of Congress until this episode, Mills had been a dominant force in tax legislation for many years. Foreign countries had sent representatives to Mills rather than to the White House to discuss export matters. But the nation roared with laughter as he appeared on a Boston burlesque stage to take a bow. Once considered presidential material, he now looked like a fool. He publicly admitted his problem: alcoholism.

I've heard many jokes about Mills from people who have never met him. But there's an unknown side to him. When a friend of mine developed a serious drinking problem, Wilbur Mills went out of his way to help him. My friend is only one of many people Wilbur Mills has helped. I do not defend Mills's capers, but I have come to know the other side of the story.

Similarly, Richard Nixon, a former member of the House of Representatives and the Senate who fell from grace at about the same time as Mills, will not receive a hero's treatment in the history books, but my guess is that history will be somewhat kinder to him than current opinion for the forward steps taken in our relations with China and the Soviet Union under his leadership. Richard Nixon's mistakes should not prevent our listening to him, for example, when he suggests that if we do not want to destroy the world we ought to be doing more to get along with the other great superpower. The public and officeholders should not be so eager to cast people as villains that we do not at least listen to them.

Wilbur Mills was not the first chairman of the House Ways and Means Committee whose personal conduct caused national controversy. John Randolph of Roanoke, Virginia (1733-1833)—colorful, unpredictable, and powerful—got an early start on his controversial career. William and Mary College expelled him when he fought a duel over the proper pronunciation of a word. A heavy drinker even as a youth, he had an unusual appearance, tall with extremely thin legs and unable to grow a beard to cover his florid face. He never married, and when some of his bitter foes made light of his high-pitched voice and charged him with impotency (which he did not deny), he responded: "You pride yourself upon an animal faculty, in . . . [which] the jackass [is] infinitely your superior!" He called himself Citizen Randolph and called others virtually every name in the book; public officials feared him. Despite his poor health, he could stand on the floor of the House for two or three hours at a time piercing the air with his high voice, bitter denunciations, and gifted oratory. Before he was thirty he emerged as the Republican (Jeffersonian) leader of the House. Jefferson, Randolph's cousin and his bitter enemy, later tried three times to have Randolph defeated. Another cousin who differed with Randolph received permanent scars from Randolph's whip. When Andrew Jackson became president, Randolph retired from the House, and Jackson named him ambassador to Russia. The Senate unanimously confirmed him, despite public knowledge of his addiction to both alcohol and opium. He died in Philadelphia on May 24, 1833, with a whip in his hand. A few days before his death, Randolph's physician told his weak patient that he would like to bring in another doctor for consultation. Randolph declined, saying, "In a multitude of counsel there is confusion. . . . The patient may die while the doctors are staring at each other."

Not a typical member of Congress, John Randolph nevertheless entered congressional halls as another of a series of strong personalities who determine the nation's future.

And sometimes the "good guys" aren't so good.

Near the turn of the century in England, Joseph Burgess, a Labour candidate for a seat in the House of Commons, refused to compromise on an issue long since obscure. Because of his intransigence, the victory went to the opposition. Burgess, editor of a publication called *Workman's Times*, apparently expected to be hailed for his refusal. But one of those who criticized him was George Bernard Shaw, who commented:

> When I think of my own character, smirched with compromise, rotted with opportunism, mildewed by expediency—dragged through the mud of borough council and Battersea elections, stretched out of shape with wire-pulling, putrified by permeation, worn out by twenty-five years pushing to gain an inch here, or straining to stem a backrush, I do think Joe might have put up with just a speck or two on those white robes of his for the sake of the millions of poor devils who cannot afford any character at all because they have no friend in Parliament. Oh, these moral dandies, these spiritual toffs, these superior persons. Who is Joe, anyhow, that he should not risk his soul occasionally like the rest of us?

Shaw's derision of the purist is well placed. Former Representative Joseph Fisher of Virginia described the process of compromise well when he paraphrased Shakespeare: "The best is sometimes the enemy of the good, and the bad must sometimes be chosen rather than the terrible."

The first time I ran for public office, for state representative, I met a woman in Granite City, Illinois, who said that she had read what I stood for and applauded my stands. "And I'm going to pray for your election," she said. "But I'm not going to vote because I don't believe in getting mixed up in politics." Those who remain so certain that only they are right, and those who remain inflexible about a particular position, unwilling to make an honorable compromise to advance toward a goal, contribute little to bringing our society closer to the ends they profess to espouse.

That is not the only failing of the "good guys." They make mistakes; they are sometimes petty. It's nice to have heroes, but real heroes are also real people.

A while ago Representative Paul Findley of Illinois introduced an amendment to a military assistance bill that would have given the president a little more flexibility in dealing with the sensitive Greek-Turkish situation. The amendment came to a vote unexpectedly and as the voting proceeded, members gathered in small knots on the floor to discuss it. There is a feeling of kinship for Greece in Congress because that nation threw off its dictatorship in 1974, because so much of our democratic heritage comes

from the ancient Greeks, and because of the political reality
that there are a great many more Greeks than Turks living in
the United States. As four of us discussed the matter—
Representatives Jonathan Bingham and Stephen Solarz, both of
New York, a nationally prominent and respected congressman,
and I—Bingham said, "The politically advantageous vote is to
vote against Findley. The responsible vote is to vote with him."
I happened to disagree with that assessment, but before I could
comment the nationally prominent legislator smiled and said, "I
thinkI'll cast an irresponsible vote." There are soft spots in the
armor of even the best.

By some standards, I'm one of the "good guys" in the House.
I disclose my income, assets, and liabilities in detail and have done
so longer than any other public official in the nation. I generally
support the types of things that Common Cause and the League
of Women Voters favor; columnist Jack Anderson in a moment
of generosity once listed me as one of the "best" members of Congress; and even most of the Republican newspapers in my district
and state have supported me, a Democrat. But I could point out
bad votes I've cast, though I thought they were good at the time.

One night, for example, the House had a debate on the defense budget. I then served on the Budget Committee's Task
Force, which deals with defense matters. The House voted $4 bil-
lion more than we had approved, $4 billion not needed. With so
many really pressing needs in the nation, I was irritated to see the
Pentagon supporters swing the House over to that extra $4 bil-
lion. A few minutes later, a proposal for $500 million for addi-
tional bonuses for World War I veterans came up. It had not been
cleared through the Veterans Committee, and we already had a
hefty deficit. World War I veterans and their widows need greater help from the federal government, but doing it on the spur of
the moment with an amendment on the floor, without knowing
the full implications or any details, was not sensible. So I voted
no. But the more I thought about that extra $4 billion wasted on
defense, and knowing that this vote would be listed by veterans'
organizations and senior citizens, I said to myself, "If we can
spend money foolishly on that, why not spend one-eighth of the
amount on these poor old people." I changed my vote to yes. It
was probably a bad vote. I cast it when irritated. Whatever program we devise ought to emerge after careful study.

From Wilbur Mills to John Randolph, from Richard Nixon to those representing you in the House and Senate, you will find the cast of characters is in many ways similar to those in the community where you live. We are similar in occupation, although members of Congress are more likely to be lawyers (261 of 535 are lawyers); we are farmers and journalists, physicians and teachers, just as you are. We have had house painters, plumbers, and pharmacists in our midst, almost any occupation you can name.

But in some ways we are unrepresentative. Two of the senators and twenty-one of the House members are women. Twenty House members are black, but there are none in the Senate. In the House there are nine Hispanics, but none in the Senate. All three groups are underrepresented, but their numbers are growing.

We are more likely to announce our religious affiliation than is the public at large. Roman Catholicism, the largest numerical religious group in the country, with fifty million followers, can also claim the largest number in Congress with 141. Episcopalians are the most heavily represented relative to membership numbers of the major denominations, with sixty-one members for three million Episcopalians. Baptists have forty-six members for thirty million, and Lutherans twenty-five for nine million. Presbyterians have fifty-four members for their ranks of four million, and Jews have thirty-eight for six million.

Diversity of background, gregariousness—these and other qualities fit the nation's legislators and legislative body. But that is only part of the story. Two thousand years ago Plutarch described what for many is the essence of politics:

They are wrong who think that politics is like an ocean voyage or a military campaign, something to be done with some particular end in view, something which leaves off as soon as that end is reached. It is not a public chore, to be got over with. It is a way of life. It is the life of a domesticated political and social creature who is born with a love for public life, with a desire for honor, with a feeling for his fellows . . .

That description fits many, but not all, in public life. There are no generalities that are universally applicable. The quest for good in public life is complex, and so is the cast of characters. . . .

The practical dilemmas that real-life politicians face do not fit into easily wrapped packages to which moral labels can be attached. This has led some to suggest that ethics and politics must be divorced completely, a notion I hear espoused occasionally by theoreticians on college campuses but not by practical politicians who know better. Churchill wrote: "A nation without conscience is a nation without a soul. A nation without a soul is a nation that cannot live." Morality helps shape the goals toward which we must strive and limits the means that can be used in reaching those goals. The goals generally must be loftier than the means. War is not an acceptable moral goal, but war as a means to achieve a goal (for example, the Afghan resistance to the Soviet presence in their country) is often recognized as morally acceptable, though sentiment on that is changing. Putting people in prison is not an acceptable goal, but putting people in prison as a means of achieving a stable society somewhat more free of crime is considered acceptable. Unfortunately, we too often disguise ignoble means with noble goals. We do not recognize what we are doing, for the good in all of us—honesty, compassion, courtesy—gets confused with the desire to get reelected, the need to send a son or daughter to college, excessive pride, the longing for revenge, the not-so-subtle temptation to say or do what will get publicity. These, and a host of other entanglements of the spirit, too often crowd out those better qualities in us. Then we need to step back and look at ourselves and our society and recognize the moral struggles we all face.

Stepping back is important to the public official. It provides some sense of perspective, of what life is all about, and of both the importance and the insignificance of many of the things we do. Part of getting a sense of perspective is simply listening. Lincoln Steffens wrote of Theodore Roosevelt what might be said of many of us: "It was hard to tell him anything; it was easy to make him talk, even about a state secret, but to reverse the process and make him listen was well-nigh impossible." Listening to those isolated voices of wisdom coming from people who may never see their name in print is part of gaining perspective. Part of that stepping back includes recognizing the progress that has been made. What is ethically acceptable is much more strictly constructed for members of Congress today than fifty or a hundred years ago. When a secretary of agriculture cracks "jokes" that degrade the nation's black population, enough people of all ethnic groups feel offended and the secretary must resign. Although some things improve, others do not. We are not revolted enough at the indecency of stockpiling weapons of incomprehensible destructive capability. Attempting to get some perspective on things is important, no matter how inaccurate and unfocused that sense of perspective may be.

The fact that there is a moral struggle within each of us does not mean that we should allow ourselves to become paralyzed. Complexity does not necessarily mean that action is impossible. The goals of peace and justice, of opportunity for employment, of dignity for senior citizens, of conquering cancer and cystic fibrosis—all can be approached even if they are not fully attained. Approaching those goals will not take place if there are no political leaders of vision and courage, two overworked words but underworked realities. "Let the prophet who has a dream tell the dream," the Lord advises Jeremiah. What this nation needs is a dream, a goal, a sense of direction and purpose. Henry Thoreau wrote: "The youth gets together his materials to build a bridge to the moon, or, perchance, a palace or temple on the earth, and, at length, the middle-aged man concludes to build a woodshed with them." There is a danger that our nation is in the middle-age doldrums, that we are planning for woodsheds instead of temples. An old Latin proverb put it differently: "An army of stags led by a lion is more formidable than an army of lions led by a stag." People working with a sense of mission and purpose are more likely to accomplish great things, and less likely to be engaged in activities that harm a society. Such leadership appeals to the best in us, and by that very action restrains somewhat the base and crude and selfish that is in us all. We need more than a woodshed mentality. "My generation lived in preparation for nothing except this war," thirty-two-year-old World War II correspondent Eric Sevareid wrote. We need to feel we are being prepared, not for a war, but for some grander enterprise; even a dull task then takes on new meaning and seems important. That requires leaders who are candid about our limitations, who do not promise too much, who recognize the complexity of the moral decisions that must be made, but at the same time know that we can come closer to understanding other nations and building a solid peace, to reducing poverty in our country and elsewhere, to conquering some of the diseases that plague us. We need leadership that nurtures the sometimes hidden flame of idealism that is a part of all humanity. In an Easter sermon, John Donne said: "All our life is but a going out to the place of execution, to death. Was there ever any man seen to sleep in the cart . . . between the prison and the place of execution? . . . [Yet] we sleep all the way, from the womb to the grave we are never thoroughly awake." We need to be awakened; we need to be lifted.

Representative Wright Patman of Texas was an old-fashioned, courtly member with whom I served. He died at the age of eighty-two while serving in the House. Television crews covering the funeral caught one magnificent line from an old woman who lived in Patman's district: "He rose up mighty high, but he brung us all up with him."

The path upward in politics is a slippery, stumbling one for both the office holder and the public. There are no sure signposts marked with guaranteed success; there are no participants enmeshed solely in virtue. But unless there are those willing to tread the slippery path, willing to stumble, willing to expose themselves, warts and all, willing to give the nation something good and noble toward which to strive, we will follow the downward path—not purposely, but just as certainly as if it were.

"He rose up mighty high, but he brung us all up with him." May some future generation say that of you and me.

LOBBYING AND LEGISLATIVE ETHICS[2]

Our system of representative democracy gives elected officials the responsibility of taking power granted to them by the voters and balancing the competing interests and demands of 230 million people to fashion public policy for the common good. For the public to have confidence in the integrity of its elected officials and government policies it must be able to trust that elected officials will freely vote their consciences while earnestly pursuing the best interests of the country and responsively listening to the concerns of their constituents. That goal, however, is threatened in the United States Senate and House of Representatives

[2]Reprint of an article by Jay H. Hedlund, director of The Grass Roots Lobby of The Common Cause, from *Representation and Responsibility: Exploring Legislative Ethics*, edited by Bruce Jennings and Daniel Callahan. Plenum Press, New York, 1985, pp. 89–107. Copyright The Hastings Center Institute of Society, Ethics, and the Life Sciences. Reprinted by permission.

by the pervasive and often invisible influence of special interest money and the lobbyists who direct its flow in Washington. Campaign contributions from political action committees (PACs), speaking fees from organized interest groups, and the often undisclosed multimillion-dollar lobbying efforts of those interests are increasingly undermining the integrity of Congress.

The elected officials we send to Washington to represent our interests there are not expected to carry out their task while blind and neutral like Justice. We expect them to be accessible to countless constituents and interest groups while being informed and articulate about complicated national problems and the intricate legislation needed to deal with those problems. We ask them to be open to all points of view but to be forceful advocates for specific legislation and policies. We yearn for statesmen who will show leadership and stay above petty political bickering and yet elect our leaders in a process that demands that they be partisans who will wade into the churning competition among political parties and ideologies.

The people elected to do this job reflect the collective qualities of their constituency. By and large more gregarious and ambitious than a typical constituent, members of Congress rise out of the diverse values, backgrounds, strengths, weaknesses, and expectations of the more than one-half million people in each House district or the larger population represented by Senators. From this constituency a member is placed on a fast track in a heady atmosphere of a powerful world capital. They lead a life of impossible demands on time, energy, and patience that few citizens would willingly choose in their own professions.

Former Congressman William Brodhead (Democrat, Michigan) describes the pressures in this life:

What kind of life do I have? How do I live? Well, I don't live very well. I'm subject to tremendous ethical conflicts all the time. Pressure all the time. A declining standard of living, traveling, working nights, on weekends. . . . The main thing is that this is a very difficult job.

Members of Congress are generally honest, open, and accessible while faced constantly with making large and small value judgments in gray areas. Congressman Thomas Downey (Democrat, New York) says, "Most issues here are not issues of conscience or morality—they are questionable calls." Each day they face basic decisions that can require the balancing of ethical choices: "Where should I be?"—back home in the district, in

Washington, on a fact finding tour; in committee, on the floor
listening to debate, back in the office; "Whom should I
see?"—constituents, the Cherry Blossom Queen, experts from an
executive agency, campaign contributors, lobbyists, the press;
"How should I act on public policy?"—on which issues of all those
before Congress to take the time needed to become expert, with
whom to align, where and how to compromise; "How should I
move politically?—to balance party loyalty with personal philosophy, to be an insider or a maverick, to seek higher office or greater institutional influence.

In this human, hectic, informal, and often unobserved give-
and-take of political and legislative process, stakes are enormous
for members of Congress, for interest groups, and for the country. A $700 billion annual budget, tax policy that determines the
distribution of several hundred billions of dollars, regulations
that can mean millions of dollars to a single company or billions
to the economy all become battlegrounds for competing philosophical, regional, economic, and political interests. In this intense and complicated arena legislators develop a unique
relationship with and often a reliance upon lobbyists for private
interests to further their objectives in both the legislative and political process.

A typical lobbyist—though clearly not all—is a white male
lawyer. He often comes to the profession after working the other
side of the street, perhaps as a former elected official, staff member on Capitol Hill, or campaign worker. Their number and
scope of activity are unknown with any precision because of an
ineffective 1946 federal lobby disclosure law. Only about 5,500
of the estimated 16,000 lobbyists in Washington are even regis-
tered with the House of Representatives. Moreover, the amount
of money spent by any one lobbyist or by all lobbyists can only be
estimated. Nonetheless, lobbying in all its forms exceeds a billion
dollars in cost annually.

A main function of all lobbyists is informative—to provide ex-
pertise to a member and his staff on some of the more than
10,000 bills and resolutions that are filed in a Congress. No single
member nor his staff can be expert or even reasonably well informed on more than a relative handful of these issues. The lobbyist aims to fill this information void as his legislation makes its
way through committee or to the floor of the House and Senate.

In this role of information trader the lobbyist represents his clients' interests, not a vaguely defined broader public interest. Although a lobbyist may often invoke higher purposes for his legislative goals, his persuasive power is designed to further the narrow interest of his client or organization. The lobbyist's role, influential in Washington, is largely unnoticed by the public. In noting the need for the public disclosure of lobbying activity the Supreme Court 30 years ago said:

Otherwise the voice of the people may all too easily be drowned out by the voice of the special interest groups seeking favored treatment while masquerading as proponents of the public weal.

A lobbyist is often valued by potential employers or clients for the political contacts he has with key people in Congress who are in a position to effect their legislative interests. This qualification for the job can help form relationships between legislators and lobbyists that give the appearance of normal social or personal friendships but are often shallower relationships of mutual professional convenience. Former Congressman Brodhead noted how the personal relationships between legislator and lobbyist are exploited:

[You have] very superficial relationships. . . . I've never been to a social occasion in this town, ever, where somebody wasn't trying to hustle me to vote for or against some piece of legislation.

The Washington Post in March, 1982, reported on how the desire for a lobbyist with good political contacts can be taken to an extreme when stakes are high. It cited the case of a lobbyist hired by the Milliken Research Company to lobby a single senator on an antitrust bill in the Senate Judiciary Committee that would save Milliken more than $14 million:

When William A. Meehan, lobbyist, marched into the office of Sen. Arlen Specter (R-Penn.) . . . no round of introductions was necessary. Meehan does not cut much of a swath in Washington; he's never lobbied here before. But in Specter's hometown of Philadelphia, Meehan has been the Republican Party boss for the last two decades, and he's the closest thing Specter has to a political godfather. . . . "He's the only one on the committee I've approached because he's the only one I know," the Philadelphian explained.

Given the barrage of issues and the countless interests contending for the attention of a legislator, a lobbyist's fundamental task is to make sure he has a chance to plead his case. He must overcome the political, policy, personal, or other barriers raised by legislators and staff that stand in the way of garnering majority support for legislative goals. Toward this end it is a truism in lobbying that "access is everything."

Political contributions from special interest groups play a crucial role for many lobbyists in gaining access to key legislators. Washington correspondent for *The New York Times* Steven V. Roberts has reported that many congressmen feel taking a campaign contribution creates an obligation that must eventually be repaid. Roberts observed further:

In one sense, power in Washington can be equated with access—the quicker your phone call gets returned, the more influence you have. And when a lobbyist calls a lawmaker who has taken his money, the return time is reduced considerably.

Legislators understand this relationship and some are open about how it works. Congressman Tony Coelho (Democrat, California) is chairman of the Democratic Congressional Campaign Committee responsible for raising funds for Democratic candidates for the House. He describes what he holds out to the larger contributors to his committee:

Access. Access. That's the name of the game. They meet with the leadership and with the chairman of the committees. We don't sell legislation; we sell that opportunity to be heard.

Increasingly, lobbyists have become a major conduit of political campaign funds for candidates for Congress. This phenomenon is directly related to the extraordinary growth in the last decade of the importance of PACs in campaigns. Since 1974, the number of PACs has increased from 608 to over 3,400. PAC contributions have risen dramatically as well, going from $12 million in 1974 to $80 million in 1982. The growth of PAC giving has surpassed even the rapidly increasing costs of campaigns. While the amount of money raised by Senate general election candidates increased roughly 180 percent from 1978 to 1982, PAC receipts increased 250 percent. The dependence of congressmen on PAC funds has also risen sharply. Although in 1974 PAC money accounted for only 14 percent of the funds for the average House candidate, in 1982 candidates for the House received fully one-third of their funds from PACs. (Unless otherwise noted, figures used in this article are based on Common Cause analyses of campaign finance disclosure statements filed with the Federal Election Commission or personal financial disclosure statements filed by representatives or senators with the Clerk of the House of Representatives or the Secretary of the Senate.) Those funds are an essential part of many lobbyists' strategies for gaining access to members after they are elected.

Although lobbyists and interest groups have always sought special legislative treatment, the extent to which organized campaign giving has dominated the political process is relatively new and arose, in part, from earlier election law changes. In 1974, Congress passed major reforms of the presidential campaign financing system as a result of the Watergate scandal. With those reforms Congress provided for presidential elections to be financed primarily with public funds while rejecting a similar system for Congressional elections. Congress also enacted new limits of $1,000 on the size of personal contributions to candidates for Congress as well as to candidates for president. At the same time that the role of private contributions was minimized, Congress also removed an existing restriction in the election law that had prohibited interests with government contracts from donating to any federal candidates through a political action committee. With the role of special interests curtailed in presidential campaigns, with no public financing of congressional races, and with restrictions removed on the establishment of PACs, a growing number of special interest groups turned their efforts toward increasing their influence in Congress.

For many lobbyists the campaign financing role is the single most important part of their lobbying efforts. One has said, "99 percent of lobbying in this city is now fund raising." Some top lobbyists refuse to represent a client unless it has a political action committee to give contributions to candidates. One of those, Robert McCandless, has explained: "Corporations can't get the attention of a congressman pulled in a thousand directions unless they go to that member and say, 'We care about your re-election.'"

This activity constructed around our system of campaign financing whereby political action committee contributions become a primary tool for the Washington lobbyist to achieve his client's or organization's legislative goals is the Achilles heel for legislative ethical standards. The threat is widely perceived. *Time* magazine goes so far as to say, "Today the power of PACs threatens to undermine America's system of representative democracy."

Elizabeth Drew, a careful observer of the interrelationships of legislators, lobbyists, and PAC contributions, suggests how the democratic process is being threatened:

The acquisition of funds has become an obsession on the part of nearly every candidate for federal office. The obsession leads the candidate to solicit and accept money from those most able to provide it, and to adjust their behavior in office to the need for money.

Legislators have an even better view of how this system works. Congressman Henson Moore (Republican, Louisiana) has said:

If he [the member of Congress] knows you aren't politically active, he may be polite to you, but if you really want to see him perk up and be interested in what you say, let him know you represent a political action committee that is going to be active in the next election.

The results of PAC giving are reflected in congressional action, whether it is specific policy decisions such as Federal Trade Commission regulations or broader policy areas of government spending and taxation. PACs are permeating the Congressional process. Here are a few examples of the relationships Common Cause found in the Ninety-seventh Congress between campaign contributions and legislative outcomes:

1. An analysis of a 1981 House vote on dairy price supports and contributions from the three largest dairy PACs showed that representatives who voted for higher dairy price supports had received on the average nearly six times as much from those PACs in 1978–80 as did representatives who voted against the daily lobby on that vote.

2. On May 18, 1982, by a vote of 69 to 27, the Senate approved S. Con. Res. 60, which struck down the proposed Federal Trade Commission used-car rule. National Automobile Dealer Association (NADA) PAC contributions to senators in their most recent campaigns equalled $435,560. The 69 senators who voted for the veto resolution received, on the average, twice as much in campaign contributions from the dealers as the 27 senators voting against the resolution.

NADA PAC contributions to House members equalled $848,846 (1979 through the first four months of 1982). The 286 House members who voted for the veto resolution received an average of five times as much from the Auto Dealers PAC as did the 133 House members who voted against the resolution. In the House, 82 percent of those who received contributions from the

Auto Dealers PAC voted for the veto resolution. Of those House members who received no NADA PAC contributions, 32 percent voted yes and 63 percent voted no.

3. During the 1979–80 and 1981–82 election cycles, the PACs of the American Medical Association (AMA) and the American Dental Association (ADA) contributed more than $3 million to House members who served in the Ninety-seventh Congress. In December, 1982, the House voted to exempt the business practices of state-licensed professionals from Federal Trade Commission jurisdiction. The 208 representatives who voted for the AMA/ADA-backed position received more than two and a half times as much from these PACs as the 195 members who voted against the professionals.

During six years from 1977 through 1982, the AMA PACs gave a total of $6,266,015 to all congressional candidates. Of that amount, $3,845,141 was contributed to candidates now serving in Congress—$3,233,656 to representatives and $611,485 to senators.

4. The 215 representatives who voted for the automobile domestic content bill in December, 1982, received $1.3 million in PAC contributions from the United Auto Workers during the last two congressional elections, eighteen times as much as the $72,000 received by the 188 representatives who voted to defeat the bill. Among House Democrats, the recipients of most of the UAW's PAC contributions, the 171 members who voted for the UAW-backed legislation received an average of $7,700 per member in UAW PAC contributions, or more than six times as much as the $1,240 per member average received by Democrats who voted against the bill.

It is not necessary to have hard evidence—a "smoking gun"—that campaign contributions actually buy votes for serious questions to be raised in the public's mind about the integrity both of individual members of Congress and of the House and Senate as institutions. PAC money has become the primary building block of a relationship that eases access for lobbyists to members of Congress and too frequently squeezes out the average citizen. As Congressman James Leach (Republican, Iowa) sees it:

You see a breakdown in citizen access. Not that a constituent isn't going to get in the door, but the guy who gave the money is going to get in first. So what you really see is a breakdown in constitutional democracy, which is supposed to be based on citizen access and constituency access. We're seeing regional politics become national. National groups determined outcomes, whereas local constituencies used to provide the crucial role. This is new.

PAC contributions, moreover, are distinctly different from most individual contributions in that PACs make their decisions about who will receive their contributions as part of their long-range sophisticated Washington lobbying strategies.

A gift from an individual citizen is a contribution from a kind of one-person multiple source: consumer, employer or employee, family member, man or woman, a certain age, experience or education. Most citizens who do contribute have more than a single interest or objective. Too often the same cannot be said of the narrow-based PACs. Typically, the PAC to Preserve the Upper Great Lakes Widget Industry cares only how the legislator votes in the subcommittee on widgets. Little if any attention is given to the legislator's vote on widows, orphans, veterans, MXs or 14Bs. Individuals generally have wider interests than PACs.

But individuals generally do not have the eleborate lobbying apparatus and the Washington representatives that PACs have. In this environment there is enormous pressure on legislators to vote with the special interests even if that may be contrary to the broader but less intense public interest.

Elected officials are increasingly open about the dilemma this system of financing poses to the integrity of the legislative process:

Former Congressman Barber Conable (Republican, New York):

I'm scared. These new PACs not only buy incumbents, but affect legislation. It's the same crummy business as judges putting the arm on lawyers who appear before them to finance their next campaign.

Senator Thomas Eagleton (Democrat, Missouri):

The current system of funding congressional elections is a national scandal. It virtually forces members of Congress to go around hat in hand, begging for money from Washington-based special interests, political action committees whose sole purpose for existing is to seek a *quid pro quo.*

Senator Robert Dole (Republican, Kansas):

When the political action committees give money they expect something in return other than good government. It is making it much more difficult to legislate.

The impact of this system of campaign financing is pervasive and poses a constant and overriding ethical dilemma for each individual member of Congress as well as the House and Senate as institutions. As Elizabeth Drew writes:

We have a system in which even the best intentioned politicians get caught up in actual or apparent conflicts of interest, in which it is difficult to avoid in effect selling votes for campaign contributions. We have a system in which even the best people do these things, not because they want to but because they are trapped.

Political action committee contributions are not the only tools lobbyists use to gain access to members of Congress and to influence legislation. In both 1979 and 1980 special interests gave $2.3 million and in 1981 more than $3.4 million to members of the House and Senate, particularly the most influential members in those bodies, in large payments that went directly into their pockets. In 1982, senators alone received more than $2.4 million in such payments. Those payments—honoraria for speeches—although legal under present provisions of law and legislative codes of conduct, raise serious concerns about real or apparent conflicts of interest.

Lobbyists who control honoraria can use them to gain an advantage in the legislative process. It is logical for groups concerned about issues that affect them to invite legislators who are expert on those issues to speak to them. Yet this creates the potential conflict of interest. Significant sums of money paid for speeches can often represent an investment by that group to develop unique access to those legislators most critical to their legislative agenda.

Senator Lowell Weicker (Republican, Connecticut), an opponent of such payments, says they "create a situation where a very small segment of the population enjoys a special relationship that is not enjoyed by the population as a whole." In addition, this pursuit for personal financial gain from honoraria may detract from the time and attention representatives and senators need for official duties. The speeches, moreover, are likely to be written by congressional staff during working hours at taxpayer expense.

The problems created by honoraria are growing. The Democratic Study Group of the House of Representatives in 1982 found that

members of Congress are not only becoming increasingly dependent on special interests to finance their election campaigns, they are also becoming more dependent on them as a source of personal income to supplement their official pay.

Evidence of the increased reliance on honoraria is seen in the fact that Senators received 47 percent more in such payments in 1982 than in 1981.

This growing dependence on outside sources of income has come less than five years after the House and Senate recognized that members relying on honoraria and other earned income beyond their official salaries posed a dangerous threat to public confidence in the integrity of Congress. In 1977, along with a substantial congressional pay increase, the House and Senate each adopted strengthened codes of conduct that included limitations on outside earned income to 15 percent of their official salary, to become effective in 1979.

The House has abided by a limitation on earned income since 1979, although raising it to 30 percent in 1981. The Senate, at the beginning of 1979, postponed the implementation of its limit for four years before finally repealing it outright late in 1982. With no overall limitation in the Senate code of conduct, the sole restriction on outside earned income for Senators in recent years was a 1976 statutory $25,000 annual cap on honoraria. After Congress repealed this sole restriction in October, 1981, no limitation at all existed on how much a senator could earn in 1981 and 1982 in outside income in addition to his official salary.

In the summer of 1983 Senator Henry Jackson (Democrat, Washington), terming the honoraria situation in the Senate "a scandal waiting to happen," forced through a 30 percent limit on honoraria in exchange for a $9,000 pay raise for senators that would bring salaries to $69,000, the same level of their House colleagues. A similar proposal had been rejected by the Senate in 1982. The salary increase was effective July 1, 1983, although the cap on honoraria was delayed until January 1, 1984. There was a predictable dramatic increase in Senate honoraria for 1983, up more than 35 percent to $3.3 million, as Senators capitalized on the unlimited system before the cap would go into effect in 1984. Recent history, however, should forewarn of efforts to amend or repeal the cap so that senators could continue to supplement their official salaries with extensive speaking fees.

The lifting of the limitations on outside earned income that were adopted in 1977 has raised questions of credibility, integrity, and public confidence in Congress. Congressman James Jeffords (Republican, Vermont) has called the practice of lobbying groups' giving honoraria to legislators "legalized bribery. When a special interest group pays $1,000—let alone $2,000—for a short speech, it is clear that the payment is made for the purpose of influencing legislation."

Lobbyists, using honoraria as a tool for access to those members of Congress who can most directly influence their legislative interests, direct the heaviest amount to members of the majority party and, more specifically, to those in leadership positions. Republican senators in 1981, the first year of their new majority status in the Senate, received nearly double the honoraria as in 1980—$1.1 million compared to $600,000. Their 1981 amount was nearly twice as much as that received by Senate Democrats. In 1981 in the House, where Democrats maintained a majority, members of that party received nearly one-quarter of a million dollars more than their Republican counterparts.

Surveying the 1981 Senate honoraria the *New York Times* found:

Only one Democrat was among the top 19 earners, indicating that the party in power, and its committee chairmen, enjoy a special advantage in obtaining lecture fees, and that it was a senator's power rather than his speaking ability that really earned those fees. Most of the senators received a large share of their speaking fees from organizations over which the chairman had jurisdiction.

Such observations fuel a growing public perception that favoritism and self-interest are more important in the legislative process than merit and the public interest. The correlation between a legislator's position of influence and the speaking invitations he receives from lobbying groups is as obvious to insiders as it is troubling to a skeptical public. Congressman Henry B. Gonzalez (Democrat, Texas) clearly describes a situation any veteran of Congress would recognize:

After I became Chairman of the Housing Subcommittee, certain people from the industry wanted to invite me to speak—for an honorarium, of course. I'd ask them how come they never wanted to hear me when I was chairman of the International Finance Subcommittee, and they don't have any answer. But you know the answer: Now I'm in a position they think can help them.

Honoraria, like campaign contributions, often are a part of an elaborate strategy developed by lobbying groups to have closer access to decision makers in Congress. Efforts by lobbyists to maximize that access and to get the undivided attention of their legislative targets also frequently lead to free trips for members of Congress. A trip to a trade association convention or a meeting with corporate executives, either to give a speech for an honorarium or to do "fact finding," may also provide the member and spouse with a holiday of sorts while giving the lobbyist who arranges the trip the undivided attention of his most important legislative targets.

A House Ways and Means Committee staffer says about that time together for lobbyists and legislators on trips:

> I would say, knowing what I do about politics, that an awful lot of business is done between people like that whether it's on the fifth green or a plane trip down to whatever it is. . . . An hour on a plane trip together, that's as significant as their spending 20 days together in Washington.

Unfortunately the "fee" to create such an efficient working environment can be so high—travel, lodging, meals, gifts, entertainment—as to be beyond the reach of nearly all but the well-financed Washington-based lobbying operations. Some members of Congress spend so much time on the road with lobbying groups that obvious questions are raised not only about the propriety of such trips but also about the adequacy of their attention to duties in Washington.

Congressman Dan Rostenkowski (Democrat, Illinois) is chairman of the House Ways and Means Committee. He is responsible for shepherding through his committee and the House legislation that may be worth millions of dollars to any single interest group. In the first two years of the Reagan Administration, his committee, among other important issues, acted on the largest tax cut bill in history and the country's largest peacetime revenue bill. Access to Rostenkowski, and his good will, is a precious commodity to the thousands of lobbyists who follow the work of his committee.

Rostenkowski is willing in the extreme to accept the lavish hospitality of some of these lobbyists. In five months spanning the winter of 1981–82, the *Washington Post* reported, he spent 30 percent of his time as a guest of various corporations, trade associations, and individuals at resorts in Florida, California, and Hawaii. The *Post* found that hotel and transportation costs for those trips, exceeding $10,000, were paid for by the sponsoring groups. He also received in the first three months of 1982 $10,000 in honoraria and more than $15,000 in campaign contributions from these same groups or their affiliates. In addition, his hosts gave him hundreds of dollars worth of gifts including a watch, radio, golf clothes and equipment, luggage, and other merchandise.

Although Rostenkowski's actions are among the most blatant, it is not at all unusual for other members to have trips provided for them by lobbyists. In October, 1981, prior to action on the defense appropriations bill, the lobbyists for Hughes Helicopter, Inc., which was concerned about funding for the production of the trouble-plagued AH64 helicopter, arranged a three-day hunting trip to Montana for two members of the House Appropriations Committee. The National Association of Broadcasters in 1981 and 1982 treated thirty-two members to all-expenses-paid trips to their conventions in Las Vegas and Dallas. Of the thirty-two, seventeen were on the House and Senate Commerce Committees, which were considering legislation to deregulate the broadcasting industry. Similar examples abound.

Lobbyists do not neglect showering similar attention on important staff members with whom they will work on a day-to-day basis as their legislation moves through the Congress. Key staff members watch over the drafting of bills and amendments, develop committee reports and floor statements for members, and are in an ideal position to advocate positions with their bosses at crucial points in the legislative process. Lobbyists constantly aim to make staff people advocates for their legislative interests. A senior staff member of an important money committee like Finance or Appropriations, in fact, may receive more attention and favors from lobbyists than junior members of Congress who have not yet risen to positions of influence.

Again, the Ways and Means Committee provides some of the clearest examples of lobbyists courting favor with key staff. The *Washington Post* points to a trip to New Orleans in March, 1982, for two top aides to Congressman Rostenkowski and a lobbyist for Nevada casino and offtrack betting groups:

It was the beginning of a three-day weekend of door-to-door limousine service, a luxury hotel, elegant restaurants, and seats in the governor's box in the Superdome for the NCAA basketball semifinals. In between was a day's visit to offshore mining operations and talk of minerals. The trip—costing more than $1,000 a person, including comparable air fare—was paid by Freeport-McMoRan Inc. Pending legislation could have a multimillion-dollar impact on the company's tax liability.

Such trips, although barely disguised whirlwind vacations paid for by special interests, are allowed under the present enforcement of the code of conduct of the House as long as a claim can be made that it is related to official duties. Although subsidized trips by members must be reported, trips by staff generally are not reported publicly unless those involved are among the relative handful of top-paid congressional staff who are required to make annual public statements of financial interest.

The examples cited may seem flagrant but they are rooted in an attitude expressed by an aide to Rostenkowski: "Washington is a casual sort of 'let's-have-lunch, let's go-to-New-Orleans' kind of town. It's all done informally. There is a steady sort of nodding of heads here." It is an attitude that exacerbates the public's suspicion that decisions affecting their lives are made more on a basis of favors and cronyism than on merit. The unchecked abuse of the relationship between lobbyists and legislators and their staffs, particularly when exploited by leaders in the House or Senate, establishes a minimal standard for what is acceptable for the institution in this area. At present it is a standard that inevitably erodes public confidence in Congress.

On a long-term basis the isolated, dramatic, and illegal violation of ethical standards by a few in Congress—as in the Abscam scandal—may be less destructive to the integrity of the institution than the failure of the House and Senate to establish and enforce appropriately high standards of conduct to guide the actions of all members during their service in office. The individual gross violation of a member trading on his office for personal gain can create a crisis for the institution. As in the case of Abscam, however, it is likely to create the impetus necessary for the Congress to address such a crisis directly and responsibly.

The more subtle deterioration of ethical standards posed by campaign money, honoraria, and excessive travel and gifts gradually reinforces a public perception that the whole legislative process is influenced more by lobbyists and special interest money than by merit. It is a perception that to the degree that it reflects reality it threatens public trust in our system of representative government.

With so much at stake in the legislative arena for interest groups and for elected officials, it would be naive to suggest that strengthened institutional standards of integrity would stamp out avarice or excessive self-interest. Indeed, draconian restrictions that hindered the vigorous competition of ideas and interests necessary in the legislative process would not be healthy. It is not too hopeful to expect, however, that progress can be made to establish standards that can maintain public confidence in the integrity of the Congress and to help assure the ethical accountability of individual representatives and senators in the face of special interests that too often have driven out ideas and competition with political money.

In fact, substantial progress has been made in recent years in elevating congressional ethical standards. In the wake of Watergate, reform-minded legislators and a concerned public teamed up to help pass open-meeting rules, campaign finance disclosure laws, and strengthened codes of conduct with improved enforcement by the House and Senate ethics committees. Additional reforms are needed, however.

First, the system of financing congressional elections must be changed. The Congress, which enacted significant and successful reforms to deal with the corruption of the financing of presidential campaigns, must set its own system of financing campaigns in order.

Comprehensive reform of campaign financing would include a system to increase the role of the small-sum, individual contributor to congressional campaigns. A system of public financing— where small private contributions to qualifying candidates would be matched with federal funds—would increase the importance of the individual contributor and lessen the role of PAC contributions. Establishing a new source of campaign funds would give a candidate an alternative to accruing the compromising obligations that are created by going "hat in hand" to the PACs.

At the same time, campaign finance reform should establish new limitations on PAC contributions. The Federal Election Campaign Act limits contributions to a candidate from a PAC to $5,000 in a primary and $5,000 in a general election. At present there is no overall limit on how much a candidate may receive from all PACs. Thus there are no checks on the aggregate influence of PACs.

In 1979 the House passed—but the Senate did not consider—a measure that would have limited the total amount of PAC contributions a House candidate could receive in any election. Such a limitation for both the House and Senate should accompany a public financing package in order to curb the growing dependence of congressional candidates on PAC contributions and to lessen the special advantage lobbyists who control those PAC contributions have in the legislative process.

Second, tight new restrictions must be placed on honoraria. Representatives and senators ought to be expected to rely on their official salaries, not payments from lobbying groups, as their principal source of earned income. To make it easier to do so, members should be supported in efforts to establish pay levels that fairly reward the demanding nature of the job and that reasonably can be expected to keep pace with inflation and to minimize the economic sacrifices demanded of those in public service.

The limited honoraria, if any is allowed, should be insulated to the greatest degree possible from a member's legislative activity. Acceptance of honoraria from any source that has legislative interests before the member's committee should be prohibited.

Third, travel and gifts provided by interest groups for members and staff should be more clearly circumscribed by the codes of conduct of the House and Senate and enforced strictly. The presumption should be that travel necessary for effective government performance should be paid for by the government. Any staff travel paid for by outside groups should be publicly disclosed. To eliminate the abuse of turning such trips into thinly disguised vacations for members or staff paid for by lobbying groups, expenses for family members, extended stays beyond the time necessary to complete government-related business, and extravagant "expenses" should be strictly and clearly prohibited.

Finally, a new, effective, and enforceably federal lobbying disclosure law should be passed. In a democratic system of government, lobbying should be a positive influence, encouraging the public's participation in political issues and congressional awareness of public opinion. Congress should ensure that such lobbying is done openly. Just as there are requirements for open congressional meetings, disclosure of elected officials' financial holdings, and disclosure of campaign contributions, a suitable lobby disclosure law should satisfy the public's right to know how organized interests are trying to influence Congress. This is consistent with the principle that the governmental process and all significant factors that affect it must be open to public scrutiny to warrant public confidence in the integrity of governmental actions and policies.

At this point neither the public nor members of Congress can determine which interests are spending how much money on lobbying for legislative goals. In late 1982 and early 1983, the banking industry spent—but did not fully disclose—millions of dollars in a successful grassroots campaign to repeal tax withholding on interest and dividends. The insurance industry spent more than

$1.8 million—much of it undisclosed—in a four-month period in 1983 in a nationwide grassroots effort against legislation that would prohibit insurers from discriminating on the basis of sex with respect to premiums, benefits, and availability of coverage. The natural gas industry has also undertaken a million-dollar grassroots lobbying campaign to secure deregulation of natural gas, and the securities industry has initiated a more modest effort to repeal a new Social Security provision relating to tax-exempt bonds. There are just part of grassroots lobbying campaigns that—apart from the money spent on salaries for lobbyists in Washington, campaign contributions, honoraria, and entertainment costs—are estimated to cost lobbying groups well over $1 billion annually, with most of it never publicly reported.

In the words of former Senator Abraham Ribicoff (Democrat, Connecticut), effective lobbying disclosure is needed "so that the voice of the few and the money of the few do not make it impossible to hear the voice of the many." To improve the present inadequate lobby disclosure, the Congress should consider three major changes to the current lobby disclosure law.

First, the provisions that designate who must register as lobbyists should be tightened. The disclosure law could be amended to include a time and dollar expenditure threshold which, when crossed, would require an individual or organization to register.

Second, the provisions that designate what must be disclosed should also be tightened. The law should be amended to define explicitly and include grassroots lobbying as a covered lobbying activity.

Finally, Congress should consider amending the enforcement provisions of the law, which are currently widely ignored. Because the existing criminal penalties are perceived by many as being so harsh that they inhibit enforcement efforts, Congress should consider adding less severe civil enforcement provisions to the lobby disclosure law. It should also consider granting specific authority to an oversight agency, such as the General Accounting Office, to audit disclosure reports and conduct preliminary investigations of suspected violations.

Richard Bolling represented the citizens of Kansas City, Missouri, in Congress for over thirty years, rising to the chairmanship of the powerful House Rules Committee. When he retired in 1982 he was widely regarded not only as a legislative giant but also as one of those members who cared most about the institutional integrity of the Congress. He warned of the growing danger of PAC contributions, honoraria, and sophisticated grassroots lobbying campaigns threatening Congress's integrity and its ability to govern:

The explosion in PAC funds and other forms of special interest money is undermining public confidence in the institution of the Congress, and for good reason. It may sound idealistic, but I know from experience that Congress must have and must appear to have integrity in order to retain the public's confidence. But the public increasingly suspects that at least a portion of Congress is no longer *pure*. Because, increasingly, what the public sees is legislation that looks like special interest wish lists. What the public increasingly discovers is that interest groups are buying the sort of access that they as voters could never dream of.

Members of Congress who have been successful in the present system may have an incentive to maintain it. The lobbyists' direction of PAC money to their campaigns will help assure their re-election. It is safer politically to take thousands of dollars in honoraria for speaking before special interest groups than it is to justify voting for a pay raise at election time. Trips to resorts paid for by lobbying groups offer a welcome respite from the rigors of a demanding job.

The personal interest a member of Congress has in maintaining the present system is in direct conflict with the broad public interest in reforming a system in which public trust in government is corroded by the lopsided influence that special-interest money gives organized lobbying groups in Washington. One Washington insider, in comments on the campaign finance system, makes the case for members acting against self-interest to curb the influence of special interest money:

My view is that if the money represents an unfair advantage it ought to be eliminated. Where is the ethics or morality in saying the system ought to be maintained because it benefits you, if the advantage is inherently unfair?

There is a special ethical responsibility for members of Congress to vote against their own self-interest and to put new checks on special-interest money. They have a moral obligation to rebuild the integrity of the Congress and reassure the public of that integrity. No one could put the need to do so more strongly than House veteran Bolling: "We can control the pernicious influence of money in politics. . . . It is essential to the survival of our democracy."

TAINTED SAINT[3]

Like the Tammany Hall bosses of old, Democratic Rep. Fernand St Germain of Rhode Island has grown rich in the business of politics.

He was reared in a working-class family during the Depression in New England's grimy, industrial Blackstone Valley. One day the young St Germain visited a dye plant where his father worked as a foreman. "He brought me into that mill on a hot summer day, 110 degrees, 115 degrees," St Germain recalls. "His purpose was to say, 'Study hard.'"

After attending Boston University Law School at night while working by day as a cloth spreader in a garment factory, St Germain found himself running for the state legislature on the side of insurgents challenging a corrupt Democratic machine in his hometown, Woonsocket, R.I. "They were trying to fill the slate and nobody would take the job," he says. He was swept into office when some of the opposition was indicted.

St Germain came to Washington in 1960. Congressmen were paid $22,000 a year, but even after the stipend was raised to $30,000 in 1964, St Germain told an interviewer he doubted that any member of Congress stayed with the idea of making money.

Congressional wages were low because congressmen were reluctant to increase their own pay, fearing they would be attacked politically. But some attempted to earn more than a salary from their political office. St Germain was one of those.

In 1971 he approached an old friend from Woonsocket, Roland Ferland, who was rising to wealth as a builder. "I said, 'If something comes along, I hope you'll consider me,'" the congressman recalls. Ferland cut him in on a 192-apartment complex in East Providence. He was the only person outside the Ferland family to invest, and he got the same terms as the relatives. He paid $3,000 for a 15-percent share of the partnership.

[3]Reprint of an article adapted from Brooks Jackson's *Honest Graft: Big Money and the American Political Process*. Alfred A. Knopf, 1988. Reprinted from *Common Cause Magazine* S./O. 1988, pp. 14-18, by permission. Copyright 1988 by Brooks Jackson.

It turned out to be a very good deal. St Germain cashed in most of his interest in 1980 for $184,798.80. His remaining 2-percent interest earned him an additional $2,400 in 1985 and $4,526 in 1986.

Here was a perfect example, updated to modern times, of the "honest graft" Boss Plunkitt had described 80 years earlier. St Germain could say he avoided the illegal forms of graft, yet he asked for and received a favor that gained him $189,000 from a developer who profited from housing subsidies that St Germain supported as a member of the powerful House Banking Committee. Ferland became one of the biggest developers and managers of federally subsidized housing in the Northeast. Meanwhile, St Germain, thanks to his spot on the Banking Committee, used his growing influence over the Department of Housing and Urban Development, which fell under Banking Committee jurisdiction, to get a larger than average share of subsidized apartments for Rhode Island.

Federal housing subsidies became a boondoggle for developers. Under the so-called Section Eight program, which became the dominant subsidy method after 1974, the federal government encouraged the construction of apartments for moderately low-income people by agreeing to pay much of their rent. In Rhode Island and other states developers could also obtain low-interest mortgages from the authority that raised the money selling bonds, whose earnings were free of federal income tax. Their low-rate mortgages were thus indirectly subsidized by the loss of taxes to the U.S. Treasury. The tax code further provided bigger write-offs for low-income housing than for other types of real estate. With federally paid rent, federally subsidized mortgage money and tax deductions, the Section Eight program for new apartments came close to a government guarantee of tax-free profits for developers.

Developers recycled some of their profits as campaign donations. The National Association of Home Builders established a political action committee, BUILD-PAC, which dispensed campaign money to St Germain and other lawmakers who voted on the subsidies. Ferland was PAC chairman for a time. He also had helped raise the funds for St Germain's first House campaign.

By 1981 the federal government had run up a $130 billion bill for Section Eight housing, which taxpayers would be paying for 30 years. Even the cost-obsessed Reagan administration required almost its entire first term to halt this subsidy for developers. St Germain—by then chairman of the Banking Committee—fought a rear-guard action against the budget cutters.

St Germain also had benefited politically from the housing subsidies. His Rhode Island office became a referral center for low- and moderate-income people clamoring to get into one of the new apartment buildings where the federal government would pay part of their rent. St Germain had little incentive to question the profits to developers like Ferland or the expense to taxpayers.

The congressman didn't invest in any of Ferland's subsidized apartments but he benefited indirectly, through the developer's other, unsubsidized deals. Both Ferland and St Germain said the deals arose from their longstanding friendship. In 1976 Ferland included him in a family partnership that developed a tract in Pawtucket, R.I. From an investment of $7,500, the congressman received payments totaling $176,250 within 10 years.

A third Ferland deal also made money, but so little that the developer apologized. In 10 years the congressman realized an $18,000 profit on an initial investment of $2,000. For a time St Germain also had to put in interest-free loans totaling $16,000. "This finally concludes one of our less profitable partnerships," Ferland wrote when sending the checks to St Germain. "I guess we can't have all winners."

The Crêpe Trust

In the early '70s St Germain found other honest graft in a string of pancake restaurants. He bought properties worth $1.3 million without putting up any of his own money, a feat made possible by friendly Rhose Island institutions that loaned him the money despite some extraordinary risks.

In 1972 International Industries was trying to raise cash by selling off some of its International House of Pancakes restaurants at below-market prices. St Germain planned to cover his mortgage payments with rents received through the company, but its financial troubles made payment uncertain.

The congressman had few assets and had to stretch his salary—$42,500 by then—to cover both an apartment in Washington and a home in Rhode Island, where his wife had returned to live shortly after the birth of their second daughter. At that point he was chairman of a banking subcommittee overseeing federal regulation of financial institutions, so bankers were in a poor position to deny his personal requests for help with the pancake house deals.

One federally regulated lender, Industrial National Bank, loaned him the entire purchase price of two Rhode Island restaurants. He bought three more restaurants in New York, Texas and Maryland on similar terms from other lenders. The Marquette Credit Union, a state-regulated bank, balked at his request for 100-percent financing. But St Germain got around that by submitting a loan application listing a selling price $15,940 higher than the true figure. (The congressman accomplished this by keeping a 5-percent "broker's commission" for himself—without telling the credit union. The institution's president at the time raised no objection when congressional ethics committee investigators told him about it 13 years later.)

St Germain soon began pressing his lenders for even more favorable terms. He induced them to lengthen the terms of the mortgages to reduce his monthly payments and increase the amount of cash he could realize from the rents. Meanwhile, International Industries ran into further financial troubles and was tardy making its rent payments for a time. St Germain extracted $20,000 in late-payment penalties in 1977, underscoring how risky the loans had been. As things turned out, despite the risks, St Germain kept up payments and the restaurants proved profitable. The congressman cleared a profit of $315,995 on the last day of 1984 when he sold one of the Rhode Island restaurants.

He kept Rhode Island voters ignorant of his appetite for honest graft. "People say I play my cards close to my vest," he once boasted, speaking of his secretive style of legislating. The same held true in business. He put the restaurant in the name of an entity called the Crêpe Trust; his own name appeared nowhere on public records.

Who's Counting?

In 1978, when members of Congress were first required to make a reasonably complete listing of their assets, debts and outside income, St Germain was forced to state his ownership of the restaurants and the Ferland real estate deals but, as the House ethics committee later found, he still failed to reveal their true value. His first annual disclosure was accompanied by a press release stating his listed holdings were worth only $236,080, a gross undervaluation. He publicly listed the total value of the three Ferland deals at less than $3,000, even though he would subsequently receive a total of nearly $390,000 from them. (The congressman said an old letter from the ethics committee itself had given him the impression he needed to report only his net equity in the restaurants rather than their full market value, as required by House regulations. The committee accepted St Germain's undervaluation as a "good faith mistake.")

The deception continued for years. In 1983 St Germain publicly put the value of his restaurants at a maximum of $300,000, but in the same year he listed their true value at $1.8 million in a confidential loan application he gave to a financial institution.

Partly because the public knew so little about St Germain's undisclosed wealth, he was able to weather opponents' charges during his 1978 reelection campaign that he was a wheeler-dealer and guilty of conflicts of interest. After that, he lived a jet-set life, golfing in the winter in St. Petersburg, Fla., and in the summer at Newport R.I. In both places he bought waterfront condominium apartments at bargain prices from savings and loan associations that were foreclosing on developers. He attended financial-industry conventions in Puerto Rico, Florida and South Carolina. Increasingly, he stayed at his St. Petersburg condominium when Congress wasn't in session, while his Rhode Island congressional staff took care of business back home.

St Germain reached for further honest graft with the help of a friend who was a major figure in the savings and loan industry, Raleigh Green of St. Petersburg, chief executive of Florida Federal Savings and Loan. St Germain had come to know him when Greene was president of the National Savings and Loan League, a trade group representing large S&Ls. Early in 1979, St Germain flew aboard Greene's jet to St. Petersburg to inspect a six-room condominium overlooking Tampa Bay. Greene was foreclosing on the developer. Florida Federal sold St Germain the apartment for $4,000 less than the appraised market price of $110,000.

Greene arranged for St Germain to invest with him and others in three Florida real-estate partnerships starting in 1980. Neither his nor Greene's name appeared on the public real-estate records. Later, when the financial links were uncovered, Greene explained the relationship nonchalantly: "It's like anything else," he said, "You sit down with your buddies and say, 'Do you want in?' And you either say yea or nay."

In January 1983, as a result of yet another foreclosure by Florida Federal, St Germain acquired a beachfront condominium in Englewood, Fla. He paid $174,000; Florida Federal lent him $173,000 to buy it.

St Germain then began reaching for honest graft that would, when exposed, trigger an official House investigation. By this time, as chairman of the full Banking Committee, he was the undisputed godfather of the S&L industry. And he tried to make a quick profit speculating in Florida Federal's stock.

The biggest S&L in Florida, Florida Federal was still a mutual association, legally owned by its depositors. Greene was pressing for permission to convert to a corporation. Newly issued S&L stocks usually provided fast money for those who got in on the ground floor.

But there was a hitch. The Federal Home Loan Bank Board in Washington had to approve the sale first. The regulators generally favored stock conversions; they got more money into the S&Ls and relieved pressure on the badly weakened S&L insurance fund. But the board denied Florida Federal's first request for quick clearance under an emergency procedure. Greene applied again using normal procedures.

As the process dragged on, St Germain's principal aide, Paul Nelson, chief of staff of the Banking Committee, contacted the chairman of the bank board and inquired about the pace of the Florida Federal application. The chairman, Richard Pratt, said Nelson called as many as three times about the matter and that Florida Federal was the only institution St Germain's aide ever queried him about. Nelson repeatedly contacted the Federal Home Loan Bank in Atlanta as well, which also had to approve the stock sale.

Though regulators later denied that Nelson's calls made them move any faster, Florida Federal got the regulatory clearance it wanted. St Germain bought 1,500 shares at the ground-floor price, paying $30,000 in May 1983. But Florida Federal wasn't one of the hot ones. St Germain sold it at a modest loss two years later, shortly after it became clear to him that an unflattering news story would appear.

St Germain at first reported only an unspecified "holding" in Florida Federal without identifying it as common stock or giving the date of purchase, as required by law. On his report the stock appeared as nothing more sinister than an insured savings account.

When St Germain learned that reporters were investigating him, he filed an amended report showing his ownership of the S&L stock. It was a prudent move; a Republican member of the Banking Committee, Rep. George Hansen of Idaho, was headed for jail because he falsified his personal disclosure forms. Hansen had completely concealed a risk-free $87,000 profit from a silver-futures trade arranged by conservative political backer Nelson Bunker Hunt and $135,000 in loans from three men whom Hansen aided in an attempt to sell an experimental hydrogen-powered vehicle to the Army.

St Germain's new disclosure forms showed he had been hiding embarrassing financial dealings. Besides his Florida Federal stock, some of his "investments" were revealed as limited partnerships in Kentucky coal-mining ventures that the Internal Revenue Service said were abusive tax shelters. St Germain had gotten more than $405,000 in tax deductions in return for a total cash "investment" of $120,000. The IRS opened a criminal investigation of the promoter but filed no charges. Eventually the IRS allowed the congressman to settle by paying the taxes he had avoided, plus interest.

On September 11, 1985, *The Wall Street Journal* published a front-page story about St Germain's wealth and tax avoidance under the headline "Making a Fortune." *The Washington Post* and others called for an investigation by the House ethics committee. Heading into an election year, St Germain suddenly found himself in a fight for political survival.

What Money Can Buy

St Germain had never had to run a modern political campaign before, and Rep. Tony Coelho (D-Calif.), chairman of the Democratic Congressional Campaign Committee, came to his rescue. To start, Coelho furnished $5,000 worth of public opinion polling.

"I said to him 'The polls are not good. Get out there right now with some bought media [advertising],'" Coelho recalls. St Germain was now officially under investigation by the House ethics committee, which began an inquiry on February 5, 1986, after months of delay. But St Germain's campaign fund continued to grow with special interest checks. Business PACs were helping him, not the Republican challenger.

No faction in the turbulent financial services industry wished to offend the chairman of the Banking Committee by failing to pay tribute. Merrill Lynch, which was keen on preventing banks from competing with the stockbrokers, gave $4,000. The Independent Insurance Agents of America donated $5,000; they wanted to keep banks out of the insurance business. And, not surprisingly, the New York–based banking giant Citicorp sent $5,000; it wanted to get into the insurance and brokerage businesses.

Some of those who gave loathed St Germain personally. "He's as arrogant and pompous and as expectant a member as there is up there," said one senior official, whose association PAC gave thousands of dollars to his campaign. "He puts the arm on you," complained the head of another trade group that donated thousands. A third lobbyist said he resented having to "kiss the ring" of the chairman, but his group gave anyway.

Meanwhile, Republican John Holmes, St Germain's opponent, found it difficult to raise money. Holmes had encountered the challenger's paradox: He couldn't win without spending lots of money, but people wouldn't donate unless they thought he was going to win. In the end, Holmes got barely $40,000 from PACs, including less than $20,000 from business groups. St Germain eventually amassed a PAC total of more than $300,000, predominantly from business interests.

As a liberal Democrat, St Germain could take business PAC money without fear of reproach from consumer groups. He was one of their favorites because he often criticized bankers for charging high interest rates on credit cards and sponsored relatively trivial but crowd-pleasing bills to regulate unpopular commercial practices. In 1986 he was pushing a measure to force banks to credit deposits quickly, trimming the long "holds" they sometimes imposed while waiting for checks to clear. The check-hold problem was of much less import than such matters as the plundering of the savings and loan industry by unscrupulous operators who threatened to bankrupt the federal deposit insurance fund.

St Germain's enormous advantage in special interest money offset his weakness in the polls. His television commercials were seen twice as often as Holmes's, and he poured additional funds into radio advertising, which Holmes couldn't afford at all. For 10 crucial days in October, Holmes ran out of money and had to stop running TV ads entirely. During that time Republican polling showed him dropping by one percentage point each day. In the end St Germain won 57.7 percent of the vote to Holmes's 42.3 percent.

After the election, Democrats chose St Germain to continue as chairman of the Banking Committee, and the ethics committee unanimously issued a report concluding he hadn't misused his office for personal gain. Throughout the inquiry, St Germain said he had done nothing that violated the rules of the House.

The ethics committee did cite him for several infractions. It found he understated his assets by more than $1 million for several years, and it cited seven trips to Florida he took aboard Raleigh Greene's company jet, despite a House rule against taking gifts of more than $100 from anyone with an interest in legislation. But it said the violations were not serious enough to warrant punishment, which the congressman accepted as vindication.

St Germain could hardly have hoped for a more accommodating jury than the 12 House members who made up the ethics committee, even though half of them were Republicans. They didn't question his income-tax avoidance or even ask for a look at his tax returns. They never troubled St Germain by questioning him under oath or even informally, communicating always through his attorney. In fact, investigators questioned nobody under oath. They failed to discover that St Germain's aide, Paul Nelson, had contacted Atlanta regulators about the Florida Federal merger. And the committee accepted Nelson's word that he couldn't remember whether St Germain had asked him to make the calls to the Federal Home Loan Bank Board chairman.

The congressman kept up a relationship with at least one of his inquisitors, Rep. George Wortley (R-N.Y.). On May 15, 10 days after the panel issued its first subpoena, St Germain appeared as a surprise guest at a Wortley fundraising breakfast at the Mayflower Hotel in Washington. "I remember being surprised as hell when he walked in the door," one banking lobbyist recalls. Wortley was a Republican whom Coelho had targeted for defeat. The event realized about $15,000 from banking lobbyists and executives. St Germain later described the appearance as just a "courtesy" to Wortley, who was a member of the Banking Committee as well as the ethics panel.

Wortley meanwhile was telling other House colleagues that St Germain would be cleared (though he would later deny violating the committee's strict secrecy rules).

Looking the Other Way

The panel most likely would have absolved St Germain in time for the election if not for a surprise visit from the chief investigator for the Rhode Island attorney general's office, Lee Blais. He told the ethics committee staff that a witness was giving testimony about bribes allegedly paid to St Germain. Thomas Broussard, a California lawyer, testified that his business partner, Rhode Island developer Ronald Picerne, claimed to have bribed St Germain for not blocking federal funds for two of Picerne's federally subsidized apartment projects.

St Germain certainly was in a position to obstruct such grants; no other member of Congress had more power over the Department of Housing and Urban Development, which administered them. Broussard testified that Picerne admitted making one cash payment to St Germain of $15,000 and a second of $20,000. Picerne, however, denied the story and St Germain said he had never been bribed by anybody. There is no indication that Rhode Island or federal authorities pursued the bribe allegations further.

Blais said later he expected the ethics committee to investigate the bribe allegation. He miscalculated. The panel never questioned Broussard. Blais's visit only slowed the rush to clear St Germain. Until the *Providence Journal* headlined Broussard's story on August 20, the committee had been preparing to clear St Germain even though it couldn't discover where he got a $28,738 deposit when he bought his first two restaurants. St Germain said he couldn't recall the source.

But eight days after the *Providence Journal* broke the bribe story, the committee issued four new subpoenas for records. The additional investigation established that the deposit money had been yet another loan from a federally regulated bank.

Besides failing to address the bribery allegation, the committee made little attempt to look into St Germain's well-known penchant for running up bar and restaurant tabs at the expense of the savings and loan lobby. His wife had moved back to Rhode Island early in his House career, and he was seen night after night in Washington eating and drinking in the company of James "Snake" Freeman, lobbyist for the U.S. League of Savings Associations. Rival banking lobbyists said Freeman's principal function at the S&L lobby was the care and feeding of his old friend, St Germain.

The ethics committee's staff had called in Freeman for questioning, but quickly backed off when his employer raised objections. The final report contained not a word about free meals or liquor.

In 1987 the Justice Department opened an investigation, questioning Freeman and issuing subpoenas for his expense-account records, which showed thousands of dollars' worth of tabs for St Germain. (St Germain denied that he improperly accepted free meals and his attorney said he was out of town on some days that Freeman listed him as a guest on expense records.) After a lengthy internal debate, the agency announced it wouldn't prosecute. Instead, officials sent a letter to the House ethics committee suggesting that it examine whether St Germain violated House rules against accepting excessive gifts from lobbyists. At press time, the committee had taken no official action.

The committee's 1987 report pleased St Germain. He said it "confirmed what my constituents, my friends and I have known all along—that I adhere to the highest standards of conduct in both public office and private business affairs."

ETHICS IN THE LEGISLATIVE PROCESS: AN OVERVIEW[4]

Fulfilling the Public Trust

Legislatures as institutions and legislators as individuals occupy an essential position our democracy and carry the burden of

[4]Reprint of an article by Daniel Callahan and Bruce Jennings, co-directors for The Hastings Center Legislative and Representative Ethics Project. Excerpted and adapted from "Ethics of Legislative Life: A Report by the Hastings Center" and reprinted by permission from *Ethics: Easier Said Than Done*, Spring/Summer 1988, pp. 64–71. Copyright 1985 by The Hastings Center.

a solemn public trust. In attempting to fulfill that trust, legislators play many different roles. Their tasks range from careful study of exceedingly complex policy questions to helping individual constituents with their personal problems.

Thus, legislators must embody our highest social ideals and aspirations without losing touch with hard reality. They must descend into the trenches of partisan dealing and in-fighting without losing their integrity and perspective.

Legislators are entrusted with significant power—the decisions they make regularly affect the lives and well-being of [thousands, and in the case of Congress], millions of people in this country and throughout the world. Their use of this power, and their respect for the public trust that stands behind it, are facts with moral implications that must not be ignored.

[While some conduct is dictated by statues or ethics codes], there is a wide variety of legislative decisions that involve important moral choices where the right course of action is not at all clear.

Toward a More Constructive and Comprehensive Dialogue

[In the present climate of scandal and growing public cynicism], legislators surely need to devote more visible and effective attention to legislative ethics. To restore public confidence, they need to demonstrate that they care about their ethical responsibilities as public servants.

Moreover, the dialogue about ethics in the legislative process should be both more *constructive* and *comprehensive*. It should be *more constructive* in that it should not arise simply as a response to intermittent scandals or focus on blatant examples of ethical misconduct. Instead, it should articulate a national conscience for legislative representation, embracing positive ideals as well as negative prohibitions. It should be more *comprehensive* than the current discussions of legislative ethics, which center on conflict of interest, misuse of office for personal gain, and public disclosure requirements.

There should be more discussion of legislative ethics within legislatures. Legislators should not only reflect upon the ethical aspects of their decisions in the privacy of their own consciences, but they should also share their ethical dilemmas with other legislators and seek the counsel of their colleagues and respected legislative leaders. Ideally, legislatures should provide an atmosphere of collegial support and respect where legislators can find positive assistance in reasoning through the moral quandaries that so often arise.

At the same time, legislative ethics is not something to be discussed only among legislators themselves; nor does it apply only to them.

Staffs. Members of legislative staffs—whose numbers and importance have increased dramatically in recent years—must have a clear understanding of legislative ethics because their conduct immediately affects legislators' ability to fulfill their duties.

Lobbyists. The same is true for lobbyists and others who play a direct role in the legislative process, and whose conduct affects the character of the political representation citizens receive from their legislators. These individuals must not lose sight of the fact that the legislative process is—and ought to be—governed by ethical as well as political and procedural rules. Their duty is not limited to promoting the political, economic, or bureaucratic interests they represent as advocates; they also have a duty to protect the ethical integrity of the legislative process. They must recognize moral restraints in their attempt to influence legislation and temper their advocacy if need be so as to support—or at least not compromise—the autonomy, accountability, and responsibility of legislators.

Journalists. Journalists are also key actors in legislative life, and the way they practice their craft significantly affects the discharge of ethical duties by legislators. Legislators realize that being watched by the media is like being watched by their constituents, and they react accordingly. Therefore, journalists are in a strategically important position to affect the ethical conduct of legislators.

Constituents. Constituents affect the state of legislative life through the civic expectations they hold and convey to legislators. Our nation cannot tolerate a state of affairs in which legislators are forced to choose between ethical integrity and political survival. We can ask that they be prepared to risk a loss of popularity and to take politically courageous stands when their ethical duties require them to do so. That is a part of what integrity and leadership mean in political life. We cannot ask that legislators routinely sacrifice their political futures in order to observe ethi-

cal standards to which their constituents pay lip service but are
not willing to endorse with their votes.

Ethics and Politics: Are They Compatible?

Some would argue that no realistic purpose is served by discussions of legislative ethics because legislators do—and must—
respond single-mindedly to political pressures. According to the
conventional wisdom, when push comes to shove legislators will
not be moved by considerations of ethical duty but will inevitably
act instead on the basis of feasibility and advantage.

There are tensions between legislative ethics and legislative
politics, to be sure. There are times when moral brakes must be
applied, times when ethical obligations do constrain political options. But these tensions do not tell the whole story. Political and
ethical considerations can also supplement and mutually support
one another.

Legislators who have a clear sense of their ethical obligations
and who know when to apply their moral brakes are usually more
effective representatives and lawmakers than those who are Machiavellian "realists."

The practice of legislative politics as the art of the possible is
an ethically legitimate calling, which serves the public interest
more often than not. Legislators who are blind to the ethical obligations of their role or who carelessly disregard those obligations
in venal or otherwise self-serving ways do sooner or later lose the
respect of their colleagues and the trust of their supporters. Having lost that respect and trust, they lose their political effectiveness and influence as well.

A Working Definition of Ethics

We define the concept of "ethics" broadly to apply not only
to individual corruption, conflict of interest, and the use of office
for personal financial gain, but also to the entire range of
"normal" legislative activities and decisions. The latter bear on a
legislator's duty to promote the public good, to represent the legitimate interest of constituents, to exercise autonomous legislative judgment, to maintain the proper constitutional functioning
of legislative institutions, and to treat other individuals with justice, beneficence, and respect.

By definition, ethics focuses on questions of right and wrong, good and evil, benefit and harm. These questions arise whenever an individual or group exercise power over others, and ethical conduct is required to transform effective power into legitimate authority.

There must be several different but mutually reinforcing factors working to support the ethical integrity of legislators:

- *informal moral traditions*
- *formal ethics regulations*
- *political incentives* in the legislative process and the electoral system, and finally
- *legislators' own personal commitment* to live up to their ethical obligations.

Types of Ethical Issues

The problems that raise moral considerations in legislative life are of two different types.

Violations of Regulations. There are instances where the activity in question is clearly unethical (e.g., taking a bribe in return for a legislative favor) and the problem is how to prevent that act. Problems of this type—which may be called *problems of regulation*—do not involve any serious conceptual or value quandaries, although they do often raise difficult practical issues concerning effective and just methods of deterrence and enforcement.

Dilemmas of Obligation. On the other hand, ethical problems may arise that do involve serious quandaries. Individuals already motivated to do the right thing cannot always know what the right thing to do is. In these cases—which may be called *dilemmas of obligation*—reasonable persons may disagree about the appropriate course of action in a given circumstance, important moral principles may require mutually exclusive courses of action, and the ethical decision maker has to choose the lesser of two evils. Here the problem is not how to deter or punish wrongdoing, but how to assist conscientious individuals in making hard choices in the most reasonable and well-informed way.

The Ethical Obligations and Opportunities
of Legislative Service

When a private citizen steps into the role of legislator, he or she takes on a second ethical identity, one composed of a structure of special obligations that are often more demanding and restrictive than the general moral obligations of private life. To assume the role of legislator is to make a special promise to the rest of us and to accept a special trust on our behalf.

We rely on legislatures to sift and balance conflicting interests, fashioning just and equitable compromises among them for the enhancement of the common good. We rely on legislatures to contain those forces that tend to pull us apart and to nourish those forces that tend to pull us together. In a world of interdependence and technological complexity, we look to legislatures to devise the rules of our collective activity, to guide the allocation of our social and economic resources, and, most fundamentally, to help channel the enormous energy and creativity of our people and our civilization toward productive, just, and humane ends.

Legislatures—the institutions that we expect to perform all these difficult tasks—are peculiar organizations. Perhaps no other institutions are so vulnerable to externally induced change; no other institutions must endure such a significant turnover in their membership every two, four, or six years and still retain stable institutional continuity.

Legislatures must continually socialize their endlessly arriving new members, but at a vastly compressed and accelerated rate. Older legislators must adjust to their new colleagues who bring new interest, ambitions, and philosophies with them and thus inject an element of uncertainty and unpredictability into legislative relationships. Legislators live by a political clock set long ago by the framers of our federal and state constitutions: every two years much that was solid melts into air—leadership positions are subject to change, new committee assignments are made, last year's coalitions dissolve and new ones form.

Legislative Ethics: An Historical Perspective

Two conclusions may be drawn from the history of Congress' handling of ethics cases: 1) legislatures cannot rely solely on the discretion of individual legislators, the standards of the criminal law, or the judgment of constituents to ensure that appropriate ethical norms are acknowledged and obeyed; and 2) the definition of an ethical issue in legislative life is relative to the institutional structure and political context within which legislators must function.

Looking at the full range of congressional and state legislative ethics reforms, one can discern two general approaches to legislative ethics:

1. **Public Disclosure.** Far and away the greatest emphasis was placed on public disclosure, a rubric that includes financial disclosure, open meetings, and disclosure of gifts and campaign contributions. The intent here was not to prohibit conflicts of interest in every form, but to give constituents the basic information they presumably need in order to judge for themselves whether unacceptable conflicts of interest are present and to react as they see fit.

2. **Codes of Conduct.** The second general approach to legislative ethics in the 1970s was a marked recourse, in those areas where disclosure alone seemed inadequate, to formal codes and rules. These rules, such as the House and Senate prohibitions on the use of the frank for political purposes, were designed to remedy some very specific, identifiable abuses. They were written in a quite detailed and technical way so that their interpretation and enforcement could become routine. . . . [u]nderstandable and laudable background considerations were at work involving notions of procedural justice and equity. These rules attempt to provide legislators with clear-cut, specific prohibitions that, once stated, can be easily obeyed without imposing undue or unfair burdens on any particular legislator.

The rules in the present codes were originally designed to reflect the legislature's institutional sense of ethical identity. They stand as a public declaration of what the institution stands for and what it expects of its members. But in practice, precisely because these rules do not include positive statements of ethical ideals and aspirations, they have an ethical "leveling-down" rather than "leveling-up" effect.

Like other professional ethics codes that are limited in the same way, these codes implicitly suggest that if a legislator has not violated any of their rules, then he or she has done all that legislative ethics requires. Beyond the confines of these rules, legislatures seem to have few valid grounds either to criticize or to praise their members.

Theories of Representation

Since the seventeenth century, political theories have developed two contrasting conceptions of representation: *"trustee"* theories and *"delegate"* theories.

Trustee Theory. According to the *trustee theory*, election constitutes a broad transfer of authority from the represented to the representatives. On this view, the representative has an almost unlimited license to make legislative decisions based on his or her own moral judgment of the best interests of the represented and the common good of the political community as a whole. The representative's fiduciary obligations to particular constituents are subordinate to more general fiduciary obligations to the public interest. What the representative as trustee owes constituents is simply his or her best effort to shape public policy wisely.

Delegate Theory. The *delegate theory*, by contrast, emphasizes a considerably more constrained and specific relationship between the representative and the represented. According to this theory, representation involves carrying out a set of express or tacit instructions. Election constitutes a specific and circumscribed transfer of authority, and the representative has a moral duty to make legislative decisions in accordance with the express interests and preferences of the represented.

In the delegate theory, unlike the trustee theory, the representative's fiduciary obligations to constituents are paramount; they must not be subordinated to the representative's responsibility to promote the public interest. In other words, the representative's duty is to promote and protect the interests of constituents—as *they* define those interests. What the representative as delegate owes constituents, then, is strict adherence to their known preferences. Their continued support in subsequent elections amounts primarily to their endorsement, not of qualities of wisdom and leadership, but of the representative's ability to deliver the benefits and protections they desire.

Applying the Theories to Practical Legislative Life. Because these theories are each simplified or abstract models of representation, they sidestep most of the hard questions of legislative ethics. These questions arise precisely because legislators are in reality both trustees and delegates, not by turns, but simultaneously in nearly everything they do.

Legislators themselves seem to recognize this. Empirical studies of legislators' own conceptions of their roles have shown that the trustee/delegate dichotomy has very little explanatory force in accounting for legislative behavior. Legislators who consciously label themselves as "trustees" do not act differently from those who label themselves "delegates." Indeed, when asked to identify themselves in these terms, most legislators respond that this distinction has little practical significance.

Three Principles of Legislative Ethics: Autonomy, Accountability, Responsibility

The ethical obligations of legislators are rooted in three basic principles of legislative ethics: *autonomy*, *accountability*, and *responsibility*.

PRINCIPLE OF AUTONOMY

This principle holds that legislators have an obligation to deliberate and decide, free from improper influence. Improper influences are those that draw legislators' use of the authority and resources of their office away from the public ends—the representation of constituent interests and the promotion of the public interest—that these offices were created to serve in the first place.

The principle of autonomy is threatened by conflicts of interest which arise when a legislator's personal or political self-interests pull in one direction, and his or her duty to serve broader public interests pulls in another. In this case, considerations of self-interest constitute improper influences, and the legislator has an ethical duty to override them in order to preserve autonomy in decision-making.

Since self-interest is such a powerful motivating force in human activities, overriding it is a demanding task. Prudence suggests that the best safeguard against unethical conduct is to avoid conflicts of interest before they arise.

Many provisions of the recent codes and ethics regulations in Congress and some state legislatures have followed this prudential approach in areas where personal *financial* self-interest is likely to conflict with the legislator's duty to serve other interests before his own.

Prohibitions on the receipts of substantial gifts and other sources of income coming from those seeking special legislative treatment are often viewed merely as restrictions on legislators. For the few corruption-prone legislators this is what they are. But for the majority of conscientious legislators these provisions are best seen, not as restrictions, but as *shields* against the exertion of improper influence by others.

However, the autonomy-based duty to deliberate and decide, free from improper influence, means much more in practice than merely avoiding financial conflicts of interest. . . . In order to preserve their autonomy, legislators must avoid becoming too dependent upon any single source of information or analysis. In their political careers legislators necessarily form close associations with lobbyists, special interest groups, and certain sectors of their district constituencies. But these special associations must not become the exclusive source of a legislator's perspective and outlook, and when they begin to distract a legislator from his or her broader democratic responsibilities as a *public* servant, their influence becomes improper.

Principle of Accountability

This principle holds that legislators have an obligation to provide constituents with the information and understanding they require in order to exercise responsible democratic citizenship. When they are in doubt about what course of action to follow, the principle of accountability recommends that legislators ask themselves: "Could I publicly justify—give good reasons for—doing this if my constituents were fully informed about and fully understood what I have done?" Simply asking: "Could I get away with this if it were revealed?" is not sufficient. The idea behind the principle of accountability is that legislators themselves ought to take reasonable steps to ensure that democratic consent is fully informed and enlightened.

The principle of accountability is the basis for the various "public disclosure" measures enacted in recent years—financial disclosure, open meeting rules, disclosure of campaign contributions, and the like. At bottom, these measures are designed to better enable constituents to judge whether legislators are fulfilling their duty to preserve their autonomy.

As with autonomy, legislators' personal or political self-interest may or may not be in conflict with their duties of accountability. Legislators are not the only source of information about their activities, but they control the flow of information that reaches constituents through the media and other sources to a significant extent.

Political considerations prompt legislators to portray their records in favorable ways and to keep some aspects of their official activities hidden from public view. This is precisely why it is important to affirm ethical considerations that oblige legislators to provide an accurate account of their record so that constituents, and other citizens too, will be in a position to evaluate it in a well-informed way.

Citizens need more than factual information; they need a context within which to interpret the significance of the information they receive from legislators. Accountability therefore requires not only that legislators should *disclose* what they have done, but also that they should *explain* what they have done. Too often, disclosure alone does not provide an effective deterrent to unethical conduct.

No matter what new campaign regulations eventually evolve, legislators must remember that the way they conduct their campaigns is a litmus test of how seriously they take their ethical obligation to be accountable.

Principle of Responsibility

This principle holds that legislators have an obligation to contribute to the effective institutional functioning of the democratic legislative process. Legislators must strike a delicate balance between accommodating themselves to the existing institutional and procedural arrangements of their chamber, and pressing for organizational change through public criticism and institutional leadership.

The principle of responsibility states that legislators have an obligation to contribute to the effective institutional functioning of the democratic legislative process.

Representation and lawmaking are collective processes; they rely on the cooperation and coordinated activities of many legislators. Therefore, individual legislators cannot fulfill the ethical obligations of their office or role merely by attending to their own activities and their own relationship with their constituents. They must be concerned as well with the activities of other legislators and with the functioning of the legislature as a whole.

The principle of responsibility adds an important element to our analysis of legislative ethics because it explains one of the features of the ethical duties of legislators that makes them more stringent than the ordinary ethical duties of private citizens. Legislators have a duty, not only to avoid wrongdoing, but also to avoid the *appearance* of wrongdoing. It is, of course, a commonplace of political prudence that legislators must be concerned with their public image as well as their public performance, the appearance as well as the substance of what they do.

Contemporary Sources of Ethical Conflicts

There are at least three features of the current electoral system that pose strong ethical conflicts for legislators by forcing them to choose, more or less severely, between their ethical duties and their political advantage. They are: 1) *electoral entrepreneurialism*, 2) the *campaign finance-lobbying complex*, and 3) *"home-style" pressures*.

ELECTORAL ENTREPRENEURIALISM

There is the growing phenomenon of electoral entrepreneurialism in legislative activities. This is directly related to the fact that political parties are less influential and are less effective instruments of interest aggregation or electoral coalitions than they once were. Voters are less likely to vote a straight party ticket, and candidates are less likely to rely on the party for campaign funds and manpower. In addition, many districts are less homogeneous than ever before, and television has become a decisive factor in campaigns.

On the campaign trail, and in the information legislators send constituents during the interim periods when de facto campaigning never stops, the electoral environment now provides less support for legislators who conscientiously fulfill their duties of accountability.

In these circumstances, it is expedient to *present one's record selectively* and to use newsletters and other direct mail appeals, sent out according to scientifically researched and classified mailing lists, to say different things to different constituents.

Moreover, legislators have devised several different techniques to cope with this free-wheeling electoral environment. For example, legislators often claim credit for projects or programs benefitting their district, whether or not their legislative efforts were actually responsible for the creation of those projects or programs.

THE CAMPAIGN FINANCE-LOBBYING COMPLEX

Congressional campaigns, and, increasingly, state legislative campaigns as well, have become exceedingly expensive. Television advertising and the professional services now associated with campaigns—consultants, managers, pollsters, and direct mail services—largely account for these costs. More important than the sheer amounts involved, however, is the fact that fund-raising has become the predominant and virtually full-time preoccupation of legislative incumbents who plan to run for re-election.

Even legislators from relatively "safe" districts have become caught up in this process for at least two reasons:

1. Raising large war chests is one of the most effective ways for an incumbent to discourage potential opponents.

2. Legislators can form their own Political Action Committees and dispense funds they do not need themselves to other legislators facing strong challenges. This, of course, is a powerful way to gain legislative influence and support that can be used later.

The campaign finance reforms of the 1970s have shifted influence from large, anonymous, individual donors to independent, corporate, and trade association Political Action Committees. PACs influence legislators in many subtle and not so subtle ways.

For these reasons alone, PACs present a concentrated set of influences that tend to make legislators responsive to special groups and interests; more responsive, we believe, than the principle of autonomy suggests they should be.

HOME-STYLE PRESSURES

Legislators develop complex conceptions of the structure of political support and opposition among their district constituents. Legislators quickly identify those whose support can be lost or won from election to election.

Generally speaking, legislators find it politically advantageous to broaden the base of their political support by moving outward from their solid base to embrace increasing numbers of marginal supports. This situation is not only politically prudent, it seems essential to legitimate and responsive democratic representation. Moreover, it is morally required by a legislator's autonomy-related duty to consider seriously the interest of *all* his constituents, and to accommodate them in a reasonable fashion.

American politics is incredibly fluid and chaotic at the present time. There is widespread political apathy combined with pockets of intense political activism, often based on unyielding single-issue orientations. Without much support from political parties to mediate their exposure to these swirling political winds, legislators often find themselves unable to move toward the middle to broaden the base of their support. Indeed, they clutch instead to their closest and firmest supporters. They find it difficult to fashion compromises because they cannot find the middle ground on which such compromises could rest.

Under these conditions, legislators are understandably inclined to adopt what might be called a "preferential orientation" toward their closest supporters. It is all too easy for them to over-identify with the interests of one relatively narrow segment of their constituency, to come to regard themselves as the representative of those supporters to whom they owe their re-election rather than as the representative of the district as a whole. And in such a conflict-ridden political environment, they easily come to regard themselves primarily as brokers for the most visible and powerful interest groups that emerge from the body of indifferent voters and from the apathetic mass of nonvoting constituents.

Legislators may owe their re-election to a majority of their voting constituents, but they owe conscientious democratic representation to all their constituents, including those who voted against them and those who did not vote at all.

Legislators cannot confidently assume that the most visible and powerful interest groups accurately reflect a cross-section of the constituency. And they cannot be content simply to act as a broker for those interests. Legislators must find ways to reach out to communicate with those who are the least visible, the least powerful, and the least well-organized, in spite of the formidable difficulties this presents today.

Modes and Methods of Ethical Leadership

Legislative leaders influence ethical behavior in subtle ways. They *lead by example*. If they so choose, they can elevate the level of political discourse, set the standard for interaction with special interests, and affect the overall moral tone of the assembly. They can especially influence the behavior of junior members. . . . If leaders abuse the legislative process for political reasons in a manner that deprives legitimate interested parties of a voice in policy-making, novice legislators come to see the abuse of the process as being ethically, as well as politically, acceptable. Conversely, if a legislative leader is an ethical role model, if he or she is an embodiment of the maxim that "public office is a public trust," if avoidance of even the appearance of impropriety guides his or her actions, then a decidedly different atmosphere is created.

The Legislator as a Counselor. Legislative leaders can also serve a salutary role as counselors. There is no reason why they should not caution junior members when they detect the beginning of a pattern of questionable conduct. The junior member surely would rather have that point made by an avuncular leader of his or her own party, in the privacy of the legislative cloakroom, than see it in print on page one of the morning papers, as the lead story on the evening news, or as the subject matter of a disciplinary proceeding.

The Legislator as an Institutional Reformer. Legislatures can support the autonomy, accountability, and responsibility of their members in more structured ways as well. For example, they can provide institutional resources, such as the Congressional Budget Office, the Congressional Research Service, and policy study groups at the federal level, that facilitate a more detailed and vigorous analysis of policy issues. They can take steps to regulate lobbying activities, and they can reduce legislators' dependence on lobbyists by employing nonpartisan, professional staff.

The Legislator as an Impetus to Dialogue. Legislatures should do more to encourage and support discussions of ethical issues among legislators. Presentations on general issues of legislative ethics, as well as discussions of the rationales behind the formal codes and regulations, should be incorporated into legislative orientation sessions and training programs conducted by universities and by organizations like the National Conference of State Legislatures. Ethics seminars have been successfully conducted in

Congress and in several state legislatures on an ad hoc basis; such seminars should be established in all legislatures on a regular basis.

Ethics Codes: Pros and Cons

One of the most visible and influential aspects of the moral ecology of a legislature is its code of ethics. Codes are too often seen as merely negative elements in legislative life—rules and restrictions that exist because legislators are unable to discipline and direct themselves.

But codes can and should have a more positive, supportive function. They can express the legislature's own sense of itself as an ethical organization; they can serve as a public declaration of ethical traditions and values that members are dedicated to serve.

At a time when legislators are increasingly being called to give a public accounting of their ethical behavior, codes can supply a common point of reference, giving legislators a standard to which they can appeal in defending their performance and giving constituents a standard to which they can refer in evaluating their representatives.

As a practical matter, codes can help legislators resist the ethical pressures they face by giving them an excuse to say no to improper influences and illegitimate demands.

We believe that legislative ethics codes ought to contain both aspirational elements, espoused ideals, and precisely defined rules of conduct. That is, to borrow the terminology of the former ABA code, a legislative code should contain the equivalent of both "ethical considerations" and "disciplinary rules." A code that contains only the former will lack bite and the possibility of adequate enforcement. A code that contains only the latter will fail to set high enough standards and will be too narrow in scope.

A legislative code of ethics ought to lay out the moral obligations of individual legislators, and of the legislature as an institution. It should cover the full range of duties and activities of legislators, addressing the collective responsibilities of the legislators as well as the responsibilities of individual legislators.

A code of ethics ought not simply to be a set of assertions. Instead, it should clearly express the philosophical, political, and ethical principles on which it rests.

The issue of enforcement is no less important. Legislators and the general public must believe that violations of a code, at least those "disciplinary" and black letter aspects of it, will be promptly, fairly, and effectively enforced. That may not always be easy to accomplish, in great part because of the requirements of due process or because of jurisdictional complications with certain kinds of violations. Nonetheless, the public is far more likely to be tolerant of those complications (and not dismiss them as mere evasions) if there are mechanisms to see that all charges are speedily investigated, that serious charges are pursued with diligence, and that an efficient and expeditious procedure exists for dealing with violations of the code.

IV. CHARACTER, MORAL JUDGMENT, AND ETHICAL LEADERSHIP

EDITOR'S INTRODUCTION

Character has emerged as a major campaign issue during the last decade. In 1980, evangelical Protestants led by The Reverend Jerry Falwell and his Moral Majority issued a call for a return to traditional values and mobilized to defeat candidates they deemed morally unfit for office. Although the character issue came to be couched in less sectarian terms as the '80s wore on, it has continued to figure prominently in the media and in many campaigns. Questions of personal morality came to the fore early in the 1988 presidential campaign. Gary Hart, then the Democratic frontrunner, dropped out of the race amid allegations of adultery, and Senator Joseph Biden's candidacy came to an end after he was charged with plagiarizing a campaign speech and cheating in law school. The Gary Hart scandal and the rash of preemptive confessions that ensued gave rise to concern that the character issue was diverting attention from matters more central to the task of choosing political leaders.

In the controversy surrounding the question of personal character, much criticism was aimed at the press, which was already under fire from certain quarters for failing to pursue with sufficient vigor wrongdoings in the Reagan administration. In "When the Government Tells Lies," published in the *Columbia Journalism Review,* Anthony Marro discusses official deception and the media's role in monitoring the honesty of government officials. In the following article, *Policy Review* asked eight scholars, public officials, and religious leaders to comment on the political relevance of public figures' private lives. The third article, by Suzanne Garment for *Public Opinion,* examines how scandals affect the attitudes and behavior of Washington officials. In the fourth piece, "Individual Character and Political Ethics," Nicholas Xenos, who teaches political theory at the University of Massachusetts at Amherst, argues that questions of character and moral behavior are largely immaterial in an age when public officials routinely refuse to take responsibility for their actions. He maintains that only responsible oppositional voices, functioning outside bureaucratic government, can practice genuinely ethical politics in the future.

The last two articles, both by United States congressmen, appeared in *Ethics: Easier Said Than Done*. Senator Ted Stevens from Alaska states in "We Need More Leadership in Ethics" that federal office holders in both the executive branch and the legislature must be leaders in raising and maintaining ethical standards, as he asserts that ethics laws cannot create ethical behavior without strong moral leadership in government. In "The Need for People of Virtue," Lee H. Hamilton, Representative from Indiana, urges high standards of moral conduct for those seeking and holding public office to restore the confidence of an American public that has come to view politics and government as "dirty" jobs in which scandals and corruption are to be expected. He stresses the need to make politics and government service honorable professions that attract people worthy of public trust.

WHEN THE GOVERNMENT TELLS LIES[1]

November 25, 1957—Dwight Eisenhower, sixty-seven years old and recently recovered from both a heart attack and abdominal surgery, is in his office. He tries to pick up a document, and can't. He tries to read it, and fails. The words, he later says, "seemed literally to run off the top of the page." He tries to get up, and nearly falls down. He tries to tell his secretary what is wrong, but she can't make any sense of what he is saying. His physician realizes almost immediately that Eisenhower has suffered some sort of a stroke.

The president has developed "a chill," the press office tells reporters. It is not until twenty-four hours later that the nation is told that its president is seriously ill.

[1]Reprint of an article by Anthony Marro, managing editor of *Newsday*. *Columbia Journalism Review*. April/March 1985, pp. 29–41. Reprinted by permission.

December 7, 1971—Henry Kissinger is briefing the press on the government's position on the India-Pakistan war. "First of all, let's get a number of things straight," he begins. "There have been some comments that the administration is anti-Indian. This is totally inaccurate." A briefing paper has been handed out at the start of the session. The first sentence reads: "The policy of this administration towards South Asia must be understood. It is neither anti-Indian nor pro-Pakistan."

A month later, Jack Anderson publishes the transcript of a meeting attended by Kissinger on December 3, just four days before the briefing for the press. "I am getting hell every half-hour from the president that we are not being tough enough on India . . . ," Kissinger is quoted as saying. "He wants to tilt in favor of Pakistan."

April 22, 1980—Jody Powell, President Carter's chief spokesman, is talking with Jack Nelson, Washington bureau chief for the *Los Angeles Times*. No military operation is being planned to rescue the hostages in Iran, Powell tells him. A blockade might be feasible, somewhere down the road, but a rescue mission just wouldn't make any sense.

The newspapers with Nelson's story, which says that the Carter White House considers a rescue operation impractical, are still scattered around in living rooms all over Los Angeles when the members of Delta Team board airplanes for the raid on Teheran.

October 24, 1983—Larry Speakes, the White House spokesman, is asked by reporters whether U.S. troops have landed on Grenada. He checks with a member of President Reagan's national security staff, and relays the response. "Preposterous," he says, and goes on to deny that any invasion is planned.

The landing takes place the next day.

For starters, Stephen Hess probably is right. The Brookings Institution scholar, who has studied both Washington reporters and government press operations, says that most government spokespersons don't like to lie. For one thing, telling the truth is official U.S. government policy. For another, they prefer telling the truth. To lie, he says, is to "fail to play fair with reporters and the public, to diminish their self-esteem, and to complicate their work."

But complications and crises are of the essence of government, and trying to put the best face on a sensitive situation also is part of the job. Political posturing, face-saving, honest error, bad judgment, and legitimate national security concerns also play a role, and so, to different degrees in different administrations, do arrogance, deceit, disregard for the public, high-handedness, and attempts to cover up stupidity and criminal conduct. The result is that reporters have come to accept some level of deception as part of the routine, and to expect, as Hess delicately phrases it, "less than full candor" on the part of their government.

In fact, Washington reporters over the years have had to deal with a steady barrage of deceptions, half-truths, and outright lies—deceptions about national security operations that were so sensitive that they probably wouldn't have published the information even if they had been able to obtain it, and deceits so petty that they wondered why anyone would bother to lie in the first place.

There was the time in 1960 when Lincoln White tried to explain away the crash of the U-2 airplane in the Soviet Union. It had been on a weather mission and had just strayed off course, the State Department's chief spokesman said. "Now, our assumption is that the [pilot] blacked out. There was absolutely no—N-O, no—deliberate attempt to violate Soviet air space. There never has been." Within days it became clear that the pilot, Francis Gary Powers, was alive, that the Soviets had him, and that he was talking. The principal attachment to the airplane was not a thermometer but a camera, and its mission was not weather reconnaissance but spying.

There was the time in 1966 that Lyndon Johnson claimed that one of his great-great-grandfathers had died at the Alamo (not true), and the time in 1971 that the White House claimed that Tricia Nixon's wedding cake had been based on an old family recipe (it apparently had been created by a White House chef).

There was the time in 1975 when FBI Director Clarence Kelley said that while there had been some warrantless break-ins by FBI agents in the past, they had been confined by and large to foreign espionage and counterintelligence matters, and had been ended by J. Edgar Hoover in 1966. In truth, there had been thousands, all of them illegal, most of them against American citizens, many of them against people never charged with any crime, and some as recently as 1972. Kelley's aides were left to explain that the head of the nation's most sophisticated police agency had been misinformed.

There was the time in 1954 when Henry Cabot Lodge, ambassador to the UN, described fighting in Guatemala as "a revolt of Guatemalans against Guatemalans," despite the fact the uprising was being orchestrated, in large part, by Frank Wisner, the deputy director for plans for the CIA. There was the time in 1981 when the Reagan administration released a white paper on Central America that attributed authorship of key documents to several guerrilla leaders who clearly had not written them. There was the time, during the Bay of Pigs invasion, when the government lied in saying that the bombings were being conducted by defectors from Castro's own air force, and then, when reporters discovered the lie, groused because the reporters did not create lies of their own to help protect the government's lie.

There was the time in a televised debate last October when President Reagan insisted that more people were receiving food stamps than ever before (actually the number had dropped by about 400,000 since he had become president), and when Walter Mondale claimed that Reagan had sought to "terminate" a housing program for the elderly (in fact, the Reagan administration had made major cuts in the program, but hadn't tried to abolish it).

There was the time that John Mitchell, the former attorney general, was indicted for lying about Watergate, the time that Richard Helms, the former head of the CIA, was indicted for lying about Chile, and the time that Rita Lavelle, a former official with the Environmental Protection Agency, was indicted for lying about the EPA's handling of toxic waste.

There was the time that Ron Nessen, President Ford's press secretary, began a response to a question by saying "To tell you the truth . . . " only to be overwhelmed by sarcastic applause.

The Manifold Forms of Deception

I.F. Stone has said that "Every government is run by liars, and nothing they say should be believed."

James Deakin, who covered the White House for many years for the *St. Louis Post-Dispatch*, pretty much agreed with Stone, but worded it differently. "Every government is run by people who seek to wield and retain power," he wrote in *Straight Stuff*, his brilliantly witty book on Washington journalism. "To do this, they must convince the public of certain things: That their policies are correct. That their facts and explanations should be accepted. That they are in control of events and situations. That sounds nicer [than Stone]. And it comes out at the same place."

To achieve these things, it's necessary not only for governments to deceive, but also to hype, slant, tilt, and gloss over, trying at the same time to present a situation in its most favorable light, while hiding, or hedging on, or deflecting reporters away from any information that might conflict with its version. Indeed, Stephen Hess has written, "It is hard to find a discussion of modern government's relations with the press that does not include the words 'manage,' 'manipulate,' and 'control.'"

It probably is a fool's errand to try to measure degrees of deception from one administration to the next, or to try to show whether Democrats are more or less deceptive than Republicans. Clearly, much misinformation was produced by the Reagan administration during its first four years, on such matters as the invasion of Grenada, revolution in Central America, its concern for the handicapped, and its commitment to civil rights. But there is no way of assessing how it compares with, or whether it's even in the same league with, the massive amounts of misinformation put out by the Johnson administration during the Vietnam War, for example, or by the Nixon administration during the Watergate years.

For one thing, it often takes years for deceptions to surface. It took congressional hearings, criminal prosecutions, and serious reporting by people like Nicholas Horrock and John Crewdson, both then working for *The New York Times*, to expose the degree to which the FBI had been staging illegal break-ins against American citizens. And even in 1985, fifteen years after the fact, we were still learning in the libel trial of General Westmoreland against CBS about the degree to which key officials in the Johnson administration knew that, despite their public statements to the contrary, there wasn't any light at the end of the tunnel.

For another thing, there is the question of degree, and the issue of whether, and at what point, numerous small deceptions begin to equal major ones.

There was a time, early in the Reagan administration, when the president's aides argued that it didn't matter whether some of his stories were literally true—his numerous misstatements of fact, his confusion about detail, and his repeated anecdotes about supposed welfare cheats that no one was ever able to confirm, for example—because they contained a larger truth.

"We've been dealing with four years of an administration that freely states—and stated early—that literal truth was not a concern," says Bill Kovach, the Washington news editor of *The New York Times*. "This is the first time I've heard that literal truth is not important to the presidency."

There also is the matter of attitude. "This administration is much more arrogant with the press," says one career government official who has served through several administrations. "The attitude is, 'Screw you, we don't need you. The Reagan administration is going to be successful despite the editorials in *The Washington Post* and *The New York Times*, and the cartoons in the *Los Angeles Times*.'"

And Morton Halperin, the director of the left-leaning Center for National Security Studies, says that many key officials in the Reagan administration have a philosophy of government that doesn't include public discussion and debate. "These guys came here straight out of nineteen forty-six," he says. "They came out of World War Two, when the government lied all the time, and it was all right to lie. The whole Normandy invasion, and the covert operations that surrounded it, are an important part of that mind-set. . . . They still think fundamentally that foreign policy should be left to the executive branch and that people shouldn't even try to find out what they're up to."

Deceptions by government officials take many forms, and it's not always easy to show what they amount to. They can include simple face-saving, such as Geraldine Ferraro claiming she felt "vindicated" by a House report critical of her failure to disclose her husband's financial interests, and routine political posturing, such as the White House announcing full support for people like Anne Burford and James Watt, when both had clearly become major liabilities and were on their way out of the government. And there is the endless, predictable attempt by administrations to portray themselves in the best light, as Reagan did in a speech to the National Council of Negro Women in July 1983. "We have authorized for filing three school desegregation cases, more than were authorized by the previous administration during its first thirty months in office," he said.

At first blush, this looks like a simple statement of fact. But when James Nathan Miller took a look at the numbers, he concluded in an article in *The Atlantic* on Reagan's civil rights record that "This seemingly straightforward twenty-four-word sentence contains three carefully crafted semantic deceptions."

To begin with, Reagan's administration hadn't actually filed more cases than Carter's. His Justice Department had filed only one, while Carter's had filed two. Secondly, while Reagan seemed to be saying that he had filed more cases, he hadn't really said that. What he had said was that his administration had *authorized* that the suits be filed. And thirdly, while he implied that he was talking about his record and Carter's on the same terms, in truth he was using an apples and oranges comparison of legal suits his people had authorized (but not yet acted on), with suits that Carter actually had taken to court.

The fact that it took Miller about twelve hours' worth of digging just to deal with that one sentence gives some notion of the problem at hand.

The Reagan Twist—and John Mitchell's Maxim

The problem, in the view of many, is very real, not necessarily because face-saving and political posturing are outrageous in themselves, but because a pattern of routine and systematic deception has very real costs, both in terms of loss of confidence by people in their government, and in terms of citizens not learning until it is too late just what it is that their government is up to. And while it is not clear that the Reagan administration is any more duplicitous than others, it unquestionably has gone well beyond other recent administrations in its attempts to bottle up information, to prevent public access to government officials and records, to threaten and intimidate the bureaucracy in order to dry up sources of information, and to prevent the press and the public from learning how their government is functioning.

This goes well beyond just shielding the president from questions (Reagan has had fewer official news conferences than any president in modern times), and doing silly things like revving up the helicopters while he's getting ready to leave for Camp David, so that reporters won't be able to make themselves heard over the din. The administration's proposals for limiting the Freedom of Information Act, censoring the public statements of government officials even after they leave office, and using polygraphs to search out people who talk to the press all have the effect of restricting access to information, and of making it harder for reporters to report on the way Reagan is running the government.

Jack Landau, who heads the Reporters Committee for Freedom of the Press, goes so far as to say that such actions by the Reagan administration constitute the greatest restrictions on public access to government information since World War II. There is no question but that the Reagan administration is seeking restrictions and kinds of censorship in peacetime that Eisenhower, Kennedy, Johnson, and even Richard Nixon didn't ask for in times of war.

There is a temptation to shrug that politicians have always lied and that the Republic nonetheless has survived. But David Wise, in *The Politics of Lying*, argues that to dwell on historical examples of lying is to miss the point entirely, because it was only in the 1960s that government deception came to be *perceived* by large numbers of citizens. Many actually were shocked to learn at the time of the U-2 incident that their government would tell such a lie. And once large numbers of people come to distrust their government, he says, a new political environment is created in which the president can no longer assume that most people believe what he says.

According to Wise, a former bureau chief for the *New York Herald Tribune*, this is a dangerous situation in a society in which the government is supposed to operate with the consent of the governed. Indeed, writing in 1972, he termed the erosion of confidence between people and government—an erosion that was documented by University of Michigan studies—"perhaps the single most significant political development in America in the past decade."

Wise laid much of the blame for this erosion on official deception, and he in turn laid the blame for much of the deception on the growth of the nation's intelligence-gathering agencies since World War II. Once the government began running covert operations it had to have cover stories to hide them, and that required government-sanctioned lies. The chief criterion thus was not truth, but just the opposite—developing lies that would be plausible enough to be accepted as truth. "Thus the standard is not truth," Wise wrote, "but fashioning lies that will be believed."

Sissela Bok, in *Lying: Moral Choice in Public and Private Life*, argues that it is dangerous to let public officials get away with even minor lies, or lies that they feel are for the public good. "Some come to believe that any lie can be told so long as they can convince themselves that people will be better off in the long run," she writes. "From there, it is a short step to the conclusion that, even if people will not be better off from a particular lie, they will benefit by all maneuvers to keep the right people in office. Once public servants lose their bearings in this way, all the shabby deceits of Watergate—the fake telegrams, the erased tapes, the elaborate cover-ups, the bribing of witnesses to make them lie, the televised pleas for trust—become possible."

And Jody Powell, President Carter's press secretary and a man who admits to at least one lie that he still believes was in the national interest, argues that while there are long-range problems for a democracy if people don't trust their government, there can be more immediate consequences, too. "An administration that has a reputation for being not credible, for evoking 'national security' to cover political embarrassments and things that don't involve any real national security matters at all, that sort of administration is going to have a harder time protecting national security secrets when there's a need," he said in a recent interview. In short, if reporters come to distrust an administration's officials, they won't believe them even when the matter is serious and the officials are telling the truth.

All three—a former journalist, an academic, and a former press secretary—would argue that it is important that the press not shrug off lies as just part of the routine, but must, instead, set out aggressively to expose them, and to hold officials accountable for them. The reason is not just to expose deceptions for the sake of exposure (although Bok, more than the others, would argue that this is an important goal in itself), but to make it possible for people to know how their government is working.

To this end, the best piece of advice for reporters was offered by John Mitchell, the former attorney general and no particular friend of the press. His words: "Watch what we do instead of what we say." In truth, he wasn't talking to reporters at the time (he was talking with a group of people concerned about the direction of civil rights law enforcement under Nixon), and he never did much to help reporters learn what his department was doing. But sorting out the difference between what a person, or a government, is saying and doing is at the heart of reporting, and central to the role of the press in a democracy. Among other things, this means getting access to information about the process, about alternatives that were debated and discarded, about how a decision came to be made, and about all the predicted results of the decision, not just those that the government sees fit to release.

This also means being able to report on the decision-making process while it is still under way, and while it is possible to show what the alternatives are. On this point, Deakin says, the press is very much like Lyndon Johnson, who when he was Senate majority leader used to complain to the White House that Congress wanted to be "in on the takeoffs as well as the crash landings."

Letting the public in on the takeoffs means telling it what an administration really is up to—whether it really has a commitment to enforcement of civil rights laws, whether it really is providing a "safety net" for the helpless, and how far it really is prepared to go in trying to prop up allies in Central America, for example—and what the likely consequence of its actions will be. And the single biggest complaint of many reporters now working in Washington is not just that the government has deceived them in major ways, but that it has taken unprecedented moves to try to prevent them from getting behind the deceptions.

Does Government Have a 'Right to Lie'?

It is not known who first argued that the government has a right to lie to its citizens, but the person who touched off the greatest furor by saying it was Arthur Sylvester, a Defense Department spokesman during the Kennedy administration. On December 6, 1962, during a dinner meeting of the New York chapter of Sigma Delta Chi, Sylvester was asked by Jack Fox of UPI what he thought about half-truths and deceptions by government spokesmen.

This was in the aftermath of the Cuban missile crisis of October 1962, and many reporters were still fuming about some of the misinformation that had been released during the crisis. For one thing, Kennedy had cut short a political trip to Chicago, and had rushed back to Washington to deal with the evidence that the Soviets had placed offensive missiles in Cuba. Instead of telling the nation that a major confrontation with the Soviets was brewing, however, Kennedy's aides explained the sudden return to the capital by saying that the president had come down with a cold.

Later in that same week, with tensions rising and questions flying thick and fast, Sylvester had authorized a press release from the Pentagon that read: "A Pentagon spokesman denied tonight that any alert has been ordered or that any emergency military measures have been set in motion against Communist-ruled Cuba. Further, the spokesman said, the Pentagon has no information indicating the presence of offensive weapons in Cuba."

The first sentence may have been technically correct. The second was false, a government-planted lie at a time when Kennedy had made the decision to confront Khrushchev, but before all the strategy for the confrontation had been worked out.

In authorizing the release, Sylvester later said, he had come down on the side of the "Lying Baptists" and against the "Truthful Baptists." His reference was to a dispute between two groups of Baptists that had erupted at Long Run, Kentucky, back in 1804. The issue was whether a man with three children who had been captured by marauding Indians was justified in lying to the Indians in order to conceal the fact that a fourth child was hiding nearby. The "Lying Baptists" argued that the father had the right to lie, and thus save the child. The "Truthful Baptists" disagreed, saying that, no matter what the consequences, the truth should be told.

This is a philosophical and ethical debate that far predates Arthur Sylvester, the Cuban missile crisis, or even the 1804 dispute among the Baptists of Long Run, Kentucky. Discussing a similar hypothetical situation, albeit one without Indians or the possibility of nuclear holocaust, Immanuel Kant argued that truthfulness cannot be avoided by any person, no matter how serious "may be the disadvantage accruing to himself or another." Samuel Johnson's view was more in line with that of the "Lying Baptists" and Sylvester. "The general rule is, that truth should never be violated; there must, however, be some exception," he said. "If, for instance, a murderer should ask you which way a man has gone."

Others have argued that the key question is whether the person seeking the information—a murderer in Sam Johnson's London or a Miami resident who suddenly has Soviet missiles aimed at him, for example—has any right to it. At what point did the American people have a right to know that their president was wrestling with a major crisis, not just a cold, and that Soviet missiles had been placed in Cuba?

Sylvester's argument was that the stakes were so high that deception, both of the Soviets and of the American people, was necessary, at least until the president had decided on his next move.

Jack Fox, in his story for UPI, gave what Sylvester later said was a fair summary of his statement at the Sigma Delta Chi dinner. "He [Sylvester] said that the government must not put out false information, but later added, 'I think the inherent right of the government to lie to save itself when faced with nuclear disaster is basic,'" Fox wrote.

Others made more of the "right to lie" part of the statement and less of the caveats, to the point where Sylvester, in an article written for *The Washington Star* in 1967, complained that they had "distorted my remarks beyond recognition, howling that they were proof that the government was not to be believed, under any circumstances."

"He got a raw deal on that," Hess said recently. "It's always been taken out of context, as though he said the government has a right to lie, period. He said a lot more than that."

In his article in the *Star*, Sylvester said that as assistant secretary of defense for public affairs he had always taken the position that the prime requisite for a government information program was that it be truthful. And he went on to argue that it was totally wrong for any press aide to lie for personal or political reasons.

Many press secretaries would agree. There is considerable evidence to back up Hess's contention that most of them don't like to lie, not just because it makes them feel bad—Lincoln White, who lied about the U-2 flight in 1960, later told Patrick Sloyan, then working for UPI, that it was "my darkest moment"—but because credibility is important to their job. To be effective, a press aide not only has to be able to generate favorable stories, but has to be able to stop bad ones. And a press aide who isn't trusted will have a whole lot more trouble trying to head off a bad story than one who is trusted. "All you need is one lie, and five years of credibility goes right down the drain," says Homer Boynton, who acted as chief spokesman for the FBI from 1973 until 1980. "So when you're giving it out, you goddamn better be right."

Sylvester's statement touched off an angry debate at the time. But the fact is that many reporters and editors agree with it, at least in principle. Philip Geyelin, for example, complained in a recent article in *The Washington Post* that the Reagan administration seemed to be squandering its credibility with a pattern of deception in its statements about Central America. But he began the piece by saying, "We will get nowhere without first stipulating that, while circumstances alter almost any case you can think of, the president has an inherent right—perhaps even an obligation in particular situations—to deceive." And he went on to argue that, when it comes to troop movements and placement of weapons, a certain ambiguity of purpose is, as John Foster Dulles used to say, "a necessary art."

Bill Kovach, who runs *The New York Times*'s Washington bureau, says that, "as a rational human being, I'd have to say yes, if lives really are at stake. But [the occasions] should be so few and far between that we talk about them for years. And it's better for [press aides] to try to avoid answering the question than to give out real misinformation, because the next time they won't be believed."

Even Jack Landau, the head of the Reporters Committee for Freedom of the Press and one of the most vocal advocates of the public's right to know, says that in some legitimate national security cases "I would guess . . . [lying] would be all right." And Jack Nelson, who was lied to by Jody Powell during the Iran hostage crisis, also thinks there are times when a government can justify some forms of deception. "I didn't like being lied to. I didn't like being used. But I didn't have a great deal of problem with [Powell's] doing it," he says. "If it was a real matter of life and death, and he thought it was, I can't argue with what he did."

What Powell did was to tell Nelson flat-out that there was no chance that a rescue mission would be launched in the near future—a lie that Powell still argues was proper, given the circumstances. At the time he told the lie the preparations for the raid were well under way, and in less than forty-eight hours the U.S. planes would be entering Iranian air space. Not only was he fearful that a story suggesting a raid was possible would alert the Iranians, but he felt that a flat statement to the contrary would "reinforce the web of deception" that had been constructed to protect the mission.

In *The Other Side of the Story*, his book on his years as President Carter's press secretary, Powell argues that there are two reasons why the government can, and sometimes should, lie. The first is that the "government has a legitimate right to secrecy in certain matters because the welfare of the nation requires it." The sec-

ond is that the press, for the most part, has a right to print what
it knows. Freedom of the press is so important to democracy, he
says, that when there is a conflict with legitimate national security
needs, it is probably better for the government to simply lie to the
press than to try to limit it, censor it, or restrict it through prior
restraint.

But Powell admits to at least one other lie that had nothing
to do with national security or life-and-death matters. It was a
question that, as Powell put it, "involved the personal life of a colleague and that of his family." Powell says he decided to lie because to respond with the truth would have resulted in "great
pain and embarrassment for a number of perfectly innocent
people." And, besides, he didn't think that the matter was of any
legitimate public interest to begin with. Powell thus goes a step
beyond Sylvester, and argues that it is sometimes permissible for
a government to lie to protect the privacy of public figures, as
well as to protect the security of the nation.

Powell, now a Washington columnist, says he has come to understand more clearly than he used to why it is that "journalists
get so damn skeptical about what people [in government] tell
them." He says he has no doubts at all that he acted properly in
the Iran situation, but has mixed feelings about the second lie.
"That's harder to defend without getting into the details, which
I won't do," he says, adding that he would probably lie again in
that situation, too.

"The minimal line you can draw there is that you can absolutely say that lying to cover up your own embarrassments is not
permissible," says Powell. "Once you get past that, you get into
areas where, unfortunately, things tend to be mixed. Then you
have to weigh in the sort of long-term impact, not just in terms
of the credibility of a particular administration, but the credibility of the government over the long haul. If you contribute to the
idea that people can't believe anything their government tells
them, that's awful. It's also dangerous."

In his book, Powell cites other cases in which he thinks a government sometimes might have a right to lie, including protection of intelligence sources and methods, protection of an
innocent person whose name had cropped up during a Justice Department investigation, and a pending decision by the Treasury
Department that could have major financial consequences to individuals and to the nation.

And it is here that he runs into conflict with many others, including Hess, who argue that there is a big difference between lying to protect legitimate national security matters and lying to protect anything less. "It's very easy to slop over into other areas . . . and I'm less sympathetic when it does," says Hess. "Just because something might concern the 'public good,' that isn't enough" to justify government lying. "It has to be to save lives, as in the Iranian hostage thing, or similar wartime activities."

But while many people in government and in the media agree that, in some circumstances, the government has a right to lie, they also agree that the people have a right to know what their government is really up to. And they argue that a chief reason that the government gets away with as much deception as it does is that the press, for all of its bluster and all its professed skepticism, is far too willing to take the government at its word.

Sylvester, for example, placed much of the blame for misinformation about government activities on the laziness and ineptitude of reporters, saying that they relied too much on handouts and failed to ask the right questions. "Every sophisticated [reporter] knows the federal government puts its best, not its worst, foot forward . . . ," he said. "That being so, it is [the reporter's] function to penetrate this protective coloration behind which all men attempt to mask their errors. If there is a credibility gap, it measures the failure of newsmen to do their job."

This is a charge that not only was valid when it was made, and remains so today, but also had been a particular matter of controversy just a decade before, when Joe McCarthy was at the height of his influence and there was much debate within the media over the lengths to which reporters should go to try to unmask deception and lies.

Joe McCarthy: Testing the Limits of 'Objective Reporting'

To understand the controversy that surrounded McCarthy and the press, it is necessary to understand not just that many of the charges by the Wisconsin senator were considered by many reporters to be reckless, but also that the press in the early 1950s was very different from what it is today. There was much less analysis and interpretative reporting in news sections (analysis and most forms of comment being reserved for the editorial pages), and almost none was provided by the wire services. The "objective reporting" standards of the day held that if a U.S. senator was going to make charges of treason, espionage, and communists in high places, that in itself was news, and it wasn't necessarily the job of a reporter to determine the validity of the charges, or to hold the senator accountable for them.

"We let Joe get away with murder, reporting it as he said it, not doing the kind of critical analysis we'd do today," William Theis, a former reporter for International News Service, told Edwin Bayley, whose book *Joe McCarthy and the Press* analyzes the coverage and finds much of it lacking. George Reedy, who covered McCarthy for United Press and later became a press secretary to Lyndon Johnson, told Bayley that his frustration at trying to cope with McCarthy's charges was a major consideration in his decision to quit newspaper work. "We had to take what McCarthy said at face value," he told Bayley. "Joe couldn't find a communist in Red Square—he didn't know Karl Marx from Groucho—but he was a United States Senator. . . . It was a shattering experience, and I couldn't stand it."

As McCarthy's influence grew, the debate over how to cover him and his charges grew also. Much of the debate was over the nature of "objective" reporting, but the debate itself tended to be partisan in the extreme. Editors and publishers who approved of McCarthy tended to argue that they wanted his statements reported as they were made, without heavy doses of analysis or perspective. And they, in turn, put pressure on the wire services, which provided the bulk of the daily coverage, to report the charges in a straightforward way.

Others, including many who disapproved of McCarthy's politics as well as his tactics, argued that reporters who simply wrote down what he said, along with the subsequent rebuttals and denials, were playing into his hands, because they were not addressing the large number of inconsistencies and proven inaccuracies that marked his attacks on supposed communists.

Some papers developed strategies specifically for McCarthy. *The Milwaukee Journal*, for example, began adding bracketed inserts to stories about McCarthy's charges, using the brackets to add explanatory information. Here is an excerpt from a May 8, 1950, article about McCarthy and Owen Lattimore, whom the senator had accused of helping to shape foreign policy to the benefit of communist governments:

McCarthy said that Lattimore has "long been referred to as the architect of the State Department's Asiatic policy."
[State Department officials and three former secretaries of state have denied that Lattimore played any part in forming policy.]
The Young Republicans guffawed as McCarthy joked about "individuals with peculiar mental aberrations as far as sex is concerned."
[The individual referred to by Mr. McCarthy here is no longer in government service.]

According to Bayley, this got to the point where, in September 1952, the *Journal* had bracketed thirteen inches' worth of such inserts into a fifty-two-inch story. "McCarthy's tactics produced lasting changes in the media," Bayley observes in his book. "Newspaper people realized that it was not enough simply to tell what had happened and what was said, but that they had to tell what it meant and whether or not it was true. By 1954, interpretative reporting and news analysis had become standard practice; these functions were no longer left to the editorial writers."

And these devices were to become more important in the following decades, not just because of the massive amounts of misinformation released by the government during Vietnam and Watergate, but because, as Wise argues effectively in *The Politics of Lying*, cover stories and deception became a significant part of government operations.

Four Kinds of Lies— and the Problems They Pose for the Press

Not all deceptions are equal, of course. There is a big difference between a Joe McCarthy making harsh, and often groundless, charges of treason, and the sort of political posturing that causes a president to defend an aide who has done something dumb. After several years of studying the press-government relationship from both sides, Hess has concluded that some reporters tolerate, even welcome, minor deceptions, because exposing deceptions helps them to display their skills. While studying the State Department press operations during Reagan's first term, he says, he found many examples of deception, most of them minor, and didn't detect much outrage on the part of the reporters there. "It is only the Big Lie, the deliberate and consistent pattern of misstatement on a matter of importance, that turns Washington reporters into inflamed civil libertarians," Hess writes in *The Government/Press Connection*.

Hess cites four broad categories of government deceptions. On a scale of decreasing acceptability to the press, he says, are so-called "honest lies," inadvertent lies, half-truths (which include many forms of political posturing and selective release of data), and flat-out lies. An "honest lie," for Hess, is a legitimate national security matter, such as Powell lying about the raid on Teheran. Even if they don't approve of such a lie, most reporters can understand the need for it, he says.

Reporters also tend to forgive inadvertent lies, because they know from their own work that mistakes happen when things are done in a hurry. Bill Beecher, a former Defense Department information officer and now a reporter for *The Boston Globe*, has said that "half the initial internal reporting within government in a crisis is wrong."

It is with half-truths, a specialty at the State Department, that some reporters begin to get resentful. The chief technique here is for a press officer to define the question as narrowly as possible and then answer it that way. Here are two examples Hess cites in *The Government/Press Connection.* Both, he said in an interview, are real examples, with the facts altered just slightly "to protect the guilty."

Q—Has the assistant secretary of state been invited to China?
A—No. (Meaning: He will go to China as an adviser to the vice president. It is the vice president who has been invited. Therefore, I am not lying. Rationale: I have to say this because protocol requires that the Chinese must first publicly extend the invitation.)

Q—Will the ambassador-at-large go to Egypt?
A—No decision has been made. (Meaning: A "decision" is made when the Secretary of State signs the cable. The cable will be signed tomorrow. Therefore, I am not lying. Rationale: I do not have the authority to give a premature confirmation.)

In the Reagan administration, examples of all four types of deception can be found in the invasion of Grenada. Larry Speakes himself may not have known that he was telling a lie when he said that it was "preposterous" to think U.S. forces had invaded, and that no invasion would take place. But Rear Admiral John Poindexter, who told Speakes it was preposterous, knew that the landing would take place the next day, and kept Speakes and other press aides in the dark about it. Speakes did not respond to a request for an interview, but Hess and Powell and a number of the journalists interviewed for this article argued that, even if he had known and then told the lie, it might have been justifiable.

The initial claim by the government that there were no civilian casualties appears to have been inadvertent. The Pentagon says that it didn't know about the bombing of a mental hospital by a Navy plane (at least seventeen persons were killed) until several days after it occurred, and no one has yet proven otherwise.

The claim by the administration that leaders of other Caribbean countries urged it to take action appears to be in the nature of a half-truth. The administration said that the urging from other leaders came after the assassination of Maurice Bishop, the Marxist prime minister of Grenada, on October 19. But Stuart Taylor, Jr., in a lengthy piece in *The New York Times* on some of the misinformation put out by the U.S. government during and immediately after the invasion, quotes the prime minister of Barbados as saying that U.S. officials had been talking about possible action at least as early as October 15, four days before the killing.

And while it's hard to determine whether the government was telling an outright lie when it said it had prevented reporters from accompanying the troops because of concern for the safety of the journalists, subsequent comments by Secretary of State George Shultz seem to give some sense of the real reason for the ban. "These days, in the advocacy journalism that's been adopted, it seems as though the reporters are always against us and so they're always trying to screw things up," he said. "And when you're trying to conduct a military operation, you don't need that."

It is difficult to know whether some of the most important misinformation was deliberate or inadvertent because the degree of the deception depends on whether there was any intent to deceive. Reagan, in a television speech to the nation, said there were an estimated 400 to 600 Cubans on the island, and that they were "a military force," rather than construction workers. The next day, Admiral Wesley L. McDonald said that captured documents showed that there were at least 1,100 Cubans on Grenada, and that they were all "well-trained professional soldiers."

Eventually, the State Department said that the Cuban government's own figure probably was right—that there had been 784 Cubans on the island. Still later, U.S. military authorities on Grenada said that, after interrogating them, they had concluded that most of the Cubans really had been construction workers, and that only about 100 had been combatants. "Thus, over three days the Pentagon estimate of the number of Cuban fighters who had met the invading force seems to have plunged from more than 1,000 to fewer than 200, including the estimated 30 to 70 Cubans who were killed," Taylor wrote.

What difference does it make whether there were 784 Cubans on Grenada or 1,100, and whether they were "well-trained professional soldiers," as Admiral McDonald insisted, or construction workers, as the Cuban government claimed? One answer, of course, is that one version suggests an attempt to take over a country and perhaps export revolution (which the Reagan administration said was the case), while the other version suggests that Cuba might only have been providing economic aid to a government that it considered an ally.

The inflation of the number of Cubans, and the initial characterization of them as a military force, was a part of the data that were used by the Reagan administration to argue that a Cuban takeover was at hand, that American students were in danger, and that, as many newspapers repeated in their headlines, "We got there just in time."

Grenada also highlighted a major problem in trying to counter deception and misinformation. The president was able to give his version on national television, to a huge audience, and was backed up by carefully selected and edited television film clips. The challenges to the official version came over a period of days and weeks, and they were fragmented and uncoordinated. One paper would challenge one statement, a second paper would challenge a second one, and a television report would challenge a third. A large number of Americans heard the president say, "We got there just in time." But it was only in a disjointed and scatter-shot way, over a period of weeks following the invasion, that the press raised the two immediate and obvious questions, neither of them yet fully answered.

Did we?

In time for what?

This issue arose again during the presidential campaign, when George Bush claimed in his television debate with Geraldine Ferraro thet Mondale had said that the American Marines who had died in the bombing of the embassy in Beirut had died in "shame." Mondale denied this, and pressed Bush for a retraction. And in the process Peter Teeley, Bush's press secretary, brought the whole problem into focus.

"You can say anything you want in a debate, and eighty million people hear it," he told reporters. "If reporters then document that a candidate spoke untruthfully, so what? Maybe two hundred people read it, or two thousand or twenty thousand."

Which makes the point that, particularly in the television age, reporters need to be aggressive in documenting and pointing out deceptions, half-truths, and outright lies, unless governments and officials are going to be allowed to lie with impunity.

How Some Journalists Cope with
Official Misinformation

There are some kinds of misinformation that quickly become apparent on their own. For example, there was Tricia Nixon's wedding cake. According to the White House, it had been based on a recipe for old-fashioned pound cake, a favorite of Tricia's, that had been in Mrs. Nixon's recipe box for years. But when the White House released a recipe for the wedding cake, scaled back down to family size, there was a problem. Housewives and amateur cooks all over the country, including food writers for several newspapers and magazines, rushed to test it. The result in many cases was a porridge-like glob that overflowed the baking pans and messed up the ovens.

When asked for an explanation, the White House first said there must have been a miscalculation in the attempt to scale down the recipe. There was hemming and hawing when it was suggested that the White House should simply produce the original recipe, from Mrs. Nixon's recipe box. There was bobbing and weaving when it was noted that most recipes for pound cake call for whole eggs (this one called only for the whites), while the White House chef was quoted as saying that his pastry chef had gotten the recipe, "where I don't know." This in itself was of no great import, except that the whole episode suggested that a White House that would put out misinformation about the origins of a cake recipe probably couldn't be expected to tell the truth about the war in Cambodia. Which it didn't.

It's not possible to test all government statements as easily as a cake recipe, of course. Some deceptions are so major and so long-running and so tightly held that it takes the combination of

Congress, the courts, and the media, working over a period of years, to unravel them. But Patrick Sloyan, a Washington reporter for two decades and now *Newsday*'s London bureau chief, argues that basic reporting, common sense, and "simple math on a pocket calculator can often deflate the biggest government lies."

One of the easiest and most obvious ways to challenge official statements is simply to go to the opposition. When Reagan claimed that his administration had made "great progress" in its efforts to protect the environment, Francis X. Clines, of *The New York Times*, made clear that officials of some of the nation's leading environmental groups didn't know whether to laugh or cry at the statement. For specifics, he went to Representative James L. Florio of New Jersey, who noted that of 22,000 hazardous waste sites identified by the EPA, only six had been cleaned up by the Reagan administration in four years, and that even as the president was trumpeting his record on the environment, he was opposing proposals in Congress to combat acid rain.

Many such claims are more a matter of opinion than fact, of course, and going to the other side is a first lesson of journalism. But some of the most basic kinds of reporting can be used to provide a second, often different, view of events and issues. And in covering an administration that works as hard as Reagan's does to control and shape the information being released, basic reporting is particularly important.

Go to the scene: During the invasion of Grenada, Reagan and the Pentagon camera crews combined to show American television viewers warehouses on the island that seemingly were stacked to the rafters with automatic weapons. The president said there were enough of them to "supply thousands of terrorists." But when reporters themselves got to the sites they found some of the warehouses half-empty, some of them stacked with cases of sardines, and many of the weapons antiquated, possibly more suited for defense by an island militia than for the export of terrorism and revolution.

Go to the people affected: The Reagan administration insisted that its changes in the Social Security Disability law were intended only to get rid of people who had no right to the government aid in the first place. The people being removed, it said, were able-bodied people who had managed to slip through loopholes and get themselves into the program because of lax monitoring and ambiguous standards. But it turned out that a third of a million persons, including many with serious physical handicaps and mental disorders, had been cut off from the payments in a massive purge of the rolls, often on the basis of reviews of their health records by doctors who had never examined them in person.

Here is how Bob Wyrick and Patrick Owens of *Newsday* began a series that grew out of a months-long study of persons whose benefits had been taken away:

"Lyle Ely was blind in one eye and had tunnel vision in the other. He could not, as he complained in one of the many forms he filled out in the last years of his life, see well enough to read, drive a car, or watch television. His partial blindness, along with the convulsive seizures that also plagued him, was caused by a tumor that grew to the size of a large orange in the front part of his brain. But claims examiners and reviewing physicians who had never seen him found him well enough to work, cancelled his Social Security disability pension, and reaffirmed the cancellation when Ely applied for reconsideration."

Go to the documents: In February 1981, the State Department issued a white paper on El Salvador, which it said "presents definitive evidence of the clandestine military support given by the Soviet Union, Cuba, and their Communist allies to the Marxist-Leninist guerrillas now fighting to overthrow the established government of El Salvador." It said that the evidence was drawn from captured guerrilla documents and war material, and had been "corroborated by intelligence reports."

The white paper was accepted by much of the nation's press, was used by State Department officials to drum up support in Europe for Reagan's Central America policy, and was used on the Hill by White House lobbyists to persuade Congress that more funds were needed to help counter the outside aid being given to Salvadoran guerrillas. But when Jonathan Kwitny of *The Wall Street Journal* began a study of the documents a few months later, and went back to the people who had drafted the white paper, he found the evidence something less than it had been made out to be.

"Several of the most important documents, it's obvious, were attributed to guerrilla leaders who didn't write them. And it's unknown who did," he wrote in the *Journal*. "Statistics of armament shipments into El Salvador, supposedly drawn directly from the documents, were extrapolated . . . and in questionable ways, it seems. Much information in the white paper can't be found in the documents at all. This information now is attributed by the State Department to other, still-secret sources."

Kwitny's article did not totally discredit the conclusion of the white paper, which was that some weapons and supplies were being sent to the rebels by communist governments overseas. But it made clear that the evidence cited by the State Department, which had been accepted at face value by much of the press, wasn't as clear or as precise or as unambiguous as the government had claimed.

So, too, with Grenada. Admiral McDonald said on October 28 that captured documents showed that "341 more officers and 4,000 more reservists" had been scheduled to arrive from Cuba as part of a plan for "the Cubans to come in and take over the island. . . . " But Stuart Taylor of *The New York Times* reported that the captured documents, when finally released, showed an agreement by the Soviet Union and North Korea to provide Grenada with $37 million worth of equipment; the only reference to more Cuban soldiers was a promise by the Cubans to provide twenty-seven military advisers to train Grenadian troops.

A senior Pentagon official was quoted by Taylor as saying that McDonald had been mistaken about the 4,341 additional troops—they were to have been Grenadians, not Cubans. And he went on to report that "there is no evidence . . . that the Cubans had planned to take over Grenada either in the documents released Friday or in any other materials made public by the administration."

Check the numbers: When James Nathan Miller set out to examine Reagan's civil rights record, he went to the data that Reagan himself had used to illustrate what he termed "our unbending commitment" to civil rights. What Miller found were not outright lies—he did not once use the word "lie" in his *Atlantic* article—but a selective use of information that told only a part of the story. For example, Reagan had touted the fact that his Justice Department had reviewed 25,000 proposed changes in the Voting Rights Act, and had vetoed 165 of them because it felt they would be discriminatory. When Miller looked at the actual record, however, he found that the veto of 165 proposed changes was not an unusually strong enforcement of the law but a dramatic reduction in the rate of objections. From 1965 until Reagan took office, the department had vetoed 2.4 out of every 100 proposed changes it had examined. But the figures that Reagan cited amounted to a veto rate of .7 per 100—a decrease of 71 percent.

Again, in a speech to the American Bar Association, Reagan said that in his first thirty months in office the Justice Department had filed more than a hundred cases charging criminal violations of citizens' civil rights. This, he said, was not just a respectable number, but was "substantially more than any prior administration during a comparable period."

In terms of *criminal* cases, the Reagan administration actually was ahead of where the Carter administration was after the first thirty months. Reagan's Justice Department had filed 114 criminal cases, while Carter's had filed 101. But the civil law has been a potent weapon for civil rights in recent decades, and when the number of *civil* cases was added, the Reagan administration fell well behind the record of the Carter administration at thirty months—a total of 225 civil and criminal suits filed by Carter, and only 156 filed by Reagan.

"Almost every one of the major points I made in the article was being made for the first time," Miller says. "The people in the daily press, even those covering civil rights, had simply printed the statements without any serious attempt to check their validity."

The Need for a More Aggressive Press

It is not necessary to challenge every statistic to make a point, and readers of most major newspapers have been told repeatedly that the Reagan administration has a philosophy about enforcement of civil rights laws that is very different from that of most recent administrations. But Miller nonetheless has a point when he says that for reporters to accept such numbers on their face is to allow themselves and their readers to be manipulated and deceived.

The challenge is likely to become greater as Reagan, immensely popular and recently swept back into office by a landslide, moves ahead with his stated goals for limiting the flow of information to the public. Already, his administration has supported bills that would exempt the Secret Service, the CIA, and most FBI activities from the Freedom of Information Act, and has imposed a rule at the Defense Department that any person with access to classified information must submit to lie detector tests whenever asked to. It has reversed the Carter administration policy and now allows the FBI and CIA to infiltrate the media if the attorney general finds it in the interest of the national security to do so, and has set regulations that allow the FBI to infiltrate and monitor domestic groups, including the press, while conducting investigations of organized crime or terrorism. It has slashed the budget of the indexing staff of the National Archives, meaning that access to historical records, including the Nixon tapes, will be delayed for years. It has created mechanisms for monitoring contacts between White House staffers and reporters, and has issued guidelines telling officials handling FOIA requests to be stingy in giving fee reductions to journalists, scholars, and authors. It has rewritten the classification system to insure that more, rather than less, information will be classified. And it has made proposals—already implemented in some agencies—that would require all officials who have had access to classified information to come back to the government for the rest of their lives and submit for prior censorship any speeches, letters to the editor, news articles, or works of fiction.

Nick Horrock, of *Newsweek*, who has worked in Washington for most of the past two decades, says that some of the changes are atmospheric, and not entirely caused by Reagan. "There has been a shift back to an atmosphere much more like it was in the early 1960s," Horrock says. "During the Vietnam War and Watergate, a lot of dissidents were in the government, and they were quick to speak out, to tell reporters that things weren't working the way they should. Now, there aren't so many dissidents. It's not popular to take risks. Being a whistle-blower is no longer popular."

In a recent article, William Greider, the former assistant managing editor for national news at *The Washingon Post* and now national editor of *Rolling Stone* magazine, argued that the press, too, seems to be in retreat. "It seems to be pulling in its lances, taking fewer risks, avoiding the hard and nasty confrontations it would have zealously pursued five or ten years ago . . . ," he wrote. "The trend I see is deep and subtle—a shift toward 'hard news,' which means narrow splinters of unexamined fact, a turning away from more provocative explorations of subjects that have not been legitimized by official sources."

If he's right, and many in the media agree that he is, it is happening at a particularly bad time. The history of the press-government relationship since World War II shows that administrations have claimed a right to lie in some circumstances, and have been unable to resist the temptation to deceive in a great many others. And this particular administration, headed by a tremendously popular president, has made clear that it wants to make information about government operations harder to get, and, in terms of threats to their careers, more dangerous for civil servants to provide.

That means that the press needs to be even more aggressive, not less, if it is to follow the John Mitchell rule for covering government: Don't watch what we say. Watch what we do.

THE SCARLET LETTER:
THE PRIVATE LIVES OF PUBLIC FIGURES[2]

Policy Review asked a number of scholars, public officials, and religious leaders to participate in a symposium on the modern version of the scarlet letter, the opening of public figures' private lives to the scrutiny of reporters, biographers, and stand-up comics. Participants were asked to write short comments on any or all of the following questions.

Public figures have been pilloried and in some cases their careers have been destroyed by reports of adultery, wife-beating, drug use, homosexuality, ethnic slurs, alcoholism, and friendships with figures in organized crime. Are any or all of these private behaviors appropriate subjects for public discussion? Is gossip of this sort simply voyeuristic and nihilistic, or does it serve an important moral purpose?

What role should private behavior and character play in the evaluation of a person's fitness for office? What aspects of private behavior and character are most important? Under what circumstances should the exposed misbehaver be given a second chance?

Should any aspects of private life be off limits to public exposure, including posthumous biography? Do individuals and families have any right to privacy, and, if so, how is this right to be balanced against freedom of the press? What are the moral obligations of family members and friends in protecting the privacy of public figures?

RANDY E. BARNETT
We are today tasting the bitter fruit of decades of agitation

[2]Reprint of an article from *Policy Review*, Spring 1987, pp. 26–33. *Policy Review* is the quarterly magazine of *The Heritage Foundation*, 214 Massachusetts Avenue, N.E., Washington, D.C. 20002. Reprinted with permission.

by activists on both the left and right to conflate the public and private spheres of life. These activists rest their respective programs on the premise that all private conduct potentially "affects" others and therefore all private matters are subject to public governance. The Left would subject every exercise of personal discretion that affects another to *judicial review*. Ideally, "due process of law" or a "fair hearing before an impartial magistrate" should extend to every decision of private life—hiring, firing, grading, ending a love affair, etc. The Right, on the other hand, wants to subject every personal choice involving vice or virtue to legislative jurisdiction. Ideally, a legislature reflecting the "public will" of the majority should impose its vision of private life on the minority.

Although activists of the Left and Right disagree about what counts as "bad" conduct and which level or branch of government should decide this issue, they vehemently agree that individuals or private groups are not to be trusted to decide many truly important matters for themselves. Consequently, much of their attention is focused on favored examples of personal or institutional "corruption" with the implicit understanding that virtuous governmental institutions can and must outperform and "check" these private institutions.

If, however, a moral or virtuous government is the solution to the immorality or licentiousness of individuals and groups, then it follows that only the truly virtuous may be "elected" to "higher" office. If the solution to human corruption is the incorruptible public official, then every private peccadillo by officials or potential officials is a matter of genuine public concern. Everything becomes public; nothing remains private. In this way, the dominant political philosophy comes full circle to ambush the political officeholder or office-seeker. It is cold comfort when truly decent persons are destroyed by the very public process they so avidly advocate.

Hyprocrisy and Power Lust

In societies where the public sphere eclipses the private sphere, two types of individuals typically survive and thrive: skillful (and lucky) hypocrites and those who so love power itself that they are untainted by avarice. Moreover, such a process is not ideologically neutral. It systematically favors advocates of "altruistic" collectivism and disfavors advocates of "selfish" private choice.

The classical liberals rested their political vision on the separation of public and private jurisdiction. Individuals and groups should be free to purse the good life in ways that do not unduly interfere with the similar pursuit by others. The "moral fabric" of a society is best woven, not by the state, but by nongovernmental institutions standing between the individual and the state—churches, schools, social clubs, charitable organizations, the creative arts, the press, etc. Such intermediate institutions are created, maintained, and constrained by the voluntary actions of countless persons. They spontaneously evolve in response to changing conditions and the growth in moral knowledge. Ideally, legal coercion is reserved to regulate the means of pursuing happiness—not to dictate ends. Individual rights—whether natural, civil, or political—define a protected domain of liberty for each person and also the boundaries of individual discretion.

In short, a world requires both general fidelity to principles of right and tolerance of moral disagreement about the good. A tolerant society in which intermediate associations are free to combat vice can expect a more virtuous citizenry. A society in which the rule of law is solely used to protect individual rights can better tolerate governance by mere human beings.

RANDY E. BARNETT *is professor of law at the Chicago-Kent College of Law and director of the Law and Philosophy Program of the Institute for Humane Studies at George Mason University.*

GARY L. BAUER

I must confess to a strong ambivalence about the recent explosion of private scandals rocking the careers of public figures. It offends my sense of decency and propriety that reporters would sneak and sniff around the lives of people to uncover something they did a decade ago that the reporter himself may have done several times last week. Then the ensuing articles destroy the public figure's reputation and make the reputation of the reporter.

The second concern I have is that scandal revelations are a chancy, arbitrary, and inequitable business. The ax falls without any apparent logic or justice. Joseph Biden's plagiarism goes unremarked for years, until suddenly it surfaces and topedoes his presidential aspirations. Gerry Studds survives revelations of pederasty, while Dan Crane pays at the ballot box for adultery with a female page. Then of course there is the sorry spectacle of Jim Wright's wheeling and dealing, which inspires only indifference among a Democrat-controlled ethics committee. Everyone knows that if all the scandals in Washington were printed, America would run out of trees. Consequently, scandal mongering becomes a very selective mode of punishment.

On the other hand, I cannot agree with those who maintain that private morals are largely irrelevant to public life. Gary Hart's infidelity certainly told me something about how I could treat his political promises: If he couldn't keep faith after a solemn pledge to a loved partner, what confidence can I as a total stranger have that he would honor his commitments—to me or to his country? Often private actions are the best evidence that citizens and voters have of what a public figure is really like. Certainly actions such as habitual drug use, wife-beating, and unlawful behavior are more reliable indices than vacuous campaign rhetoric, often forgotten the day after the election. They tell people what their leaders are, not just what they pledge to be.

Finally, I feel that the American people have an ample fund of shrewd judgment, common sense, and tolerance so that they can assess the relevance of the publicized information to the candidate or public official's performance in office.

GARY L. BAUER *is Assistant to the President for Policy Development.*

ALLAN C. CARLSON

Recent embarrassments among our political caste have spawned calls for a new silence over the private lives of our public officials. The angst-ridden pundits tell us that this attention to personal matters is an unworthy development, and a break with a long tradition of propriety. They argue, too, that private, usually sexual, matters have no tangible relationship to public judgment.

Neither response bears much scrutiny. The first reply ignores the truly raucous political history of the nation, where political scandal has been the rule, not the exception. Among the sainted Founders, for example, Alexander Hamilton came under attack for an adulterous liaison with Mrs. Reynolds, to which he finally confessed in a published pamphlet designed to save his political hide. Thomas Jefferson faced those rumors (apparently false) of frequent trysts with slave Sally Hemmings. Grover Cleveland acknowledged his probable paternity of an illegitimate child (he at least had the decency to support the lad financially). It is true that a few politicians—notably John F. Kennedy—received curious dispensations from the press. But they have been the extraordinary ones, chosen by the gods.

The second reply, moreover, is premised on a radical split between "public" and "private" that is impossible to sustain. Several of JFK's midnight assignations in the White House, for example, were intimately involved with his politics, including his reported affair with a Mafia moll. The character of politicians—their ability to remain faithful to commitments, their courage under attack, their fortitude in periods of stress—must also bear some relation to their fidelity within a marriage and their ability to control libidinal drives. Even the skill shown by politicians as parents—their degree of success in raising responsible children to adulthood—offers solid insights into their leadership qualities (here, George Bush, Richard Nixon, and Walter Mondale look good, Ronald Reagan . . . well perhaps we can blame it on California).

With this said, there do remain limits to inquiry that should be governed by taste and a code of honor. There is a great moral divide, for example, between Gary Hart's liaison with Donna Rice and Pat Robertson's attempt to protect the secret of his marriage date. The former is a stupid, sordid matter (according to the tabloids, Hart used the old line, "I'll make you First Lady . . . after the election"); the latter, an understandable, forgivable attempt to protect one's wife and children from the consequences of youthful indiscretion. The relevant question, perhaps, is whether the press is still able to tell the difference.

ALLAN C. CARLSON *is president of The Rockford Institute.*

JOSHUA O. HABERMAN

The wrong way of putting the question is: "What do you want, high private morals or competence?" It should not be an either/or question. The American people want both, at least as much as possible. We should avoid harsh Puritanism and cynical pragmatism. What we need is a heavy does of moral realism in judging the fitness of a candidate for public office. It makes little sense to say: "What, he has a character defect? Only people of perfect character should hold public office." Absolutist standards would effectively disqualify all but saints from holding public office.

Equally mistaken is the assumption that one's private life is irrelevant and that the only thing that matters is competence.

The importance of one's private life varies from very little to very much according to the particular vocation or position. Few people, for example, would be concerned with an electrician's sexual mores when a switch needs to be repaired. It is quite different when we choose a teacher, police chief, or political leader. Those in respected positions of responsibility who work with people in the community are not only responsible for performance but, like it or not, serve as role models. Whatever that means, it implies, at the very least, personal conduct in conformity with the values that are upheld by the community and, in the case of the political leader, by his constituency. Society is destabilized by a leader guided only by his own "moral preference," overriding the moral conventions sanctioned by the community.

Create in Me a Clean Heart

The classic biblical example of a transgressor's rehabilitation and recovery of credibility came after the prophet Nathan confronted King David with the fact of his scandalous adultery with Bathsheba. David's reaction was recorded in Psalm 51, surely one of the most moving documents of repentance in literature. It helps us understand why posterity still regards David as a hero. Three points stand out: 1) Honest acknowledgment and confession of the delinquency without ifs or buts or the slightest attempt to shift blame or explain it away; 2) profound remorse; 3) convincing evidence of a radical change of heart. The psalm resonates with the outcry of moral anguish from the heart of the penitent, as suggested by the following phrases:

Be gracious unto me, Oh God, according to Thy mercy . . . Wash me thoroughly from mine iniquity, and cleanse me from sin. For I know my transgressions; My sin is ever before me . . . Thou desirest truth within . . . Purge me . . . and I shall be clean . . . Create in me a clean heart, Oh God, and renew a steadfast spirit within me . . . Let a willing spirit uphold me. Then will I teach transgressors Thy ways, and sinners shall return unto Thee . . . The sacrifices of God are a broken spirit; a broken and contrite heart, Oh God, Thou wilt not despise.

David was forgiven because he established credibility by his seriousness, his instant and abject confession, and the persuasive expression of his penitence. Most important, he was convincing in his change of heart.

The American people in judging human character and conduct usually will apply the two-dimensional measuring yard of justice and compassion so typical of the biblical tradition. We believe in forgiveness if circumstances warrant it and if the transgressor merits it. This means that a second chance is not given automatically but must be earned.

JOSHUA O. HABERMAN, *formerly senior rabbi of the Washington Hebrew Congregation (Reform), is visiting professor at Wesley Theological Seminary and Washington Theological Union, and president of the Foundation for Jewish Studies.*

CARL F. H. HENRY

Public figures are entitled to some privacy at least. They are under no necessity to bare their private thoughts to the world or to fully expose their private lives to the media. After all, my inner ideas—and yours—are private property on which we need pay taxes only to God; and our private behavior—insofar as it involves ourselves alone—is seldom our neighbor's business. Family members or trusted friends who may shatter that privacy and prattle publicly about our personal thoughts and behavior forfeit our confidence.

In God's sight, lustful imagination or contemplation of crime justifies His moral condemnation. But statute law deals not with inner but with outward behavior. When crimes are alleged against state and society, public discussion of a person's conduct and premeditation may be not only proper and important but imperative.

But even here there are limits. Unfortunately, reporters and biographers often peer through every available peephole of one's life, expecting, even hoping, sooner or later to find adultery, homosexuality, drugs, criminal contacts, alcoholism, spousal abuse, or some other vice. The press subtly prejudges public figures by anticipated guilt. Sad to say, an author's voyeuristic imagination can add sales potential to biography; if such narrative is posthumous the subject is beyond his or her day in court. Can such cowardly character-assessment justify itself as serving an ethical purpose?

Morals of the Media

That investigative reporters, media anchormen, and biographers seem exempt themselves from the scrutiny they impose on others is remarkable. Should public trust require that before assignment to a permanent post media personnel be subjected to public grilling and review of their private lives? Do anchormen reveal their after-hours indulgences? If not, why should the public servant be inordinately scrutinized? One answer is that we expect officeholders to be role models because they serve their country and represent constituencies. But cannot an anchorman in quite different ways honor or dishonor the public trust? Are not all of us morally responsible whoever and whatever we are? Should we expect more of a presidential candidate or of a televangelist than of an investigative reporter?

Once a society exempts certain classes from universally shared moral imperatives it is in trouble. To expose anyone's immorality is hardly a titillating pastime to be undertaken with glee. But for the grace of God all of us have the same potentiality for ethical compromise.

To destroy confidence in a public figure may indeed at times be legitimate and necessary. Not to do so may undermine confidence in the very democratic processes that the Free World treasures. But there is a proviso: the prosecutor dare not arrogate to himself or herself the prerogatives also of judge and jury. Such arrogance also undermines respect for those same democratic processes. The press has not yet, happily, displaced Congress, the presidency, and the Supreme Court. It will best serve the legality and morality of its profession and of the nation if its personnel manifest the same integrity that a just society expects, and rightly expects, from all of us.

CARL F. H. HENRY *is the founding editor of* Christianity Today *and author of some 35 works including the six-volume* God, Revelation, and Authority.

RUSSELL KIRK

Private probity and public virtue.

Must people in public office be always exemplary in their private lives?

From Alexander Hamilton's affair with a woman client to the amours of Gary Hart, the American democracy frequently has rejected public men when it is said of them that they have promiscuous appetites or who have in some other fashion offended against what Marxists delight to call "bourgeois morality." The conspicuous rectitude of George Washington or John Adams remains the standard of political conduct for most Americans.

America's liberal intellectuals, on the other hand—Robert Maynard Hutchins, for one—often have asserted that competent performance of public responsibilities is everything, and that private vices or virtues are not proper concern for the electorate or the molders of public opinion. In Lear's phrase, "Let copulation thrive"—King Lear that is, not Norman Lear—as long as the public interest be not adversely affected.

Public Good, Private Turpitude

Plato raised such questions of rectitude in the public man some 2,400 years ago. These issues grow serious again in our closing years of the 20th century, so like Plato's age in its incertitudes about moral standards. Can public good consist with private turpitude?

Take adultery—a term Gary Hart preferred not to define. A good many eminent statesmen, in many countries, have fallen into that slough. Even John Morley, the Victorian [statesman] and sober man of letters, kept in his house for years a woman who was not his wife, whom he had rescued from a brutal husband.

We lack space here to touch upon the amatory exploits of British World War I Prime Minister David Lloyd George, President John F. Kennedy, and other possessors of power in a democracy. Does a politician's adulterous habit impede him in his public duties?

The answer to that question depends upon circumstances. A statesman's infatuation with the female agent of a foreign power may have consequences very grave indeed.

Or, as T. S. Eliot once remarked in a letter to me, the secret homosexual appetites of senior officials in the British intelligence services—two such had fled to the USSR for fear of arrest as Soviet agents not long before he wrote—scarcely are matters of indifference to the realm. Eliot added that a teacher teaches as much by what he is as by what he says. And that principle may apply to people in high authority.

President Galahad

So I think that the American public does well to take some account of a public man's private character and habits. Yet the public would be foolish to expect every influential politician to live as a Galahad or a Parsifal, without stain or reproach. Chiefs of state and leaders of the crowd have to be men of the world.

President Richard Nixon remarked to me once that he did not think the people wished him to become a preacher of sermons, an issuer of moral rescripts. "I can speak to some effect on drug abuse," he added—but he took it, rightly, that a president's duties are not those of *pontifex maximus.* Later, when the Watergate tapes were examined, certain hardened newspaper men affected shock at some rough phrases employed by Nixon and his kitchen cabinet.

The press, somewhat sanctimoniously, expected the public to wax indignant.

But why so? Abraham Lincoln had told off-color stories in the White House. Let us not pretend, ladies and gentlemen of the press, that the sort of men who seek great political power are notable for their chastity of thought and expression. Let us be grateful, rather, when such a rare politician appears among us.

Although it is unreasonable for the public to expect perfection of soul in every candidate for office, still Americans' frequent disapproval of politicians' private pecadilloes is founded upon something sounder than mere prissiness. It is not silly to ask one's self whether a public man, false to his wife, might not play fast and loose with his party and the public interest on convenient occasion. Nor is it absurd to suggest that servitude to what once was called "unnatural vice" might subject a public man to corrupting political pressures.

I offer an illustration of this principle. Some years ago, the character and fitness committee of the Michigan Bar Association was examining a candidate for admission to the bar. It was found that he had once been convicted of rape. The following dialogue occurred:

Examiner: "Why did you rape her?"

Candidate: "The opportunity presented itself, and I took it."

At the very least, it may be legitimately suspected of such an applicant that he might do with a client's money, on opportunity, the sort of thing he had done to the woman.

And so it is with a politician: The public entertains the legitimate presumption that the illicit lust for women's bodies might be paralleled in a public man's soul by an illicit lust for acquiring possessions, what we call cupidity, and by an illicit lust for power, what St. Augustine and Thomas Hobbes called the *libido dominandi*—the lust for power, the appetite for absolute dominion. The public does well to try to safeguard itself against the conjunction of corruption in these three allied forms.

Then why think the American public pharisaical in making amatory decency a condition for election to high office?

If a candidate were notorious for having committed, as a private act, fraud or armed violence, would anybody hold that such private vice is irrelevant to candidacy for a higher public trust? What a person is accustomed to practice in private, he is all too liable to apply to his conduct in public concerns.

A Tyrant's Lust

Public wrath at erotic misconduct by men in power is no new phenomenon. A principal reason for the old Greeks' hatred of tyranny was the tyrant's power to gratify his lust upon the bodies of his subjects. What undid King John and compelled him to sign the Magna Carta was his relish for the wives of his vassals.

And in the present circumstances of society, it is not unhealthy for the electorate to take a hostile view of adultery in high places. The family, which Cicero called the foundation of all other social institutions, notoriously is in a decaying state. If those in high political authority do not stand as tolerable examples of familial loyalty, who will?

Practical politicians, like single men in barracks, don't turn into plaster saints. But to argue that private character bears no relationship to fitness for the exercise of political trust and power—why, many centuries of human experience in community refute that liberal notion.

RUSSELL KIRK *is the author of* The Conservative Mind. *This article is reprinted with permission from* Newsday.

ERNEST W. LEFEVER

"If men were angels," said James Madison, "no government would be necessary." And, we might add, politics would be less complex and more boring. Eighty years ago John Dewey said,

"While saints engage in introspection, burly sinners run the world."

Neither Madison nor Dewey was counseling despair. They were merely underscoring the plain truth—all men are sinners and government is not run by angels or saints.

This should come as no surprise to anyone observing the current presidential campaign or, for that matter, to anyone who looks honestly in a mirror. We are all sinners? So what?

The voter should distinguish between those vices and imperfections that bear directly on the behavior of one who holds (or aspires to) high office from those that do not. To speak of vices, we must also speak of virtue. High in the list of virtues essential to statesmanship are wisdom, prudence, integrity, courage, and a commitment to a free and just society. We associate Winston Churchill with these attributes, but even he was not without flaws.

Among the serious character flaws—if a pattern persists—that should disqualify a candidate for president or a lesser office are lying, stealing, bribery, and brutality. Little white lies, stealing paper clips, and "bribing" someone with a box of chocolates may be regarded as trivial. Lying on one's resumé, plagiarism, cooking one's income tax returns, or being at either end of a bribe are serious.

It is the absence of integrity—oneness—that disqualifies. But integrity is not enough. It must be buttressed by the courage and wisdom to translate one's commitment to the good society into practical policies. This involves prudence, pragmatism, and a willingness to compromise.

This suggests that there is a quality we call civic virtue that should characterize citizen and statesman alike. Civic virtue must embrace a sense of history and an understanding of the requirements of freedom and decency in the face of a totalitarian challenge.

In practical terms, the citizen should vote for the candidate who is best prepared to support and promote civic virtue. In many cases, such a candidate may have flaws in his personal life and his opponent may be singularly free of such flaws. But the responsible voter must vote policy, not personal perfection. I prefer a burly sinner who supports aid to the Nicaraguan freedom fighters over a saint who supports the Sandinistas.

ERNEST W. LEFEVER *is founding president of the Ethics and Public Policy Center.*

FORREST MCDONALD

In this matter, as on most, I am in accord with Alexander Hamilton. Though he had been personally victimized by a partisan press considerably more vicious than the media are today, Hamilton was nonetheless an effective champion of a free press and of the right of the public to know—within limits. In one of his last and most celebrated cases as an attorney, he defended Harry Croswell, editor of a small upstate New York newspaper. Croswell had printed a charge that Thomas Jefferson had paid a notorious pamphleteer "for calling Washington a traitor, a robber, and a perjurer . . . and for most grossly slandering the private character of men who [Jefferson] well knew were virtuous." Croswell's charge was true, but under the common law truth was not a defense in cases of seditious libel, and Croswell had been convicted.

On appeal to the state supreme court, Hamilton argued that truth must be a defense, because "malicious or mischievous" intent was crucial to determining whether a writing was libelous, and truth was relevant to determining intent. It was not an absolute defense, however. The truth must not be used "wantonly; if for the purpose of disturbing the peace of families; if for relating that which does not appertain to official conduct," there is no right to print and no right of the public to know. But if it is within the domain of what the public should know in order to behave responsibly at the polls—including anything that pertains to the character of a candidate or an officeholder—then the truth should be printable without fear of retribution. If, Hamilton concluded, "you cannot apply this mitigated doctrine . . . you must forever remain ignorant of what your rulers do. I never can think this ought to be; I never did think the truth was a crime; I am glad the day is come in which it is to be decided; for my soul has ever abhorred the thought, that a free man dared not speak the truth."

Hamilton lost the case, but virtually all the members of the legislature had come to hear his argument, and forthwith a bill was enacted making Hamilton's position the law of the state. Eventually it became the law of the land, forming the legal foundation, firmer than the First Amendment, for the ideal of a press that is both free and responsible.

It must be emphasized that responsibility is quite as important as freedom, and the key to responsibility is truth. Reporters, biographers, historians, and other chroniclers have the right to inquire into the private affairs of public men and women, but only if they report the truth—not half-truths, innuendoes, suspicions. If they record other than the truth, they betray their responsibility and thereby subvert the justification for the freedom.

FORREST MCDONALD *is the author of* Novus Ordo Seclorum *and the Jefferson Lecturer for 1987.*

ELLEN FRANKEL PAUL

Perhaps *Policy Review*'s invitation to reveal my thoughts on "the modern version of the scarlet letter" has uncovered a hideous moral weakness lurking in the innermost recesses of my being, but I must confess that I have rather enjoyed the recent journalistic revelations of the peccadilloes of such public figures as Gary Hart and Joseph Biden. It is always pleasant to see one's ideological adversary unmasked as the mountebank and prevaricator one always suspected that he was, but what if the ox being gored happened to be one of our own?

Certainly, then, the enjoyment would be much diminished, even eviscerated. I can recall quite vividly my horror when all of those stories on Spiro Agnew's bribe taking and rigged contracts—inspired, I had thought, by pure malice against the press's prime tormentor—turned out to be true. Conservatives have had their share of fallen idols, Congressman Bauman being one of the more recent and saddest examples.

Thus, no one in public life apparently, Left or Right, is immune these says from the scrutiny of the Fourth Estate. Are these tawdy revelations proper, or rather symptomatic of the decay of journalistic ethics and, more generally, of the endless fascination of the American public with scandal, especially of a salacious nature? I must conclude, and this may be a highly idiosyncratic view, that the former is closer to the mark.

Would it be preferable for the press to shield its favorite public figures, each reporter or editor taking upon himself a determination of whether or not to publish information damaging to a public figure? Indeed, this is how the press did function in the not too distant past, with such luminaries as presidents Franklin Roosevelt and John F. Kennedy only posthumously revealed as the philanderers that the Washington press knew them to be in their lifetimes. An informal gentleman's agreement that the moral lapses of those in public office ought not to be exposed to those who elected them seems a far more dangerous ethic than the somewhat seedy one prevailing today, where reporters lurk in bushes in the hope of catching a senator and his paramour.

Individuals who willingly put themselves forward for high public office deserve all the scrutiny that a free, competitive press can provide. Who can recall a president who ran on a platform of unbalancing the budget even more, or of getting us into war; yet all in recent memory have done the former, and many the latter. The much maligned "character issue," is of much importance, and we need to know if those who offer themselves as candidates for the highest office in the land are liars, plagiarists, hypocrites, or corrupt, because character will determine quite a lot in the way a president handles his office, especially in a crisis.

Outrageous Intrusion

What is unseemly, if not outrageous, is the intrusion of the press into the lives of ordinary citizens faced with catastrophe. Do reporters really need to ask the sole survivor of a fire how she feels as the paramedics remove the bodies of her children from the wreckage? I think not.

As libel law has developed, courts have distinguished between public figures and private individuals. In the case of the former, much more demanding standards must be met by a plaintiff who considers himself defamed, thus making it very difficult to convict any publication of having committed libel. A nonpublic figure must meet less rigorous criteria in order to prevail. What I wish to suggest, is that this distinction from the libel law may be useful in demarcating the permissible from the impermissible in investigative journalism. If someone is, in contrast, a public official or a seeker after public office, he deserves full scrutiny, no holds barred, because he has invited the public to know him and to trust him. For private individuals suddenly thrust forward on the public stage through inadvertence or bad luck, reporters ought to show some self-restraint and respect for these people's privacy. Other public figures—movie stars and the like—deserve the gossip columnists that their publicists so voraciously seek.

ELLEN FRANKEL PAUL *is deputy director of the Social Philosophy and Policy Center at Bowling Green State University.*

ERNEST VAN DEN HAAG

A "public figure" is a person who has volunteered for an elective office, and thus has volunteered to give up his privacy, to allow his life to become public. He may or may not cooperate with the media, which want to scrutinize his life. But the media have a right to scrutinize and publish on their own. And while a public figure is protected by laws against trespass and malicious libel, it is not up to him to determine what part of his life qualifies or disqualifies him for the office he seeks or holds.

The most titillating aspects of a candidate's life—*e.g.* his sexual behavior—are least likely to be relevant to his office. But they are not privileged information. Gary Hart succeeded in making sex relevant. Not because 1) he had affairs (which is neither here nor there), but because 2) he lied about them (which says something relevant about his character), and 3) because his lies were demonstrably lies (which says something important about his judgment. Come to think of it, the lack of restraint and discretion demonstrated by the affairs themselves also does). Do we want a president who, when cornered, lies, and does so even when the lies will be demonstrated in short order to be lies? And who then attacks those who revealed his lying?

Mr. Hart could have refused to discuss the matter. "No comment" is fine when no comment would help. He could have refused to discuss his private life. He probably would still have had to withdraw, but he could have done so with dignity. This is where Judge Ginsburg did better. He preempted what his enemies would have disclosed and withdrew, his veracity, his honor, and his ability to perform his duties unimpaired. He admitted a past lack of judgment thereby showing a current presence of judgment.

The courts have held that persons who do not run for, or hold, public office, may nonetheless become "public figures" enjoying less protection against libel than others do (they have to prove malice) if they voluntarily enter the public arena. If someone publishes a book attacking homosexuality, or upholding the gold standard, it is quite justifiable for the press to point out that the author is a homosexual, or a dealer in gold. But most cases are less clear-cut. I can understand the public curiosity, but not the public interest, in the sex life of a famous actress or baseball player. I should like more protection of privacy here. Yet the "celebrity" often cooperates in these invasions of privacy. After all, nobody is compelled to discuss anything with the press. Those who seek favorable publicity, and complain when the publicity turns out to be unfavorable, should have known that they cannot dictate the *kind* of publicity they get.

ERNEST VAN DEN HAAG *is John M. Olin Professor of Jurisprudence and Public Policy at Fordham University.*

PAUL M. WEYRICH

In the current confusion about private lives and sins versus public morality and disclosures, most people talk as if the dilemma were a new one. The fact is, it only seems new because we have largely abandoned our moral rule of thumb for dealing with it. Like all moral guidelines, it is not always easy to apply in practice, but in formula it is fairly simple. This moral standard is found in various forms in various traditions, but as spelled out for us by Jesus Christ, it goes as follows:

If your brother does something wrong, go and have it out with him alone, between yourselves. If he listens to you, you have won back your brother. If he does not listen, take one or two others with you. But if he refuses to listen to these, report it to the community; and if he refuses to listen to the community, treat him like a pagan or a tax collector. (*Jerusalem Bible*, Matt. 18:15–17)

It does not require the faith of a Christian to recognize the wisdom of these words. It might require experience, however. I myself learned the hard way that it serves no good, either for the individual or the community, to overlook or conceal the immorality of public figures. In every case where I thought it best to remain silent so as to avoid division and scandal, subsequent events forced me to rue my decision. Such things have a way of making themselves known, and time usually only serves to exacerbate the situation.

Matthew's Gospel definitely implies that the community has an interest in the private morality of its members. But the rule also respects human weakness and the private nature of that weakness, and gives ample opportunity for offenders to mend their ways before risking public exposure. In short, the application of this rule to our public men and women would ensure that, though they are fallible creatures, they at least hold the same standards and ideals as the community they serve. This is obviously a desideratum: Would we want as senator or president someone we wouln't trust to baby-sit our children for one evening? Would we choose for the Supreme Court a man we wouldn't hire to do our taxes?

In the present cases, we cannot expect journalists to accept the burden of fraternal correction. The role of the journalist seems to come in when it's time to "report it to the community." But if the rest of us took on the responsibility of charitable and fraternal correction of our colleagues, we would avoid most, if not all, of the newsworthy scandals.

PAUL M. WEYRICH *is president of Free Congress Foundation.*

POLITICAL IMPERFECTIONS:
SCANDAL TIME IN WASHINGTON[3]

There were only four at the dinner table one night not long ago in Washington, so the talk turned naturally toward the subject nearest to everyone's heart: recent, current, and future government scandal. "The climate has become impossible," said the cabinet member in the group. "It's gotten so that even when you're up on the Hill for a budget hearing, they treat you like a criminal."

That Secretary's complaint was typical of the way people at high levels in the federal government talk these days. Scandal—personal misconduct, financial chicanery, or political controversy with criminal overtones—has come to occupy more of their conversation and energy than policy questions or even conventional, horse-trading, vote-getting politics.

It is hardly an exaggeration to say that scandals and investigations now dominate the agenda of much of Washington's political elite. How did this happen, and what does it mean?

Some would say that our obsessive hunting after political miscreants is quite unremarkable and healthy. They would further say that the whine of a high official complaining about the hunt is the sound of a properly functioning republic. Human beings have enjoyed being scandalized by one thing or another about

[3]Reprint of an article by Suzanne Garment, a resident scholar at the American Enterprise Institute for Public Policy Research. *Public Opinion*, no. 1, vol. 10 (1987), pp. 10–12, 60. Reprinted with permission.

their governor's behavior since humanity first oozed up out of the swamp. The slaves who hauled bricks for the pyramids probably spent their water breaks gossiping about the Pharaoh's lewd antics with his latest concubine.

Our modern democracy is in fact less scandalous in some ways than other regimes at other times, though it's more scandalous in others. Only an American, for instance, could summon up moral outrage (or even interest) over the peccadilloes that pass for sexual scandals in this country. On the other hand, because a lot of un-rich but ambitious and ingenious folks make their careers in U.S. politics, we have always generated financial corruption of a most inventive and luxuriant sort. A corollary of this is also undoubtedly true: As government grows in scope and changes its shape, the opportunities for corruption grow and change along with it. Willie Sutton used to say that he robbed banks because that's where the money is. *Mutatis mutandis*, the same is true in politics.

Other changes in society affect both the prevalence of scandal and the public's awareness of it. Some would insist that American public officials simply have lower ethical standards than they did, say, a decade ago, because the idealism of the late 1960s and early 1970s has given way to selfish Yuppieness. But in fact it is quite implausible that official standards have declined far or fast enough to explain the increase in our preoccupation with scandal news over the decade. It's more likely that mass communications magnify the scandal phenomenon by trumpeting the news of sin far and wide, giving the impression that there must be even more of the stuff lurking in the closet. As the influence of television increases, the trumpet sound grows louder.

Finally, some experts in the shiny new ethics-in-government field explain with satisfaction that we have more lawbreakers and rule violators today because our standards have *risen*. The rules are tougher now, so that people who would have been called law-abiding yesterday are outside the pale today. This change is the price that we pay for civilization's moral progress, and we must accept it as such.

Scandalous Conventions and Inventions

The "business as usual" arguments cannot fully account for the large and increased role that scandal and criminal or ethical wrongdoing now play in current public discussion.

To be sure, venerable "human nature" and "price of democracy" factors do explain a good part of the decade's sex and drug scandals. Crooks in high places have always been with us and always will be. Representative Gerry Studds's homosexual involvement with a congressional page was revealed in 1983, but it would have caused a stir had it become known in just about any American decade. And a Paula Parkinson is a Paula Parkinson whenever and wherever you find her.

But some of our current scandals involving conflict of interest, or alleged executive branch violations of Congress's laws, belong disproportionately to this time and place. Standards of behavior in this area have indeed changed. Just as important, the pursuit of this kind of wrongdoing has not only expanded and intensified but also has become institutionalized.

Some kinds of criminal investigation into the behavior of public officials have long been fairly routine in American public affairs. By now you can rest assured that at any given moment in the life of your town or city, some local officeholder is getting probed, indicted, or sentenced for an act of corruption.

Frequent as these occurrences are, though, they have remained essentially local—that is, circumscribed. Sometimes they do engage the attention of the entire country, or have a major effect on how the nation as a whole thinks about its political health—but only sporadically.

What is new is the growing institutionalization of investigative politics at the federal level. Partly this is a matter of sheer volume. The number of federal ethics prosecutions going on at any one time has increased enormously. In fact, it has increased tenfold over the past decade. Even more such investigations will never make it into the open records. The number of federal investigators at work has mushroomed as well—departmental inspectors general and their staffs, Justice Department probers, congressional staff sleuths, and the investigators of the General Accounting Office.

Numbers, though, cannot tell the whole story. To say that a practice has become institutionalized is to say more than that its incidence has grown. Instead, the term means that a pattern of incentives has developed to keep people following the practice routinely, out of habit or for their own benefit.

That is what has happened to our pursuit of public wrongdoing.

Creating a Scandal

Let us examine the hypothetical case of a typical, garden-variety Washington scandal—not a five-star production like Watergate or Iran, but just a few allegations that some official has used public office for the private benefit of his or her friends. In other words, the stuff we hear about every week in present-day Washington.

The attentive public will most likely get its first word of this scandal from a newspaper headline. The initial information is much less likely to emerge first from the mouth of an anchorperson on the nightly news. Newspapers dig up stories more often than TV news programs do, though the tube is unsurpassed in its ability to spread the tidings once they have been announced.

The initial newspaper headline may have originated in the work of some lonely print reporter sifting diligently through public records, following weeks of false leads, and finally forcing knowledgeable and heavily sweating government officials to confirm what he has found. There are fine investigative reporters who do indeed work this way.

But it is far more likely that the story originated in a leak.

Let us try to be more precise about this. A great deal that appears in newspapers comes from leaks, in the sense that reporters have extracted it in one unofficial way or another from public officials or institutions. But for present purposes, we are talking about leaks of a certain sort, cases in which the leaker is an active party in the transaction because he or she has a personal interest in having the story become news.

The "active leak," as opposed to the "passive leak" or even the "coerced leak," is nothing new under the journalistic sun. But remember, there are more investigative agencies at work now. Critics may contend that some of these agencies are not vigorous enough, but an awful lot of people working for these organizations no longer think of themselves as mere bureaucrats dispassionately checking out the latest charge against the Deputy Under Secretary of Whatever. No, these modern investigators think their job is to pursue the alleged crooks energetically and nail them securely to the wall.

This change has come about not so much from alterations in the structure of various government agencies as from basic shifts in their culture—that is, in the values that animate the officials working inside them.

So on any given day you can bet that someone will be running
around town trying—public-spiritedly, of course—to peddle an
investigative story to an appropriate newsperson. The objective
is to fire the engine that will lift the investigation into orbit
against the vast inertial resistance posed by recalcitrant institutions and individuals.

Among investigative reporters, there has always been and
continues to be competition for the good stories. There has also
developed, by now, a parallel competition among leakers for the
ear of a hot reporter.

In all this bargaining, it should be noted, would-be government sources have one particularly valuable benefit to offer: The
investigation they are dangling in front of the reporter is already
official at one level or another. A reporter who chooses to pursue
the story is safer than he would be if he were following a random
rumor, because he will be standing shoulder to shoulder with the
U.S. government.

Some of the scandals bought and sold in these source-
journalist exchanges would have been juicy news stories at any
time in the history of the country's modern press. But these days
a number of important newspapers have been assigning more
people to pursue investigative projects—to spend the time on
them that a beat reporter does not have, to cultivate the people
who give out the crucial pieces of information, and to plow
through the required documentation.

When newspapers allocate resources to these projects, they
do so because they consider it their job to bring their readers
more investigative news. In part they are simply responding to
the pressures of business competition. Not much beats a scandal
or a declaration of war for making bombshell headlines and getting people to buy those papers or turn on that tube. Even in the
more high-minded professional competition for journalistic
prizes and reputation, a good scandal series makes a news organization a real contender. If the paper next door has one, you as
a newspaper manager would do well to get one too.

But newspapers do not respond to competition mindlessly in
this area or any other. Editors carry other standards in their
heads about what news should be in their papers and what should
not. Your run-of-the-mill ax murderer, sensationally interesting
as he may be, will find it hard (though not impossible) to get his
story onto page one of the *New York Times*. When newspaper edi-

tors deliberately decide to pursue and be specially receptive to government scandal stories, they are operating according to a theory—largely unspoken and even unthought—of how government should work and how it actually does work. When they actively seek to uncover scandals, they are assuming that the government is still shot through with as-yet-secret, evilly glittering ore waiting to be mined. They think a great deal is going on in government that should and will outrage the public. They think that the cost to them of pursuing these stories will be outweighed by the journalistic benefits of the investment.

For these reasons, journalists agree to become part of the process rather than simply recording it.

When journalists behave this way, they are acting in part as the cultural heirs of Watergate; their behavior is not wholly unprecedented. At the most general level, by definition a reporter can never be a strictly neutral observer. Almost any political event is changed at least a little in its meaning and consequences when it stops being private and becomes public. The Heisenberg principle has its political equivalent.

More specifically, since the end of the nineteenth century, U.S. investigative reporters have directly helped to create the stories they were covering. Muckraking journalists were no detached observers of corruption and scandalous conditions in post–Civil War America. They were tools of the reforming legislators and arms of the prosecution. To a certain extent this kind of connection is in the very nature of modern investigative reporting.

In recent years the pace has changed, though, and the political communications system has developed a noticeably increased appetite for a continuous diet of facts and news about the scandal of the moment. In part this appetite comes, once again, from the pressures of business and professional competition. More interesting, it also seems to stem in part from a conviction among newsmen and government investigators that the scandal will die if journalists do not hook it up to a powerful life support system. Normal investigative processes, they think, will not prove unrelenting enough if they are allowed to take their course, away from the constant light of publicity. Instead, investigations moved out of sight of an unblinking journalistic eye will fall into their natural state, which is death. They will, for practical purposes, cease to be investigations at all.

This increased appetite, and the pressure it produces, have at least two sorts of consequences. For one thing, in order to keep up the sense of movement required of them, reporters must sometimes write stories containing little new information. In the same way, they may be forced to make a lead out of facts whose probative force is quite untested and whose real significance to the investigation has come nowhere near being determined.

Second, when the breathless stories about a given scandal appear in quick and steady succession, they have their intended effect: People who are politically attentive become transfixed by the march to the guillotine. They spend a significant chunk of time reading and talking about each day's new shock, even if they are fortunate enough not to be personally affected by it.

To the extent that our minds are on this sort of news, we stop thinking of public life as an arena for public policy debate or even a smoke-filled room for old-fashioned horse-race politics. We begin to see political life as a high-stakes obstacle course. At each stage of the contest, some will prove vulnerable to investigation and some will turn out to be safe. Of those who are in imminent danger of being "gotten," only a portion will be nimble enough to escape.

The Codes of Indecency

A heightened sensitivity to these particular dangers in public life has, in turn, consequences for the way the political community does business. Anyone who writes about national politics, for instance, has gone through the following experience more than once: A scandal story surfaces in the papers. The initial item may not seem very damaging. If it does look disturbing, you might ask the target of the story to explain the item and find that he does so easily. If you are at all predisposed to think that he or she is not a crook, you will conclude that the newspaper has been caught in a grave and embarrassing error or a huge act of injustice. "Aha!" you think. "The charge is false! The vultures have their facts wrong! They must be made to retract and apologize!"

You may even write some such thing in an editorial, op-ed piece, or column.

But then, day by day, the newspaper starts producing more and more information on your friend the target. As he gets to be a hot subject, the investigations really get rolling, and the flow of information about him increases. In the end, he may turn out to be criminally guilty of something after all. Perhaps his violations consisted only of trying to obstruct the investigators' efforts to flush him out. No matter—these secondary crimes are quite enough for an indictment these days.

So you, the commentator—or the supporter who has been defending the poor guilty slob at dinner parties all over town—end up with a large amount of egg on your face. In fact you may have bought yourself even worse trouble: People may begin to charge you, plainly or snidely, with the egregious crime of being insensitive to the pernicious existence of sleaze in government.

If you are a person of normally fearful temperament—if you do not enjoy a fight, and do not relish living outside the pale of respectability—you soon enough begin to look before you leap. You learn not to spring so quickly to the defense of your friend, your political ally, or the man in the news who merely happens to look innocent. You know that tomorrow, or maybe the day after that, as the investigators keep pressing and the accused gets a more extended chance to put his foot in his mouth and his hands around his own throat, the odds of his unharmed survival will keep on dropping.

You may decide to make a statement of solidarity with the accused, but it will be formulaic: "My heart goes out to him in his time of trouble," for instance. Everyone in the community knows by now just what a sentiment like that is worth. You may write something nice about him, but it will always include some version of the by now well-known "Watergate disclaimer": "It is always possible, of course, that new facts may emerge. But for now . . . " Everyone can translate that one, too.

During any scandal, many onlookers feel some of these anxieties and make some of these calculations. The collective effect of all this hedging of bets is to make the accused weaker as the contest proceeds.

But democratic politics has never been famous for the nobility of the characters who populate its halls of power or the generosity with which they are treated in their hours of need. Even if this is a time when the rules of the game are particularly rough, why the concern?

People worried about scandalmongering in Washington usually point to several bad consequences. The best people, they say, will no longer be attracted to public service. Embattled government officials will begin to practice more secrecy rather than less. Officials will be afraid to say controversial things.

From the other side of the fence, those pushing for still higher moral standards in politics say that the worriers are, in truth, merely crying wolf.

The judgment will not be in for some years, of course. But certain consequences of the new style have started to emerge.

The capital city in a democracy, and the capital's outposts in other sections of the country, always have a lot to answer for. The city turns policy thinkers into mush-heads. It makes healthy partisans into mealy-mouths aching for the establishment's dinner table. On the other hand, a political establishment is a political community, whose members can make some judgments about one another's character according to a set of more or less common standards. This virtue may seem small but is not to be sneezed at; heaven knows it has been hard enough in recent years to keep in operation at all.

Nowadays there is less and less of that sense of common language and common standards. It is not that people are yelling at one another over policy, or that electoral contests are unprecedentedly bitter, or even that there is some Watergate-style paranoia—the "us" camp versus the "them" camp. Instead, what you will hear if you listen closely is that communications have become increasingly veiled. There are controversial words that political types will not utter in public or commit to paper. They use code words to one another instead. There are certain arguments they will not make to strangers. Instead, they substitute others, false stand-ins for the real thing. Even to their close organizational associates they will refrain from disclosing their true political agenda. They become inscrutable or talk in bureaucratese, saving their real thoughts for more private gatherings.

In short, they are coming to base their behavior on the conviction that there are two relevant categories in government: the hunters and the hunted.

Will the results of the change be permanent or disastrous? No one can yet say. But anyone who tries to deny that the change is taking place either has not been listening hard enough or is no longer being allowed into the places where he can hear the music.

INDIVIDUAL CHARACTER AND POLITICAL ETHICS[4]

Gary Hart's lasting contribution to American politics may well turn out to lie in the area of political iconography. Home-video images of Hart on the *Monkey Business* with Donna Rice have become a staple of the network news programs, displayed whenever they set out to explore the higher reaches of public morality. Such is the nature of politics in the affluent society, with all those minicameras flowing through the market and into the hands of the citizenry.

What legitimates this media excursion into the hitherto British domain of politics and sex is the famous Character Factor, invented to focus on Hart's personal weirdness—the functuations in his name and age—rather than on the vacuity of his political being. The Character Factor was tailor-made for voters considering a candidate living on the dangerous edge of compulsive sexual appetite: would you want a guy like that to have his finger on the button? The reporter who publicly asked Hart if he'd ever committed adultery justified himself by reference to the Character Factor, and he had the super-serious ruminations of academic and journalistic pundits to back him up. Since then, we've seen the Character Factor dent quite a few more characters, from other presidential hopefuls to Supreme Court aspirants.

Most of the Character Factor talk has had to do with journalistic ethics and whether or not someone's private life is or should be off limits. In an age when it is a commmonplace that the only persona that counts in politics is the public one—that there is no reality behind the fabricated personality designed by media consultants and propped up before the cameras—this questioning might be taken as a hopeful sign: at the least, it may show a popular dissatisfaction with the cardboard-cutout school of politics. On the other hand, it may only reflect the sad realization that accompanies a *People* magazine view of the world.

The discovery of so little in the domain of character troubles the pundits because of that nagging button question, the question of the awesome power—ultimately the awesome violence—of

[4]Reprint of an article by Nicholas Xenos, who teaches political theory at the University of Massachusetts at Amherst. *Grand Street*, vol. 7 (Summer 1988), pp. 154–160. Reprinted with permission.

the state. It is difficult to contemplate such power without the belief that it will be exercised responsibly, and any shred of doubt concerning character tampers with that belief.

Long before there were such buttons, but at a time when Europeans had had some considerable recent experience of people killing each other over political goals, Max Weber gave this issue of responsibility some thought. In his essay published in 1919, "Politics as a Vocation," Weber went so far as to claim that the essential characteristic of the state was that it was the repository of legitimate violence in the modern world. Whoever became involved with politics, he wrote, must necessarily become involved with violence. But this did not mean that Weber, any more than Machiavelli, felt that politics should be shunned: on the contrary, he held the true politician in high esteem as one who was willing to tread in this moral minefield. (Weber was himself an active and influential political figure in Weimar Germany.) In describing that terrain, Weber distinguished between what he called an "ethic of responsibility" and an "ethic of ultimate ends." The first is constructed around the full knowledge of the implications of employing violence toward some political end and carries with it accountability for "the foreseeable results of one's actions," while the second is concerned only with the ends themselves, even at the expense of destroying them through means in fundamental contradiction to them. Weber the Machiavellian and anti-utopian wanted us to see that there could be no heaven on earth, that "he who seeks the salvation of the soul, of his own and of others, should not seek it along the avenue of politics, for the quite different tasks of politics can only be solved by violence." And yet only the person who combined the ethic of responsibility and the ethic of ultimate ends, he thought, could truly be said to have the "calling for politics." This characterization of the political life as a calling—a term that Weber borrowed from his investigation into Calvinism in *The Protestant Ethic and the Spirit of Capitalism* (1904–5)—is very beautiful and indicative of just how singular and important Weber thought such a life to be. It is also very likely of little real value in assessing the situation of political ethics in America today.

If the idea of a calling for politics is a little far-fetched in the contemporary domestic setting, it is for reasons Weber recognized, because the specter of crazed utopians running amok was not the only vision that haunted him. Far more menacing in its implications was the imagery of the "iron cage" he employed at the end of the *Protestant Ethic* to represent a modern world trapped by the desire for material wealth and the routinization and bureaucracy that go along with it. The Calvinist felt called to the worldly asceticism that Weber—rightly or wrongly—thought to be the foundation for rational capitalist behavior. But powerful forces were unleashed, desire was now turned loose and the pursuit of wealth took on a life of its own, no longer justified by reference to higher principles. In the modern world, Weber wrote in the closing pages of the *Protestant Ethic*, "the idea of duty in one's calling prowls about in our lives like the ghost of dead religious beliefs."

In place of the calling, one might say, we have the job classification. The triumph of capitalism and the growth of the state have resulted in the establishment of bureaucratic, rational organization on an unprecedented scale. The responsibility that goes along with occupying an office in a bureaucracy is quite unlike the ethic of responsibility Weber ascribed to the political figure. The responsible officeholder is someone who abrogates responsibility for his or her actions—carrying out orders is the essence of the bureaucrat; doing it with conviction is the mark of true talent. When the time comes, if it comes, to ascribe responsibility to the actions that are taken by bureaucracies, the trail leads into a maze of office cubicles and usually disappears. We persist in believing that someone must be responsible, but the rationale of government and corporate bureaucracy is "deniability," whether it is the Iran-Contra scandal, the E. F. Hutton bank fraud scandal, the NASA-Challenger scandal, or any typical screw-up by a commercial airline or the Pentagon that is in question.

If we return now to the button question, we can see the difficulty all this presents for any coherent notion of political ethics and why the Character Factor is an escape from the real issues involved. The obsession with character hides the suspicion we feel that, like the penultimate scene in *Apocalypse Now*, no one is in charge. But with this big difference: in the case of the state, unlike Coppola's Vietnam nightmare, the result is not chaos but normality. The state's power is managed, administered, its violence hidden by the indifference of managers and administrators who seldom have to face up to the human consequences of their actions. The lack of responsibility is recognized even as the language of responsibility is occasionally invoked. When the Congressional committees investigating the Iran-Contra affair got down to trying to find someone to point a finger at, they concluded that "the ultimate responsibility" rested with President Reagan, since he had created the general policy the National Security Council bureaucrats thought they were carrying out, even if he then took a nap for the duration. That reasoning—the notion that political leaders set the ends and the bureaucracy provides the means—is close to Weber's ideas about political leadership and political responsibility. The problem is that, in practice, responsibility doesn't mean very much. As the Congressional committee members themselves noted, President Reagan on several occasions declared that he accepted responsibility for various aspects of the affair. The committees found that "fundamental processes of governance were disregarded and the rule of law was subverted," but they shunned any idea that the "ultimate responsibility" for these things carries with it any cost. As long as Ronald Reagan, didn't personally break any laws, or conspire to, he is immune from any real responsibility for his actions—he simply says, "Okay, I'm responsible," and goes about his business with, at the worst, the loss of some points in popularity polls. Whatever political power he lost in that latter part of 1987 was in all probability more a function of his lame-duck status than of his responsibility for subverting the rule of law.

The earlier Tower Commission criticized President Reagan's management style, and in doing so it was closer to the mark than the Congressional committees. The notion of responsibility is tied to political leadership; management to the techniques of bureaucratic control. While it is probably absurd to assume that anyone can really manage the state's bureaucracy, the Tower Commission at least acknowledged what has been a fact for some time: the presidency has been transformed from a political office into a chief executive officer. CEOs are, for the most part, faceless, soulless people who have risen to the top of a corporate bureaucracy. They are judged as to what are called their management skills in the only way they can be: by the bottom line. Recent obsession with the federal budget deficit represents an effort to apply the same management standards to government as are routine in business. When a CEO is found wanting in his or her management skills—i.e., when the company loses money—he or she is generally given a few sacks full of stock and cash and either made Chairman of the Board or sent packing to become a CEO someplace else. Presidents have a different sort of contract, so when they get critized they shuffle their Cabinet while the stockholders interview candidates for the succession, each of whom puts his best manager's face on and tries to look tough.

The parallel carries through to all levels. The corporate bureaucracies have the Harvard Business School to train young would-be executives, while the government recruits eager staffers from Harvard's Kennedy School of Government. Both schools specialize in teaching management skills. Apparently, the ghosts of the calling haunt the halls of both institutions, as they do the élite medical and law schools, since all these places now employ what are called ethicists. The professional ethics racket specializes in teaching lawyers, doctors, business executives and government officeholders how to appear virtuous. Its arena is one of judgment, but it is judgment of a particular kind. The professional ethicist looks to examples drawn from past practices within a profession to establish rules of conduct which can then be applied to specific instances to judge whether or not a particular action is within ethical bounds. This judgment is essentially the judgment of a specialist observer relating the actions of an individual to the rules of conduct of an office. What this represents is the bureaucratization of political ethics, its entrapment within an office cubicle of its own. It is recognition of the fact that the actor is subservient to the role, without an independent moral bearing and without responsibility. All that is important is the appearance of ethical propriety, not the relationship between an individual's action and the moral and political principles upon which he or she acts. Don't be surprised when every government agency, like every hospital, has its resident ethicist whose job it is to dispense advice on how to look clean while doing the dirty work.

The transformation of political office into management thus renders the question of character moot. If we are to find an arena in which the practice of political ethics makes sense, one in which an ethic of responsibility tied to an ethic of ultimate ends might mean something, it will have to be outside political office, which is another way of saying that it will have to be outside the state. What this might mean can be glimpsed by looking at the situation of political activists in Eastern Europe today, particularly in Poland, Hungary and Czechoslovakia, where there is no question of involvement with the state. There, political action takes the form of opposition in the face of the state's power. While the bureaucrats who react to these activists do so with the utmost lack of responsibility, following orders, the dissidents act with definite ends in mind, ones relating to freedom and autonomy. And they act with responsibility, knowing that the consequences of their actions can mean imprisonment or physical assault and can have consequences for their fellow subjects. What their example shows is that it is in confronting or circumventing the power of the state, rather than in exercising it, that political ethics can still have meaning today.

But the example of Eastern European dissidents also points up the problem we face in establishing an oppositional ground for political action in this country. The violence of the state is rarely seen anymore here, except in foreign policy, and even then only infrequently. All our attention is focused these days on the nuclear button, but that is an abstraction. The thought persists that if only the right people were in office the state could accomplish much that is good and worthwhile, that the state is a neutral instrument to be wielded for some purpose. This is a residue of the Progressives and the New Dealers and has led to the destruction of whatever oppositional culture preexisted the consolidation of power in the federal government. As a result, armies of pragmatic, well-intentioned people have gone off to wage their wars on the terrain of conventional politics, have fought their way into the cubicles within the fortress and are now missing in action.

Max Weber wanted to believe that the person with the calling for politics would be able to direct the vast power machine that is the modern state, give it some sense of ends toward which its power would be directed and take responsibility for it. But in the world of the iron cage, Weber's solution is a dangerously ambiguous one. That world is one of interests, not vision, and the political leader, as Weber also recognized, is a representative of interests. The only coherent ends political leaders can bring to the task of directing the state are the interests they represent, interests which, in the nature of things, will not conflict with the state organization's irresponsible interest in power. The most effective political leader will be the one who manages to bring the interests he or she represents and the interests of the state into the closest possible harmony. If by chance good is done, it will doubtless be coincident with an extension of the state's power into some new domain and very likely incidental to it in the long run.

At present, oppositional voices in America, particularly those of intellectuals, are largely without consequence and therefore without responsibility. Happily, few have turned to violence in frustration, which is its own form of irresponsibility, and which is anyhow the state's field of battle. Many more have been tempted by the allure of power or the right candidate. Twenty-odd years ago, an oppositional culture seemed to be forming, though incoherently and without lasting effect, as it turned out. But the effort was worthwhile. To do it right will take intelligence, a nuanced sense of tactics and a commitment to opt out of the iron cage. It may take a renewed sense of a political calling tied to opposition as an office. Only then will we be able to speak of character and political ethics in the same breath.

WE NEED MORE LEADERSHIP IN ETHICS[5]

Throughout the last 20 years, the Congress of the United States has spent a considerable amount of its time in various attempts at addressing the perception that the ethical standards of federal office holders and employees must be substantially heightened if the republic is to survive. This perception of low ethical standards and the dire necessity of corrective legislation has been chronicled by the media and commented upon by self-proclaimed guardians of morality.

In response, Congress passed measures such as the Ethics in Government Act of 1978, the Code of Official Conduct of the Senate and House of Representatives of 1977, and recent amendments to federal conflict of interest laws which now bar a broad range of post-employment lobbying by many former federal office holders.

[5]Reprint of an article by United States Senator from Alaska Ted Stevens, a member of the Senate Rules Committee. Reprinted by permission from *Ethics: Easier Said Than Done*, Spring/Summer 1988, vol. 1, no. 23, pp. 110, 145.

In spite of this flurry of legislative activity, "ethics in government" is still a leading topic of public policy debate in Washington.

The problem is that these laws have not fixed the issue because morality cannot be legislated. Unfortunately, this truism has been lost on many in Congress, the media, and among the community of so-called "public interest" groups.

As the chairman of the Senate's Select Committee on Ethics from 1982 to 1984, I saw at close range the results of congressional attempts to mandate morality, both for members of Congress and staff (via Standing Rules of the Senate and House) and for employees of the executive branch (via civil and criminal statutes). This experience has made me more skeptical about the value of rules designed to create ethical behavior.

While I do not argue that minimal standards of acceptable conduct should be eliminated from existing federal statutes (such as the proscriptions against bribery and the acceptance of illegal gratuities), I am convinced that some of the Senate's rules merely add a layer of confusion and uncertainty to existing legal standards.

For example, the Senate has adopted a rule which prohibits the receipt of a "gift" of over $100 in value from a "prohibited source." The practical effect of this rule is to sanction the receipt of gifts valued at less than $100. For some, rules like these alleviate the need to make a personal, reasoned, moral judgment as to the propriety of accepting a $98 gift from a lobbyist or a $500 gift from a "non-prohibited source."

Instead of promulgating narrowly drawn legislative restrictions, prohibitions and criminal sanctions, we should focus on the dramatic need for positive leadership on ethics issues. Congress could begin by implementing a series of in house conferences for senators and staff at which ethical standards would be discussed and common moral values would be outlined.

I am pleased that the Josephson Institute has begun to undertake such conferences for Senate staff. As anyone who has been involved in legislative ethics issues can attest, preventive medicine before the fact is far preferable to after the fact remedial action.

Congress should provide guidance to its own members and employees, as well as to the federal government, by providing a standard, an example by which government staff and citizens generally can guide their decision making.

There are a number of ways Congress can play a constructive role in the establishment of a more ethically sensitive environment. For example, the leadership of each party in the Senate could enhance the moral tone of the institution by assigning senior members of the Senate to act as members to younger senators on troubling ethics issues. Such a procedure would help to minimize political considerations and result in the sharing of experiences and wisdom, which could significantly aide younger colleagues to perceive and to deal with the ethical dimension of their work. The collective advice and wisdom of senior senators could generate an institutional consensus as to appropriate mores and conduct, and a positive moral tone would be established for the institution.

Similarly, the president of the United States must take a position of leadership on "government ethics" and speak out on the need for very high standards of personal conduct. Historically, the president has served as a moral force in American life, establishing a tone for the standards of conduct of all Americans. The White House and the Congress must become a "bully pulpit" for governmental leaders to argue the necessity of a return to traditional values and high standards of morality.

Today, on the issue of "government ethics," America needs less restrictive legislation and more positive leadership.

THE NEED FOR PEOPLE OF VIRTUE[6]

Americans are uneasy about morality and ethics in high places. Unfortunately, there seems to be good cause.

At least 21 members of Congress have been indicted in the last decade. Over the last seven years, more than 100 Reagan administration officials have been in the news for alleged ethical or legal misconduct—an unprecedented number. During the past five years, almost every state and major city has confronted a

[6]Reprint of an article by U.S. Representative from Indiana, Lee H. Hamilton, chairman of the House Select Committee to Investigate Covert Arms Transactions with Iran. Reprinted by permission from *Ethics: Easier Said Than Done*, Spring/Summer 1988, vol. 1, pp. 94, 136, 137.

scandal among its public officials. In 1986, the Justice Department obtained more than 1,000 convictions in cases of public corruption. This kind of behavior has led to a broad cynicism—if not ridicule—among Americans. It has made them uneasy about the health of our system of government.

Some say that politicians just reflect a looser moral climate in America, where sexual indiscretions, selfishness, "white lies," and an "enrich-thyself" philosophy—though not praiseworthy—are not that uncommon. Others say that public officials today face stricter standards and tougher scrutiny than in the past. My view is that things are not as they should be and that "ethics questions" are important ones to ask.

While not every action of candidates or public officials should be open for scrutiny, the public does have a legitimate interest in activities which could impair the ability of officeholders to carry out their official duties or which would bring discredit on the institutions of government.

The misconduct of any government official reflects on all government officials, even those who, often under the most difficult circumstances, have conducted themselves according to high ethical and professional standards.

Public leaders face a crisis of confidence. There are significant social costs when the public trust is violated. Opinion polls indicate that a lack of confidence in the integrity of elected officials is a major reason for the low voter turnout in recent elections. Without trust, democratic government just does not work.

Moreover, dishonesty and deception lead to bad policy. That was one of the major lessons of the Iran-contra hearings. During the testimony we heard people claim that the ends justify the means, and that lying to Congress and to the American people is an acceptable practice.

Such attitudes almost guarantee policy failure. Lying and deception about our sale of arms to Iran led to confusion and disarray at the highest levels of government, undermined our credibility with our key allies, and harmed the president's ability to gain and sustain congressional and public support for his policies.

So often during the hearings I was reminded of President Jefferson's statement: "The whole art of government consists in the art of being honest."

Our Founding Fathers recognized that no matter how well-structured government is, it will not work unless its offices are held by people of virtue. Public officials, they said, should possess a "disinterested attachment to the public good, exclusive and independent of all private and selfish interest."

Clearly, they were right. No matter how carefully we draft the laws, no matter how precisely we structure our democratic institutions, and no matter how meticulously we set up checks and balances, if we do not have leaders with high ethical standards the results can still be disastrous.

I have come to the view that we *should* apply a higher standard of accountability to those seeking and holding public office than to those in private life. Are we thus applying a different standard of morality to public officials? In one sense, no. The kinds of standards we apply to public officials—such as veracity or fidelity—obviously apply to other people as well. However, because top government officials have both visibility and influence, my feeling is that we probably do, and should, apply a higher degree of accountability to their conduct. I think we are right to expect our leaders to reflect high personal integrity and exercise good judgment in both their public and private lives.

Although we need to make sure that we have people of high moral standards in office, my sense is that our efforts have generally been too one-sided. We focus our efforts on trying to "push out" of the process those whose standards of conduct do not quite measure up. This is, unfortunately, necessary at times. But to improve the standards in government, we must also try to "pull in" to the process Americans of fine character and sound judgment in both public and private matters.

We have an enormous pool of talented individuals with high standards in this country. No doubt many of them are turned off to a career in public service. They are, rightly, concerned about: pleading with special interest groups to get the enormous sums of money needed to run for office; enduring harsh, negative campaigning and personal attacks; hearing their job portrayed as "dirty" and downgraded even by other politicians; deserting their families for the long months of running for elected office; answering questions from the media which poke and pry into every aspect of their personal lives; and having their real contributions ignored, while their minor mistakes are magnified.

These factors work against drawing good people into government service. We must work to reduce them and show that public service can be honorable.

Changing the major disincentives to public service in the American political system will certainly not be easy. But we must strive to make a career in politics and government service appealing and honorable.

We should tend to the wisdom of our Founding Fathers by consciously seeking to draw into politics people of virtue. If we do not succeed in doing this, we place in jeopardy our future. Government, like many other institutions, is only as good as the people who comprise it.

BIBLIOGRAPHY

An asterisk (*) preceding a reference indicates an excerpt from the work has been reprinted in this compilation.

BOOKS AND PAMPHLETS

Beitz, Charles et al., eds. International ethics. Princeton University Press. '85.

Bok, Sissela. Lying: moral choice in public and private life. Pantheon Books. '78.

Cockburn, Alexander. Corruptions of empire. Verso. '87.

Davis, Harry R. and Good, Robert C. Reinhold Neibuhr on politics. Macmillan. '60.

Denhardt, Kathryn G. The ethics of public service. Greenwood Press. '88.

Eisenstadt, Abraham S. et. al., eds. Before Watergate. Brooklyn College Press. '78.

Ellis, Anthony. Ethics and international relations. Manchester University Press. '86.

Fain, Hashell. Normative politics and the community of nations. Philadelphia University Press. '87.

Fleishman, Joel L. and Payne, Bruce L. Ethical dilemmas and the education of policymakers. The Hastings Center. '80.

French, Peter. Ethics in government. Prentice Hall. '83.

Gaede, Erwin A. Politics and ethics. University Press of America. '83.

Gutman, Amy and Thompson, Dennis, eds. Ethics and politics. Nelson Hall Publishers. '86.

Hampshire, Stuart et al., eds. Public and private morality. Cambridge Univ. Press. '78.

Haughey, John C. S.J., ed. Personal values in public policy. Paulist Press. '79.

Heidenheimer, Arnold J. et al., eds. Political corruption. Transaction Publishers. '89.

Horwitz, Robert H., ed. The moral foundations of the American republic. University Press of Virginia. '86.

Jackson, Brooks. Honest graft: big money and the American political process. Knopf. '88.

*Jennings, Bruce and Callahan, Daniel, eds. Representation and responsibility: exploring legislative ethics. Plenum Press. '85.

Jones, Donald G., ed. Private and public ethics. Edwin Mellen Press. '78.

Keller, Elizabeth K. Ethical insights, ethical action. International City Mgt. Assn. '88.

Keohane, Robert O., ed. Neorealism and its critics. Columbia University Press. '86.

Kipnis, Kenneth and Meyers, Diana T., eds. Political realism and international morality. Westview Press. '87.

Klitgaard, Robert. Controlling corruption. University of California Press. '88.

Lipsett, Seymour M. and Schneider, William. Confidence gap: business, labor and government in the public mind. Free Press. '83.

Myers, Robert J., ed. International ethics in the nuclear age. University Press of America. '87.

*Neely, Alfred S. IV. Ethics-in-government laws. American Enterprise Institute. '84.

Niebuhr, Reinhold. Moral man and immoral society. Scribner. '60.

Noonan, John T. Bribes. Macmillan. '84.

Nye, Joseph S. Ethics and foreign policy. Aspen Institute for Humanistic Studies. '85.

Pennock, J. Roland and Chapman, John W. Compromise in ethics, law, and politics. New York University Press. '79.

Pennock, J. Roland and Chapman, John W. Justification. New York University Press. '86.

*Roberts, Robert N. White House ethics: the history of the politics of conflict of interest legislation. Greenwood Press. '88.

*Simon, Paul. The glass house: politics and morality in the nation's capital. Continuum Publishing. '84.

Stern, Philip M. The best Congress money can buy. Pantheon. '88.

Thompson, Dennis F. Political ethics and public office. Harvard University Press. '87.

ADDITIONAL PERIODICAL ARTICLES WITH ABSTRACTS

For those who wish to read more widely on the subject of ethics in politics and government, this section contains abstracts of additional articles that bear on the topic. Readers who require a comprehensive list of materials are advised to consult the *Readers' Guide to Periodical Literature* and other Wilson indexes.

'A stone in one's shoe': running with integrity. James M. Wall *The Christian Century* 104:843 O 7 '87

Presidential candidates Gary Hart and Joe Biden were not brought down by their actions but by the public perception that they lacked integrity. Their withdrawal from the race illustrates that the system of nominating presidential candidates has become a referendum on character. Character, however, is too vague a term with which to evaluate a candidate. Scruple, which is derived from a Latin word meaning a small, sharp stone in one's shoe, or an uneasiness, is a much better evaluative term, indicating as it does that a candidate should be judged on his sensitivity to his own imperfections and to the need for honesty.

All the president's friends. Harold Smith *Christianity Today* 32:15 Ap 22 '88

Attorney General Edwin Meese's involvement in the Wedtech scam raises questions about voters' responsibility for such embarrassing situations. As media exposure of White House scandals has shown, executive-branch appointees chosen for their apparent ideological purity may not have the common sense or moral integrity to carry out administrative assignments. The American electorate should not throw its wholehearted support behind an appointee on ideological grounds alone, and the next U.S. president should likewise look beyond ideology when making decisions to hire or fire.

Seeking solutions to the ethics crisis. Ann McBride *Common Cause Magazine* 14:44-5 Mr/Ap '88

News stories about ethical lapses by governmental officials are shockingly commonplace, but the current sleaziness could prompt fundamental reform. Lawmakers in both the House and Senate intend to push legislation designed to discourage the revolving door syndrome, in which former public officials cash in on the access and information they have gained. Good laws will be of no avail, however, without strong and effective enforcement. When Congress reauthorizes the Office of Governmental Ethics in 1988, it should compel the OGE to fulfill its mandate of enforcing ethics standards. The independent counsel provisions of the Ethics in Government Act are also critical to the effective enforcement of the law, but the constitutionality of that act has been challenged. Common Cause chairman Archibald Cox is preparing a friend of the court brief defending it. As Congress attempts to clean up after the Reagan administration, it must also reform its own ethics codes.

A recipe for respectable government. Fred Wertheimer *Common Cause Magazine* 14:43-4 S/O '88

The next American president must strive to improve public attitudes toward government. During the Reagan years, ethical principles were ignored amidst a general disdain for government, compensation for governing lagged behind that for leadership roles in the private sector, and young people were dissuaded from public service, particularly by the

weight of education debt. It is critical that the American public come to
acknowledge the necessity of having government as a mediating force and
that it be willing to pay salaries to public leaders that reflect the importance of their responsibilities. College students must be given innovative
types of financial assistance and ways to repay education debt.

Countdown on corruption (Common Cause campaign to re-form congressional campaign funding; special section).
Common Cause Magazine 14:50–4 S/O '88

Common Cause is launching a major congressional campaign-finance reform effort called the Common Cause Ethics Agenda during the current
election. Growing contributions from special interest PACs are skewing
elections in favor of incumbent senators and representatives, and honoraria serve to subsidize these officials' personal incomes. In the 100th
Congress, a minority of senators managed to block action on a historic
comprehensive reform bill. Common Cause aims to get candidates for the
House and Senate on the record on the issues of redressing campaign finance practice and banning honoraria. Recommendations for involvement in the effort and information regarding the Common Cause
campaign are provided.

It's time to reform Congress. R. Cort Kirkwood *Conservative Digest* 14:39–43+ S '88

Congress is in urgent need for reform. Capitol Hill has been corrupted
by money, power, and special privileges and co-opted by special interests.
While the cost of running Congress has ballooned to $1.9 billion a year,
congressmen spend less time working today than they did ten years ago.
There are currently at least eleven laws that Congress has imposed on the
rest of the nation but from which it exempts itself. Republican congressman Hank Brown of Colorado has introduced legislation that would end
congressional exemption from these laws and implement a host of other
reforms. Fellow Republican congressman Howard Coble of North Carolina has introduced a bill to reform the congressional pension system, one
of many ways in which Congress indulges itself at the taxpayers' expense.
It is up to the voters to break the cycle and elect principled men and wom-
en and turn the profligate out of office.

The aides virus (ex-congressional aides working as lobbyists).
Jeffrey L. Pasley *The New Republic* 197:22+ O 19 '87

Growing numbers of high-level congressional aides are turning to influence-peddling when they leave Congress, where they are well schooled in
the ways of interest group politics. Capitol Hill aides tend to be more effective lobbyists than former officials from the executive branch, in part
because they are not bound by legal restrictions like those that have
caused trouble for Michael Deaver. On the Hill, where people tend to believe that even the grubbiest interest deserves an advocate, the idea of

conflict-of-interest appears to have been lost. When James Madison envisioned a government that mediated among conflicting interests, he did not intend that the interests and the mediators would be the same group of people or that the ability to pay would determined which interests would be represented.

The school for scandal. J. L. Pasley *The New Republic* 199:20 Jl 4 '88

The kind of "professional politics" that the Graduate School of Political Management (GSPM) is hoping to promote is so fundamentally flawed that even an added emphasis on ethics cannot redeem it. The GSPM, which started holding classes September 1987 at City University of New York's Bernard Baruch College, is the brainchild of Neil Fabricant, a lawyer who became a sort of political entrepreneur in New York State. Although the faculty seems to lean toward the Right, Fabricant stresses that the school has no ideological program and is committed instead to "stimulating professional identity and discipline in what is de facto a profession." The professional politics that the school is designed to promote appears to be practiced, like law, by disinterested mercenaries. Even with a code of ethics, a political profession serving the goals of whomever can pay, regardless of the merits of a cause, is the last thing this country needs.

Last testament (independent counsel's report on E. Meese). *The New Republic* 199:4 Ag 8-15 '88

Edwin Meese's disingenuous reply to independent counsel James McKay's report confirms that Meese either doesn't know right from wrong or doesn't care about the distinction. McKay decided not to issue any indictments but determined that Meese did break the law in two small matters. He also raised questions about the attorney general's propriety and sensitivity on a variety of other matters. In response, Meese claimed that McKay had no right to make any ethical criticism because he was only supposed to decide whether to bring criminal charges. In addition, Meese has claimed that he is completely blameless because no charges were brought against him. In essence, the attorney general's brief boils down to the contention that, by his own standards, he has done nothing wrong. Now that he has established what his standards are, we can judge him by our own.

Congress faces an ethics gap. Mickey Kaus *Newsweek* 112:16–17 Jl 4 '88

Increasingly, conduct that Washington, especially Congress, has deemed normal and ethical is striking the rest of the country as corrupt. House Speaker Jim Wright, for example, received an unheard-of 55 percent royalty for his book, copies of which were bought in bulk by people who might have an interest in lining Wright's coffers. Wright is correct, however, in stating that he did nothing illegal. A number of common Washington practices that are entirely legal but ethically questionable are described.

The foul stench of money (financial abuses by congressmen). Margaret B. Carlson *Time* 132:21 Jl 4 '88

Despite rules aimed at preventing financial abuses, U.S. congressmen frequently receive free vacations and meals, large campaign contributions from lobbyists, and exorbitant fees for delivering speeches or just appearing at an event. Legislators supposedly accept money from lobbyists to help finance their campaigns, but House incumbents have so many advantages that they are usually reelected; many are not even challenged. Upon retirement, a congressman elected before 1980 can keep his accumulated bounty for personal use.

Implausible deniability. Mortimer B. Zuckerman *U.S. News & World Report* 103:68 Ag 3 '87

The Iran-contra hearings have turned Washington into the City of Lies. Paradoxically, the man who gained the most credibility during the hearings, Lt. Col. Oliver North, is a self-confessed liar. Although it is not clear whether the president knew about and approved the Iran-contra transactions, he may have avoided knowing too much so that he could take shelter behind the doctrine of plausible deniability. Congress is right to be shocked by the revelations of covert dealings in the affair, but it must examine its own role in the conduct of foreign policy. It must ensure that elected representatives are fully informed about executive decisions and must recognize that its role in foreign policy requires consistency and candor.

Moral judgment and political action (address, October 26, 1987). Peter L. Berger *Vital Speeches of the Day* 54:115–22 D 1 '87

In a lecture delivered at Boston University in Massachusetts, professor Peter L. Berger describes how a social-scientific perspective can help citizens of a democracy face the political challenges of the modern world: Max Weber's advocacy of an ethic of responsibility, which was set forth one year after Germany's defeat in World War I, is relevant to anyone today who wants to act politically in a morally defensible manner. The social sciences offer four contributions that facilitate taking morally responsible political actions: intellectual detachment, clarification of normative and cognitive presuppositions, identification of the social location of actors and their interests, and the assessment of political and moral trade-offs.